Praise for
David Horowitz and *The Enemy Within*

"Though he doesn't know it, David Horowitz was central to my education. Despite growing up in the heartland of the New Left, I knew little about them until I discovered Horowitz—easily our greatest chronicler of their thought and deeds. *The Enemy Within*, like all Horowitz's work, combines front-row eye-witness experience with careful research. While the gravity and horror of what he writes can sound too incredible to be real, it's all real. He knows these people like no one else. Believe him and prepare."

> —**MICHAEL ANTON,** author of *The Stakes: America at the Point of No Return*

"In this powerful new book Horowitz shows how the Democrat Party has embraced a world view that is anti-constitutional, anti-American, racist, and totalitarian down to the pronouns we are permitted to use. This new Democrat Party is at war with the First Amendment, the independence of the judiciary, the separation of powers, and the two-party system. *The Enemy Within* is a book for all patriots who understand that our country is in a fight for its life."

> —**MARK LEVIN,** author of *Unfreedom of the Press*

"Keen and searing historical insights into the division and demonization that mark so much of today's politics—David Horowitz does it again in a must-read for any American concerned about where we're headed as a nation."

> —**LAURA INGRAHAM,** #1 *New York Times* bestselling author of *The Obama Diaries* and *Power to the People*

"David Horowitz, like a highly skilled surgeon, explores and dissects the frightening ideas and individuals behind the hard Left's push to change America. This one is not to be missed. I highly recommend it."

> —**PETER SCHWEIZER,** author of *Clinton Cash* and *Profiles in Corruption*

"Today, America is in our greatest crisis since the Civil War. We have never needed the clarity, wisdom, and fog-lifting ability of former 1960s radical and now great American champion David Horowitz. His new book, *The Enemy Within*, is a must-read, no-holds-barred, courageous guide to understanding the threat and equipping Americans to defend their country."

> —**CONGRESSMAN LOUIE GOHMERT**

"How did our country get here? The courageous David Horowitz offers this lucid examination of the movements that have pulled our nation toward totalitarianism."

—**ERIC METAXAS,** #1 *New York Times* bestselling author and nationally syndicated radio host

"Urban insurrections go unpunished by municipal authorities, the First Amendment is under relentless assault, the two-party system is the target of unprecedented attacks, and a racialist agenda has supplanted the once liberal outlook of the Democrat Party. In these dark times, David Horowitz's new book shines a needed light on the sources of the crisis and a guide to an American renewal."

—**RICHARD GRENELL,** former Acting Director of National Intelligence

"*The Enemy Within* does not describe some distant, faraway threat. It describes a threat to America that comes from within America, from the ideological Left. David Horowitz has firsthand knowledge of who these people are, how they act, and how they think. Here he lays out their diabolical scheme, rooted as it is in Marxist-Leninist ideology, and shows how we can get rid of this scourge once and for all. A great book!"

—**DINESH D'SOUZA,** bestselling author of *What's So Great about America* and *The Big Lie*

"David Horowitz is an American patriot who has dedicated his life to understanding the existential threat to our country posed by the radical Left. The crisis he has been warning about for half a century is here. To survive, Americans must take the threat Horowitz describes in *The Enemy Within* seriously and get actively involved in fighting the dark forces he identifies so eloquently in this book."

—**GLENN BECK,** host of *Glenn Beck* on TheBlaze and of *The Glenn Beck Radio Program*

The Enemy Within

DAVID HOROWITZ

THE ENEMY WITHIN

HOW A TOTALITARIAN MOVEMENT IS DESTROYING AMERICA

REGNERY PUBLISHING
A Division of Salem Media Group
Washington, D.C.

Regnery® is a registered trademark of Salem Communications Holding Corporation

ISBN: 978-1-68451-054-2
eISBN: 978-1-68451-113-6

Library of Congress Control Number: 2020952234

Published in the United States by
Regnery Publishing
A Division of Salem Media Group
Washington, D.C.
www.Regnery.com

Manufactured in the United States of America

10 9 8 7 6 5 4 3 2 1

Books are available in quantity for promotional or premium use. For information on discounts and terms, please visit our website: www.Regnery.com.

Dedicated to the millions of inner-city kids forced into Democrat-run failed public schools, which year in and year out deny them a shot at the American dream; the inner-city inhabitants of America's violent-crime zones run by the Democrat Party and its criminal-friendly officials; the innocent victims of criminal aliens in this country thanks to the Democrats' sabotage of America's borders; the European and Asian Americans denied equal rights and opportunities by the systemic racism of "woke" institutions; the small-business entrepreneurs and employees of all ethnicities whose lifework and livelihoods have been destroyed during the virus by Democrats' dictatorial shut-down orders; and American patriots betrayed by Democrats' contempt for America's constitutional order and shameless support for its foreign enemies—Islamic jihadists, China, and Iran.

"At what point then is the approach of danger to be expected? I answer: If it ever reach us, it must spring up amongst us. It cannot come from abroad. If destruction be our lot, we must ourselves be its author and finisher. As a nation of freemen, we must live through all time, or die by suicide."
—Abraham Lincoln, *Lyceum Address*

"We are not carrying out war against individuals. We are exterminating the bourgeoisie as a class. We are not looking for evidence or witnesses to reveal deeds or words against the Soviet power. The first question we ask is—to what class does he belong, what are his origins, upbringing, education or profession? These questions define the fate of the accused. This is the essence of the Red Terror."
—Cheka official during the time of Lenin

CONTENTS

PART ONE

FOUNDATIONS

1

White Male Christians

Americans are more divided today than at any time since the Civil War. So deep and intractable are the divisions that our most fundamental rights—to religious liberty, freedom of speech, and the presumption of innocence until proven guilty—are under relentless attack. We can no longer even agree on so basic a principle as the need for a legal immigration process to protect our sovereignty and civic culture. Even more ominously, we cannot count on the commitment of one of our major political parties to honor the results of a presidential election or adhere to the rules that prevent election fraud.

The two parties are now guided by outlooks so divergent that their supporters seem to inhabit alternative universes. For four years slander has been a weapon of first resort for the "Resistance" to President Trump—its goal his removal from office by any means available. This is a political agenda at odds with the core premise of our democratic system, which was designed by the Founders to promote compromise and mutual respect. The effect of the anti-Trump obsession and the strategy of obstruction has been to deepen conflicts and make them all but unresolvable.

Another casualty of the Democrats' "Resistance" has been patriotic loyalty, which is now suspect as loyalty to "white nationalism" and "white supremacy." The presentation of a common front to America's enemies and the idea that "politics stops at the water's edge," were once hallmarks of a loyal opposition. But they have been cast aside by Democrats bent on sabotaging Trump's presidency, regardless of the effects of their defection on America's national security.

In the course of the anti-Trump wars, we have become two nations with little shared ground on the core issues that previously defined us: Whether individuals should be judged on their merits, or on the basis of their skin color, gender, and sexual orientation. Whether "Resistance" to a duly elected government is compatible with a democratic society or a dagger aimed at its heart.

The source of these divisions is a reactionary ideology usually referred to as "Identity Politics," which has engulfed the Democrat Party and undermined its liberal instincts. It is an ideology that is racial and collectivist, that privileges groups over individuals and demonizes those who fall on the wrong side of its social equations. As a worldview, Identity Politics is fundamentally at odds with America's core principles of individual freedom, accountability, and equality, which have been the foundation of the nation's progress for more than two hundred years.

Identity Politics is often referred to as Political Correctness, but it is more accurately understood as Cultural Marxism—the idea that American society is characterized by oppressive hierarchies, and thus divided into warring races, genders, and classes. Political Correctness is a term that describes a left-wing party line. It was coined by the mass murderer Mao Zedong in the 1930s to keep his followers under the heel of the Chinese Communist Party. Adherents of the progressive party line today regard white Americans, males, Christians, and Jews as "oppressors"—enemies—and themselves as warriors for social justice.

The Communist Origins of Identity Politics

According to Wikipedia, the phrase "Identity Politics" first appeared in a 1978 manifesto written by self-described black feminist "revolutionaries," who were members of the "Combahee River Collective."[1] The manifesto proclaimed their unalterable hostility to the American system: "Black women's extremely negative relationship to the American political system (a system of white male rule) has always been determined by our membership in two oppressed racial and sexual castes. . . . [F]ocusing upon our own oppression is embodied in the concept of *identity politics*. We believe that the most profound and potentially most radical politics come directly out of our own identity. . . ."[2]

Citing their debt to lifelong Communist *apparatchik* Angela Davis, the Combahee radicals paid homage in their manifesto to the Marxist roots of their outlook and its anti-American agenda: "We realize that the liberation of all oppressed peoples necessitates the destruction of the political-economic systems of capitalism and imperialism as well as patriarchy."[3] In other words, Identity Politics originated as an anti-American, Marxist ideology dedicated to America's destruction.

Identity politics is a totalitarian ideology that depicts all aspects of human activity—down to the use of pronouns—as political, therefore requiring management and control. It erases individuals by assigning them to categories that ignore their particular circumstances, achievements, failures, and choices. Individuals are judged first and foremost on the basis of their race, gender, and sexual orientation. These categories take precedence over their individual origins, attitudes, and achievements.

Modern progressivism, which embraces Cultural Marxism, is a reactionary movement whose goal is to return to the status societies of the pre-capitalist era—when individuals were born into an unalterable hierarchy ranging from peasant to aristocrat. This was the situation that existed before the revolutions of the eighteenth century created liberal democracies with their concept of individual freedom and their opportunities for upward mobility facilitated by market capitalism.

Identity Politics is based on the false premise that America is a society in which people are consigned to castes that define their roles and stamp them for life. In reality, the opposite is true. America is the most upwardly mobile society in human history. All its citizens are afforded the right to climb the ladder of opportunity, and also to fall from its economic and social heights.[4]

Identity Politics is a collectivist ideology that is the antithesis of America's self-conception and aspiration since its Founding—the belief that individuals are created equal and are to be judged on their merits, not by their origin or other unalterable characteristics. Identity Politics ignores the dedication and sacrifices that millions of Americans of all races and genders have made to defend the principles of "created equal" and "born free." It also ignores the actual American achievement: the creation, through two centuries of struggle, of a nation that is today the most inclusive and tolerant, multi-ethnic, and multi-racial society in human history.

The Racist Premise of the Progressive Left

In one form or another, Identity Politics now forms the core conviction of America's political progressives and the Democrat Party. Its reactionary outlook was recently on display in an ABC News column by Matthew Dowd, a sometime Republican, current Democrat, and charter member of the Washington establishment. Dowd's column appeared—not coincidentally—two days after the conclusion of a ferocious party-line battle over the Supreme Court nomination of Justice Brett Kavanaugh, in which Identity Politics played an ugly and defining role (see chapter 5).

The headline of Dowd's column was a summation of its thesis: "Us White Male Christians Need to Step Back and Give Others Room to Lead."[5] In normal times, the transparent bigotry of this remark and the agenda being pushed in his column would have been sufficient to make American hairs stand on end. But bigotry on behalf of groups that are designated victims of oppression has become so ingrained in the politics of the Left, and so influential in the political culture at large, that Dowd's comment passed unnoticed. In Dowd's view, which is the view of leftists generally, what is wrong with America is that there are too many white males—white Christian males—occupying positions of power and influence and, allegedly, keeping diverse, "marginalized," and "under-served," minorities "in their place."

The very idea that blacks are "marginalized" is absurd. They are obviously front and center in America's culture and consciousness, as well as in the distribution of race-based privileges and benefactions. Recognizing these facts is not to deny that a significant minority segment of the black population is poor and lives at the social margins. But skin color can hardly be an explanation for their plight when the majority of black Americans are comfortably in the middle class and better off than the populations of any black-run society on earth.

The view that blacks still suffer systemic racist oppression in America—that in order to advance they need white elites "to step back"—is a fiction that provides an excuse for failure, while also imbuing social justice advocates with a false sense of moral superiority. The Matthew Dowds of the world assume the posture of soldiers against injustice, which leads them to condemn not only the American present but the American Founding and its framework of individual freedom.

Progressives dismiss the creation of America as the malicious work of slave-owning white Christian males. This is an incitement to dismantle the most successful project in creating a multi-racial, multi-ethnic society on record. It is also historically false. White Christian males were responsible for the first moral condemnation of slavery in world history. And the founding generation pioneered the abolition of slavery in the Western hemisphere and created a political framework that laid the groundwork for the integration of all Americans in a diverse polity with equal rights for all citizens regardless of creed or color. Unfortunately, the attack on these ideas and this legacy is now the core curriculum of America's schools and the reigning bias of its popular culture, thanks to the dominant presence of leftists in the nation's teaching professions, entertainment industry, tax-exempt advocacy culture, and media.

Even though America is an electoral democracy whose Constitution guarantees that the rights of any citizen are equal to the rights of any other, progressives believe—and believe passionately—that America is actually governed by racial and gender "hierarchies" that keep non-white, non-male citizens down. These hierarchies are said to oppress minorities and exclude them from rising by means of "glass ceilings" and other invisible barriers erected by a white male "patriarchy" to keep them "marginalized" and subordinate.

These claims are as factually baseless and politically destructive as the Marxist ideas that inspired them. Nothing could constitute a more direct assault on America's founding principles, which regard every citizen as unique, equal before the law, and accountable for himself. Is it actually the case that whites stand in the way of blacks and women? That white males need to step back to make room for others to solve the nation's problems? These are peculiar claims about a democracy in which women and minorities constitute a majority of the population and—thanks to the patriarchal Founders and subsequent male majorities—are constitutionally guaranteed rights identical to those of other citizens, whites and males included. They are even more peculiar coming on the heels of an eight-year presidency whose chief executive, Barack Obama, national security chief, Susan Rice, and chief law enforcement officers, Eric Holder and Loretta Lynch, along with thousands of elected officials at the national, state, and local levels, were all black Americans. Among the women and blacks who have administered America's foreign policy as secretaries of state in the last two decades are Colin Powell, Condoleezza Rice, Madeleine Albright, and Hillary Clinton.

As a measure of this achievement, consider that there is not a single majority black or brown or Asian nation in the world that has elected a white president, made a white person its chief law enforcement authority, or entrusted one with its national security and foreign policy.

To justify his hostility to white Christian males and America's founding principles, Matthew Dowd offered this sweeping, historically illiterate
statement: "In the great span of world history, nearly all change and
progress has come from an under-served and out-of-power group pushing,
prodding, and pounding on those who hold power to expand it to include
a wider and more diverse population." These are clichés of the Left, commonly deployed to energize its troops. However, few statements so brief
in nature can be said to contain so many obvious falsehoods. Factually
speaking, the opposite is nearer to the truth. In the great span of world
history, virtually all civilizational advances and social progress have been
the work of groups that were already socially powerful, and that shared,
ethnicity, religion, and gender with the ruling groups they overthrew.[6]

The forces of progress have generally not been what Dowd describes
as "under-served," or representatives of a more "diverse population." In
the West, unquestionably the greatest social progress of the last 250 years
has been the creation of liberal societies that support the principles of
individual liberty, equality, tolerance, and inclusion. The groundwork of
liberty was laid by documents like Magna Carta, which was the work
of a group that belonged to the same social stratum as the authority
whose power it curtailed: white, Christian, male, and aristocratic. The
general progress of liberty was advanced by England and America,
majority white Christian nations that led the world in abolishing the
3,000-year-old institution of slavery, which is still practiced in black and
Muslim Africa today.

This progress was made possible by principles and actions that
originally were entirely the work of white Christian males, who were
under no pressure from "diverse," "under-served," and out of power
groups to do what they did. There were no successful slave revolts in the
United States. Once slavery was abolished by white males, freed black
Americans spear-headed a Civil Rights Movement that eventually ended
segregation and institutional discrimination. But they did so in an indispensable alliance with white Americans, who put their lives on the line

and provided the financial and political support that made it possible to overthrow the Southern regime of segregation and Jim Crow.

The U.S. Constitution does not contain the words "white," "black," "male," or "female" precisely because the Founders believed they were creating a society in which equality would eventually prevail. It took nearly two hundred years, hundreds of thousands of lives, and the greatest social revolution in history to bring about the changes necessary to realize that dream. It is a grim irony, therefore, that for the last fifty years so-called progressives and the Democrat Party, which claims to represent "under-represented" and diverse communities, have been working to turn back this clock and reverse the gains of the Civil Rights Movement by introducing racial and gender categories and quotas into virtually every aspect of social life, from college admissions to job applications to positions on the United States Supreme Court.

It is this regressive attack on America's fundamental principles by the Left that is the source of the irreconcilable conflicts and ugly passions that are currently tearing the nation's fabric apart, and that is the subject of this book.

An Anti-American Creed

Karl Marx was intent on fomenting war between economic classes; Cultural Marxists have expanded the scope of his target to races, genders, and religious Christians.[1] Identity Politics, or Cultural Marxism, has been the core curriculum of American public and private schools for several generations now. To distance themselves from the Communist atrocities they made possible, and to absolve their ideas from responsibility for the catastrophic results, radicals have changed the name of their utopia to "social justice." But their political mission—civil war in pursuit of a totalitarian ambition to remake the world and dominate its inhabitants—remains the same.[2]

Every university ethnic- and gender-studies program created in the last sixty years is based on the discredited Marxist model of oppression—a model that portrays American democracy as a sham designed to obscure the reality of domination and control.[3] All these academic "studies" programs promote the belief that races and genders are not biologically grounded but "socially constructed" and thus open to revision and repair by revolutionary parties backed by the power of the state. All the ethnic- and gender-oriented academic fields frame their subjects as victims of oppression—with one exception, the field of "Whiteness Studies," which is devoted to the proposition that "whiteness" is evil and needs to be "abolished."[4]

The racist perspective of the Whiteness Studies field was summarized in these self-abasing terms by Jeff Hitchcock, executive director of the Center for the Study of White American Culture, at the Third National Conference on Whiteness held in 1998: "There is no crime that whiteness has not committed against people of color. There is no crime that we have not committed even against ourselves.... We must blame whiteness for the continuing patterns today that deny the rights of those outside of whiteness and which damage and pervert the humanity of those of us within it."[5]

This is obviously not a framework for scholarly inquiry, but a political diatribe that is both historically ignorant and bigoted. White people have created a civilization that abolished slavery, gave minority populations unprecedented opportunities, afforded women equal rights, and set standards of civil behavior that benefit all. Despite this, a pioneer publication of the academic movement of "whiteness studies," the magazine *Race Traitor*, edited by Harvard faculty who were also members of the Communist Party, featured this motto: "Treason to whiteness is loyalty to humanity."[6]

What began in the 1970s as a racist movement directed against whites by fringe leftists in the academy has now become a central organizing theme of the progressive left and the leadership of the Democrat Party. Today it is so powerful an ideology that it has spawned indictments of the president and his supporters, and of America itself, as "white supremacist," a perfectly ludicrous charge. What could be a more baseless slander when applied to the most inclusive and tolerant nation in the world, sixty years after the passage of the Civil Rights Acts, and in the wake of the election—and re-election—of a black president, whose margin of victory was secured by white majorities?[7]

An Oppression Curriculum

A sign of the "whiteness" movement's success has been the insertion of its anti-white, anti-male, anti-Christian bigotries into the curricula of the nation's K–12 schools both public and private. One of many left-wing organizations involved in this sinister effort is "Just Communities," which operates in thirteen states.[8] The following chart is taken from a K–12 curriculum provided by Just Communities, called "Forms of Oppression."[9] This curriculum was authorized and underwritten with a budget of $1 million by the Democrat-run Santa Barbara, California, school district.

There are many similar curricula and teacher resources for K–12 students available at internet sites such as the Orwellian "Tolerance.org." These sites promulgate racist stereotypes about so-called white oppressors, emphasizing the "invisibility" of white racism and privilege, while describing it—absurdly and without evidence—as "systemic."[10]

Forms of Oppression	Privileged Oppressor Group	Target/Victim Group
Sexism	Men	Women
Racism	White People	People of Color
Heterosexism	Heterosexual People	LGBTQ People
Classism	Wealthy People	Working Class & Poor
Religious Oppression	Christian People	All Others

"Forms of Oppression." *Just Communities*

This slanderous list imposed on schoolchildren is designed to incite feelings of envy, resentment, and outright hatred towards the targeted "oppressor" groups, regardless of what the individuals who compose them think or actually do in their lives. It is the antithesis of the principles enshrined in America's Declaration of Independence and Constitution. But that is the totalitarian point of blaming alleged "structures of oppression" for individual behaviors rather than judging the individual behaviors themselves. The focus is always on the imaginary "structures," and away from the specific acts of individuals, who are effectively erased. It is a Morality Play in which people are damned by their race, gender, religion, and economic status before they have committed a single act.

It is also a vision in which the social order is a zero-sum game, where the deficits of individuals belonging to one social group are alleged—without evidence—to be caused by the successes of another. This is a destructive lie designed to create envy, resentment, and hatred towards individual members of the target groups—for example, Christian males like Bill Gates, whose immense wealth is actually made possible only by Gates's successful efforts that created jobs and wealth for millions of others on a global scale.

A leading academic figure in formulating the Left's oppression perspective and inciting hatred of racial and gender groups was the late University of Chicago feminist professor Iris Marion Young. Her seminal book, *Five Faces of Oppression*, is based on the collectivist idea that concepts of justice should not be applied to individual actions and deserts. According to Young, membership in a social *group* is the primary factor in establishing what is just and what is not. This membership is essential to addressing "structural inequalities," because social rules and institutions allegedly "constrain" individuals as a group. This is collectivism run wild; it is an unreconstructed Marxism refuted by the millions of individuals who rise every day out of circumstances that might be expected to constrain and disadvantage them, and succeed.

The Cultural Marxism pervasive in America's K–12 schools teaches students to view their social environment as a world divided between black and white, good and evil, oppressed and oppressor. It is a totalitarian vision that actively suppresses such vital bourgeois principles as individual responsibility, accountability, and freedom.

Although the curriculum cited above has been simplified by its creators for teenagers, it is an accurate guide to the attitudes of progressives at all levels of authority, achievement, and sophistication. Its crass bigotry, simple-minded ideas, and general lack of touch with reality can be gauged by its description of Christians as the sole religious oppressors of all other religions, who are described as their "victims." The victim groups evidently include Muslims who have recently slaughtered over half a million Christians and Yazidis and other non-Muslims solely for the crime of having different religious beliefs. And atheists who, acting as Communists and Nazis, murdered millions for their ethnicity and religious faith.

In the eyes of the progressive Left, Christians are responsible for white civilization with all its alleged iniquities bared and its miraculous achievements hidden. Remove the metaphysics of "oppression" from this equation and what is left but a curriculum of hate that justifies aggression towards groups guilty by virtue of their skin color, class, gender, and religion?

The victim category "people of color" used by adherents of the oppression creed is itself a racist term designed to demonize its targets, specifically whites, who are the only people in the world who are not "of color," and therefore not victims but oppressors. The term and its usage are not grammatical English but of French provenance, indicating their wholly ideological nature. "People of color" is designed not only to demonize white people but to excuse those "people of color" who are imperialists and dictators, run the most oppressive social systems in the world, and have historically enslaved more black Africans, for example, than have white Europeans. And still do.

The term "people of color" defines no real-world group with common interests. The principal enslavers of black Africans, over more than a thousand years, were other black Africans and brown Arabs. Black Hutus in Rwanda recently massacred a million black Tutsis. Mexicans are descended from Spanish conquistadors but also from the indigenous Indians they oppressed and slaughtered. In the framework of Identity Politics, however, both groups are "people of color," therefore by definition oppressed (by whites). If the term "people of color" isn't racist, what is?

Identity Politics is not only racist but totalitarian. It encompasses and defines the totality of individuals and their life paths, while erasing their biographies and their individual wills, character traits, and actual deeds, submerging them into group identities. This deprives people of human agency. In the progressive view, the destinies of the oppressed are determined by others beyond their influence and control. Similarly, the guilt of the oppressors lies first of all in their genes, not their ideas, choices, and actions.

The oppression curriculum explicitly states that white people are racists because they are white. An abstraction called "whiteness" causes them to collude in an alleged global system of privilege and oppression. According to the oppression curriculum, they collude by "working together to make it happen," "intentionally or unintentionally," "consciously or unconsciously," "by action, inaction, or silence." In other words, being racist oppressors is their unalterable *status*. In the hands of ideologues, "white privilege" is one's essence regardless of what one actually does—or suffers. Nothing that one achieves is the result of one's actions or talents but is the unearned fruit of being white.

According to the oppression curriculum, "white people privilege" is "unearned access to the resources that enhance one's chances of getting what one needs to influence others in order to lead a safe, productive, fulfilling life."[11] You might try telling this to all the white people who lost the opportunity to attend elite universities, qualify for scholarships, or secure jobs and promotions because of affirmative action programs that discriminate against them on the basis of race.

The Dangerous Fiction of White Skin Privilege

"Forms of Oppression" is a reliable guide to the basic architecture of Identity Politics and its racist agendas. Under its aegis, individuals disappear, along with their achievements, abuses, failings, prejudices, attitudes, and actions. Both oppressors and oppressed are viewed as passive objects of racial and gender powers—influences beyond their control. All the dimensions of human intentions, actions, and interactions are flattened into crude and narrow categories, whose moral implications are predetermined. And the bottom line is that white people are condemned for imaginary sins, while "people of color" are exonerated for presumed victimizations.

The informational website Wikipedia, which reflects commonly held opinions and prejudices, defines white privilege this way: "White privilege (or white skin privilege) is the societal privilege that benefits people whom society identifies as white." It then explains "societal privilege" this way: "In anthropology, privilege is a special right, advantage, or immunity granted or available only to a particular person or group."[12]

But the inconvenient fact is that for nearly sixty years it has been illegal in America for any social institution or authority to grant special rights or advantages or immunity to any particular person or group based on skin color—unless one is black or brown or the member of a "victim" group specifically designated to receive affirmative action benefits (a clear violation of the Fourteenth Amendment).

In short, "white privilege" is a fiction convenient to the Left, whose real agenda is to demonize white people and remove from all others responsibility for what they do or fail to accomplish in life. "White privilege" is not an analytic category; it is a weapon designed to cripple and destroy white people who get in the way of the leftist agenda.

The website Tolerance.org is a resource for K–12 teachers put together by the Southern Poverty Law Center, a notorious left-wing smear site and blacklist organization (see chapter 7). An article on the website titled "What Is White Privilege Really?" explains the invisible powers of white privilege this way: "It seems logical that a person should have the chance to prove themselves individually before they are judged. It's supposedly an American ideal. But it's a privilege often not granted to people of color—with dire consequences. For example, programs like

New York City's now-abandoned 'Stop and Frisk' policy target a disproportionate number of Black and Latinx [sic] people."[13] The suggestion
that black and Hispanic people are targeted for their skin color is false.
The policy would have been illegal if it were true.

"Stop and Frisk" was originally a New York law enforcement practice designed to make random checks for illegal concealed weapons, and
thus to prevent potential robberies and worse. It was instituted by conservative Republicans and subsequently cancelled by left-wing Democrats
who claimed it was "racist." To make "Stop and Frisk" a racial issue,
opponents of the policy such as Tolerance.org suppress the details of its
rationale, and in particular the profiles of the individuals it was designed
to target. In all their analyses, Identity Politics ideologues are careful to
eliminate the individual details, including the motivations for policies
and their specific applications. The purpose of this is to bring into focus
the racial Morality Play of the Left: black, victimized and good; white,
privileged and bad.

The racial categories obscure from view all the actions of individuals
that might account for the disproportionate number of blacks and Hispanics affected by "Stop and Frisk." For example, 97 percent of the
homicides in New York are committed by blacks and Hispanics.[14] While
blacks constitute only 23 percent of the population, they commit 70
percent of the armed robberies. By contrast, whites commit only 4 percent of robberies.[15] In other words, the "Stop and Frisk" policies that
"disproportionately" discover concealed and illegal weapons among
blacks and Hispanics have an explanation that is behavioral, not racial.

So-called white privilege is a reflection of the fact that whites are
only 3 percent of the homicide problem and 4 percent of the robbery
problem. Therefore, law enforcement officials are sensibly less interested
in them. The privilege is not a privilege. It's earned. On the other hand,
87.5 percent of the homicide victims of blacks and Hispanics are other
blacks and Hispanics.[16] Taking into account all these statistics, the now
abandoned "Stop and Frisk" policy is realistically seen as a privilege for
the black and Hispanic citizens who are the potential targets of lethal

criminal behavior and were therefore favored for protection. From the vantage of the black and Hispanic victims of criminals carrying illegal weapons, the *elimination* of "Stop and Frisk" is actually racist.

Of course, it is quite possible that the procedures were unjustly applied and that some people who were stopped did not fit the profile of suspects whom police were supposed to search. And perhaps the practice was so intrusive that it was not worth the gains. But this still would not be a case of white-inflicted injustice—let alone "oppression"—since the majority of New York City's police officers are black, Hispanic, and Asian minorities, and the rationale for the law had nothing to do with racism. The effect of the Identity Politics creed is to remove all the complexities of the real world in favor of a policy that meets ideological criteria to satisfy progressive hostility to whites. It is proposed as a measure to protect minorities but actually results in adverse consequences for the minority victims of inner-city crime.

The Myth of Systemic Racism

Most arguments offered by proponents of the "white skin privilege" doctrine depend on attributing all disparities between races to "systemic racism" rather than the habits, attitudes, and actions of individuals. For example, the Tolerance.org article tells us that "the ability to accumulate wealth has long been a white privilege—a privilege created by overt, systemic racism in both the public and private sectors." Typically, Tolerance.org doesn't actually identify any overt racist policies or acts (which are illegal under American laws). Nor does it examine any of the individual behaviors that lead to wealth accumulation. Its premise that the ability to accumulate wealth is a white privilege would be news to Oprah Winfrey, daughter of a sharecropper, raised in segregated Mississippi, whose net worth is $2.9 billion or to billionaire basketball player and TV host Shaquille O'Neal; billionaire icon Michael Jordan; centimillionaire LeBron James; hip-hop mogul, clothing magnate, and outsized celebrity Sean "P. Diddy" Combs; mega-millionaire entrepreneurs Tyler

Perry, Robert Johnson, and Kanye West—or any of the many other blacks who have managed to accumulate tens and hundreds of millions of dollars in a single lifetime.

"Inherited wealth" is often invoked as an insuperable advantage—a privilege that allegedly whites alone can take advantage of. But 80 percent of all millionaires are first generation millionaires.[17] In other words, they earned their good fortunes. On the other hand, 70 percent of black children are born out of wedlock—a nearly insuperable *dis*advantage— thanks to a policy of the welfare system inflicted on America's poor by Democrats, which cuts off welfare benefits for homes where a father is present. All other factors being equal, including race, a child raised in a single-mother household is four to five times more likely to be poor than a child raised in a household with two parents.[18] Factors such as father-lessness are generally excluded from the "studies" that claim the wealth gap is intractable. Attempts to introduce such uncomfortable facts are summarily dismissed by advocates of the "systemic racism" myth as "blaming the victim."

The advice offered to teachers on the Tolerance.org site is to encourage whites, who are said to be unconscious of their racism, to have compassion for the black people they "unwittingly" victimize. Racism, according to the self-proclaimed "anti-racists," is unconscious and invisible. Otherwise, of course, it would be prosecutable under America's existing laws. Because there are only a minimal number of such prosecutions, ideologues are forced to rely on the preposterous claim that white racism is pervasive but unintentional—simply a product of being white. It is part of the alleged "structural oppression" that afflicts everyone who is non-white.

According to the white privilege ideologues, "blacks can't be racist." The actual rationale for this absurdity is that recognizing black racism— which is the central creed, for example, of the Nation of Islam—is too embarrassing to their claims. The formal argument they propose—that "blacks have no power"—is so ridiculous they don't even bother to present a case for it. Since it's directed against whites, merely asserting the claim is sufficient.

Because the allegedly "systemic" problem of racism cannot be attributed to overt racists and is thus invisible, it has to be explained to people by a multi-billion-dollar industry of "diversity experts," whose arguments are as elaborate as they are malicious—focusing on collectivities like "people of color" while ignoring the individuals within the collectivities. If blacks as a racial group earn less than whites, that must be the result of racism. But if the majority of blacks have actually been able to enter the middle class, what accounts for the failure of inner-city blacks to do the same? If this disparity were mainly or exclusively a matter of race, how to explain the successes of the black majority? More likely it is individual bad choices, including absent fathers through multiple generations, off-the-charts crime rates and drug abuse that have shaped the circumstances of those still trapped in poverty. If white racism and white privilege are the answers, how is it that Asian Americans from India and Japan are richer ethnic groups than whites?[19]

The effect of a Cultural Marxist outlook is to create guilt on the white side of the scale and grievance on the black side, leading to emotions that can be corrupting for both. The alleged oppressors are burdened with a guilt that may be unconnected to anything they have actually done, but can do serious damage to their judgments nonetheless. It can, for example, encourage the abandonment of merit standards because they are alleged instruments of "structural racism," while promoting tolerance for behaviors that are destructive to the very individuals they may be seeking to help.

Nobody argues such drivel where athletes are concerned because it is obviously ridiculous. But the success of the war against standards in institutions of learning has had a devastating effect on the minorities it is alleged to protect.

On the "victim" side, the idea that there is a system of racial privilege that is rigged against them encourages feelings of resentment, fatalism, and entitlement that can prevent individuals from taking responsibility for their behaviors and actions, stripping them of the power to change and succeed.

Radical Abuses of Race

These problems are compounded by the fact that Cultural Marxists in the university have been working for decades to persuade Americans that an elaborate structure of "intersectional" oppression organizes society into a series of overlapping hierarchies that only a "social justice" revolution can correct.

Intersectionality Theory was the brainchild of a radical leftist, Kimberlé Crenshaw, a disciple of the founder of "Critical Race Theory," Harvard professor Derrick Bell. Critical Race Theory is a radical legal framework that maintains that because the structure and history of America are allegedly founded on racism and oppression, the nation's laws and legal institutions are necessarily unjust, invalid, and undeserving of non-white minorities' respect."[20] This presumably includes the Thirteenth Amendment freeing the slaves, as well as the Fourteenth Amendment and the Civil Rights Acts, which guaranteed equal rights to all citizens regardless of color.

Not surprisingly, Bell was an acolyte of Louis Farrakhan, America's most notorious racist and anti-Semite. Bell has described Farrakhan as "smart and super articulate" and "perhaps the best living example of a black man ready, willing and able to 'tell it like it is' regarding who is responsible for racism in this country." Among Farrakhan's telling-it-like-it-is statements, is this: "I wonder, will you recognize Satan. I wonder if you will see the satanic Jew and the Synagogue of Satan . . . because Satan has deceived the whole world."[21] In a 1992 interview, Bell elaborated: "I see Louis Farrakhan as a great hero for the people."[22] The kitsch analyses and conclusions of Critical Race Theory and its offshoot "Intersectionality" faithfully reflect the virulent racism of its creator.

An entire academic industry in Gender Studies, Black Studies, Ethnic Studies, Gay Studies, Critical Race Studies, Post-Colonial Studies, and similar politically conceived fields is devoted to elaborating Bell's hateful views, organized by the theory of "Intersectionality." This is the claim that multiple "interlocking" oppressions are inflicted on multiple victim groups by a "matrix of domination." The matrix is a *fata morgana*, an ideological fiction concocted out of the familiar group of alleged "oppressors"—white Christian heterosexual males.

Using the Intersectionality model, the specifics of what actually constitutes oppression become ever more remote, and the reality ever more distant and obscure. The sheer piling up of alleged racial and gender injustices—abstract, unconsciously committed, invisible, and dependent on disparities that have multiple non-racial or gender causes—becomes the demonic fiction that provides its adherents with a convenient weapon to indict and/or destroy anyone who deviates from opinions and behaviors that are "politically correct."

According to Professor Jonathan Haidt, in the framework of Intersectionality Theory, "America is said to be one giant matrix of oppression, and its victims cannot fight their battles separately. They must all come together to fight their common enemy, the group that sits at the top of the pyramid of oppression: the straight, white, cis-gendered, able-bodied Christian or Jewish . . . male. This is why a perceived slight against one victim group calls forth protest from all victim groups. This is why so many campus groups now align against Israel."[23] It is why advocates for women's "liberation" and gay rights support Islamic terrorists, misogynists, gay-bashers, and Jew-haters in Gaza and the West Bank, who actually oppress women and regard homosexuality as a crime punishable by death.[24]

The intellectual incoherence of Intersectionality Theory, and its undefended and indefensible premise that there are groups in America that are actually oppressed, haven't been obstacles to creating a national academic industry; or to providing an anti-liberal ideology for the Democrat Party; or to gaining government support for its unwarranted, racist agenda. As of 2018 the National Science Foundation had supported 101 programs devoted to combatting Intersectional oppression in the sciences (!) at a cost of $62.5 million. The programs were designed to identify alleged "systems of discrimination and disadvantage" against women in the STEM fields (Science, Technology, Engineering, and Mathematics) and offer assistance in combatting them.[25] Of course the willingness of the oppressor caste to provide hundreds of millions of dollars annually to helping and advancing these individuals produces no second thoughts for the Intersectionalists about their paranoid fantasies of sexual hierarchies and oppressions.

A One-Party Culture

That real-world facts are no obstacle to advancing these ideological slanders was demonstrated in July 2017, when a Google engineer named James Damore wrote an internal memo addressing the assumptions behind such programs, specifically the claim that women were blocked from entering STEM fields because of patriarchal oppression. His memo, which he called "Google's Ideological Echo Chamber," examined the many factors besides possible anti-female bias that might lie behind the lower number of women programmers.[26] These included biological factors leading to psychological differences between men and women that might influence the latter's choice of fields to enter.

Studies show, for example, that women are generally more interested in people, while men are more interested in things, which could account for some of the difference. Moreover, the generous incentives provided by Google, the National Science Foundation, and universities to lure women into engineering, along with the general left-wing attitudes of Google employees as revealed in their subsequent attacks on Damore, provide strong evidence that choice rather than gender discrimination is the decisive factor in determining women's presence—or lack thereof—in STEM fields.

Google's response to Damore's internal memo was to fire him for promoting "gender stereotypes"—an indication of how Cultural Marxist myths and authoritarian practices now dominate the tech giant's company culture.[27] But a scientific study published in February 2018 served to vindicate Damore's conclusion.[28] The study was called "The Gender-Equality Paradox in Science, Technology, Engineering, and Mathematics Education." It was based on research in sixty-seven countries and found that men and women had roughly equal capabilities in STEM fields. The "paradox" referred to the fact that in more gender-*equal* countries *fewer* women entered STEM fields, while in countries where there was more pronounced gender *in*equality *more* women pursued STEM careers.

The researchers' conclusion—supplemented by additional surveys and studies—was that economic conditions in countries where there was pronounced gender inequality tended to be much worse, so that women had an incentive to choose higher-paying STEM careers, whereas in the richer countries, which had more gender equality, women had greater options and therefore gravitated towards fields that were more attractive to them. In other words, just as Damore had concluded, *choice*—inadmissible to the oppression commissars—was the decisive factor in determining their career paths and the reason that, despite massive efforts to encourage women to pursue STEM fields, they resisted the option.

The abuse heaped on Damore by Google executives and employees, who called him "sexist" and "anti-diversity," merely confirmed his observation that the Google community was an ideological monolith, incapable of discussing real issues or examining dissenting views. Google's hostility towards Damore was only the tip of an iceberg of hate inspired by Intersectionality Theory, and directed towards individuals said to make up the "matrix of domination," which, according to the Intersectionality theorists, is composed of a "patriarchy" and "white supremacists."

Google's own dictionary defines "white supremacy" as "the belief that white people constitute a superior race and should therefore dominate society, typically to the exclusion or detriment of other racial and ethnic groups, in particular black or Jewish people."[29] Wikipedia concurs: "*White supremacy* or white supremacism is the racist belief that white people are superior to people of other races and therefore should be dominant over them."[30]

At its height, roughly a hundred years ago, the Ku Klux Klan openly embraced these views which defined its mission. At that time the U.S. population was 106 million and the Klan had 4 million members, including eleven U.S. senators and over seventy-five members of the House of

Representatives who received Klan assistance in winning their seats.[31] Currently, the Klan is estimated to have 3,000 members in a country of 330 million, and there is not a single elected official or prominent public figure who belongs to it.[32] The Ku Klux Klan remnants, and the "white nationalist" followers of racists like Richard Spencer, are an insignificant fringe who cannot hold a demonstration where they are not outnumbered a hundred-fold by those who show up to protest their presence. They are, moreover, shunned throughout the nation, including by conservatives.

Yet the term "white supremacist," without any visible anchor in reality, is thrown around wildly by Democrat politicians and so-called progressives, for whom it is simply a means of demonizing, demeaning, and delegitimizing political opponents. When White House strategist Steve Bannon was given a permanent seat on the National Security Council, the Democrats' House Minority Leader, Nancy Pelosi, went on the attack with racial slanders. "It's a stunning thing, that a white supremacist would be a permanent member of the National Security Council," she said, adding that the move was "making America less safe."[33] Pelosi did not provide a shred of evidence for any of her slanderous claims—that Bannon is a racist, or a "white supremacist," or that he was endangering America—because none exists. But none of the Democrats attempted to distance themselves from Pelosi's slanders. On the contrary, her gutter attack was seconded by other Democrats and by a leftist media equally unconcerned with real-world facts, and Bannon's appointment was eventually withdrawn.

Cultural Marxism is not just a weapon in the arsenal of Nancy Pelosi but a core doctrine of the Democrat Party, guiding both its policies and its tactics. Its 2016 platform vowed "a societal transformation" (that is, a revolution) that will "end institutional and systemic racism in our society." Its 2020 platform was even more radical. Yet institutional racism as a systemic American problem is mostly a political fiction. Institutional racism was outlawed more than half a century ago with the passage of the Civil Rights Acts. Any incidence of such racism today is actionable in the courts, including the leftist appeals courts that have thrown out multiple Trump executive orders on ideological rather than constitutional grounds. If institutional racism were a serious problem, the courts would be jammed with lawsuits to correct the injustice. But they are not, because the charges of institutional and systemic racism are baseless left-wing slanders.

There are two exceptions: the euphemistically named "affirmative action" race preference programs, and the inner city public schools that year in and year out fail to keep 40 percent of their students from dropping out, and 40 percent of whose graduates are functionally illiterate. These are glaring examples of systemic racism that won't be addressed because of the support of the Democrat Party and its teachers' unions, and because until Trump came along Republicans turned a blind eye towards these social atrocities.

With these exceptions, "systemic racism" and "institutional racism" are anti-American myths spread by oppression-model dogmatists. Ever since the ascendance of Bernie Sanders, the platforms of the Democrat Party have been shaped by these myths. Thus the 2016 platform regards social and economic disparities as *prima facie* evidence of racial or gender oppression and attributes such disparities not to individual decisions, capabilities, and performances, but to unidentified "policies" which, if they actually existed, would be illegal.[34] Consider this plank:

> *Closing the Racial Wealth Gap*
> America's economic inequality problem is even more pronounced when it comes to racial and ethnic disparities in wealth and income. It is unacceptable that the median wealth for African Americans and Latino Americans is roughly one-tenth that of white Americans. These disparities are also stark for American Indians and certain Asian American subgroups, and may become even more significant when considering other characteristics such as age, disability status, sexual orientation, or gender identity [i.e., intersectionality categories—D. H.].[35]

The platform goes on to explain: "The racial wealth and income gaps are the result of policies that discriminate against people of color and constrain their ability to earn income and build assets to the same extent as other Americans." In fact, there are no such policies. To repeat: if such policies existed, they would be illegal under the 14th Amendment, the Civil Rights Act of 1964, and many, many other laws enacted since then. The income disparities are actually explained by the facts of individuals' lives, for example the presence (or absence) of two-parent families, the degree of education, the presence of substance abuse, or whether (in the case of Hispanic Americans) English is spoken in the home.

More generally, the ability to accumulate wealth is determined in large part by genes and by cultural attitudes that guide the choices families and individuals make. Otherwise Indian and Japanese Americans, who are "people of color," would not be America's richest (and therefore most "privileged") economic groups. By taking away the agency of individuals to determine the outcome of their lives, the Democrat platform turns people into puppets of social forces beyond their control, victims of "oppressors" who must wait to be liberated by "social justice warriors" and ultimately government *diktat*. It is a malevolent vision that has been tested on a billion people under Communist regimes with catastrophic results.[36]

3

A Racist Culture

Since the election of Barack Obama as America's first black president, racist doctrines—including the preposterous claim that America is a "white supremacist" country—have become the currency of progressive politics. This irony, as poignant as it is disturbing, is highlighted by the pampered career of Ta-Nehisi Coates, an African American racist whose bilious tract *Between the World and Me* won the National Book Award in 2015 and established the author as the cultural elite's authority on the subject. Five years after its publication, Coates's book is still high up on the *New York Times* bestseller lists, and Netflix has made a feature film based on its malicious and mendacious claims.

On the subject of race relations in America, Coates comes to this conclusion: "White supremacy was so foundational to this country that it would not be defeated in my lifetime, my child's lifetime, or perhaps ever."[1] In Coates's view, it is as if the Ku Klux Klan had actually won the political and cultural wars that consigned them as white supremacists to the dustbin of history.

Nor is this arraignment of white Americans, and what Coates regards as *their* country, an idiosyncratic lapse. His hatred of whites and

America is expressed throughout his pronouncements and writings: "I view white supremacy as one of the central organizing forces in American life, whose vestiges and practices afflicted black people in the past, continue to afflict black people today, and will likely afflict black people until this country passes into the dust."[2]

A Celebrated Black Racist

Ta-Nehisi Coates is the son of a former member of the Black Panther Party, a violent political gang of the 1960s, which made the chant "Off the Pigs!" (death to the police) famous and made good on that threat on several occasions.[3] The Panthers were responsible for the murders of several law enforcement officers, members of their own party, and more than a dozen ordinary citizens—all but one of them black.[4] Coates, himself a beneficiary of racial preferences, is the only member of his family who failed to earn a college degree, but because of his leftist views (and no doubt his race), he was made a *New York Times* op-ed columnist, a visiting lecturer at MIT, an editor of *The Atlantic*, and the recipient of a $625,000 MacArthur Foundation "genius award." So much for the marginalization of black people in America.

Following the National Book Award Coates received for *Between the World and Me*, he became America's most celebrated black author, in fact the most celebrated author of any ethnicity or race. In the words of George Packer, another National Book Award–winner, "Coates has become the most influential writer in America today; [his] latest *Atlantic* essay is already being taught in college courses."[5]

When Coates was appointed an editor of *The Atlantic*, one of America's oldest and most respected liberal journals, he reacted this way: "I knew by then that I was not writing and reporting from some corner of American society, but from the very heart of it, *from the plunder that was essential to it*, and the culture that animated it" [emphasis added].[6] In other words, according to Coates, America, which has showered him with privileges about which most other people—white or black—can only dream, is not only a racist enterprise; it is a criminal one. As Coates puts it in *Between the World and Me*, "'White America' is a syndicate, arrayed to protect its exclusive power to dominate and control our bodies. The power of domination and exclusion is central to the belief in being white, and without it 'white people' would cease to exist for want of reasons."[7] Coates and his "liberal" sponsors should be ashamed of promoting crackpot views and racist poison like this.

Instead, Coates's ravings have not only won him the National Book Award but allowed him to make the finals for the Pulitzer Prize and the National Book Critics Award. *Between the World and Me* was listed as one of the "finest books of the year" by the *New York Times Book Review*, *O: The Oprah Magazine*, the *Washington Post*, *People*, *Entertainment Weekly*, *Vogue*, the *Los Angeles Times*, the *San Francisco Chronicle*, the *Chicago Tribune*, *New York Newsday*, and *Publishers Weekly*.[8] *Publishers Weekly* described the book as "compelling . . . indeed stunning, rare in its power to make you want to slow down and read every word. This is a book that will be hailed as a classic of our time."[9] *New York Times* columnist David Brooks, whom one would expect to know better, called it "a great and searing . . . mind-altering account of the black male experience." In *Vogue*, Megan O'Grady exclaimed that "Coates has penned a new classic of our time," a book that is "urgent, lyrical, and devastating in its precision."[10] In other words, if you're black and hate white America, you can count on the elite culture to provide you with rich rewards.

There were dissenters. Columbia University professor John McWhorter, the noted black linguist, was willing to identify *Between the World and Me* as the noxious claptrap it obviously was. "My issue with the Coates phenomenon," McWhorter wrote, "is that I find it racist." White critics, he observed, "are letting pass as genius something they never would if it was not a black person doing it."[11] In response to which, Tucker Carlson wryly observed, "This is a deep point. . . . Why would a racist nation try to pretend that *Between the World and Me* is a smart book?"[12] It was a good question. The praise for the book was a reflection of the anti-white attitudes that now pervade progressive communities, which patronize black racists like Coates as if blacks can't be expected to observe the same standards and decencies they expect of whites.

Coates's prominence as a public intellectual and the extraordinary respect he receives from the political Left and so-called liberals, including an invitation to the Obama White House, are the only reasons that his anti-white racism and virulent hatred for America are noteworthy, or that anyone should pay any attention to him at all.

One explanation for Coates's sudden and extraordinary celebrity is that his racist attacks, not only on whites but also on law enforcement, resonated with outrage on the Left over a series of police shootings that occurred around the time of his book's publication. These shootings in Ferguson, Baltimore, and other urban centers became the focus of national protests promoting extreme claims that would be key themes of Coates's book.

A central event in *Between the World and Me* is the police shooting of Coates's friend, Prince Jones, who was killed by a Montgomery County officer who claimed that Jones, who was black, had attempted to run him over with his car when the officer was trying to arrest him for dealing drugs. On the surface, it seemed like a classic case of what leftists across the nation were portraying as a genocidal war against innocent and unarmed blacks. There is no such genocidal war.[13] But Coates's explanation of the shooting of Prince Jones was a more extreme example of cognitive dissonance than even this unjustified claim.

"Here is what I knew at the outset," writes Coates. "The officer who killed Prince Jones was black. The politicians who empowered this officer to kill were black. Many of the black politicians, many of them twice as good, seemed unconcerned. How could this be?"[14] In other words, given the presence of black law enforcement officials at the center of this case, how could it be made to fit the Intersectionality framework of black oppression, let alone the Left's indictment of police for allegedly conducting a race war against blacks? How could Coates justify his hatred for the country that had integrated blacks into its society at all levels and bestowed on Coates himself such privileges and rewards?

Brace yourself for the answer. Coates understands that many of the black "victims" of police shootings have criminal records, or like his friend were dealing drugs and resisting arrest. He understands that "black on black" homicides claim many more black victims than police shootings. So he knew that only an outrageous twisting of the facts could justify his malice. His bigoted hatred of white America turned out to be up to the job.

To answer the question as to how black criminality as judged and combatted by black law enforcement could still produce black innocence and white guilt, Coates dismisses the notion that "black crime" is the responsibility of blacks at all, or that it even exists. According to Coates, it is white supremacists who are responsible for black crime. White supremacists pull the strings behind the scenes and manipulate black puppets into committing criminal acts.

According to Coates,

> "black-on-black crime" is jargon, violence to language, which vanishes the men who engineered the covenants, who fixed the loans, who planned the projects, who built the streets and sold red ink by the barrel. And this should not surprise us. The plunder of black life was drilled into this country in its infancy and reinforced across its history, so that plunder has become an heirloom, an intelligence, a sentience, a default setting to which, likely to the end of our days, we must invariably return. . . . The killing fields of Chicago, of Baltimore, of Detroit, were created by the policy of Dreamers [Coates' name for white believers in the American Dream], but their weight, their shame, rests solely upon those who are dying in them.[15]

These ravings are a psychotic fantasy. By blaming whites for every suffering and every deficiency in the black community, even criminal acts, while ignoring the fact that most blacks don't inhabit inner cities, don't commit crimes, and long ago joined the middle class, Coates proposes to answer the question of how it is possible that a black cop killed his criminal friend: "The Dream of acting white, of talking white, of being white, murdered Prince Jones as sure as it murders black people in Chicago with frightening regularity."[16] In other words, whites are racist plunderers and murderers, and the black officer was "thinking white" when he committed what Coates describes as a racist execution of his friend. Whites are responsible for every so-called "black on black crime." Even though the cop who pulled the trigger was black, his aspiration was to be a good cop, therefore white. This is the twisted logic by which whites are supposed to have murdered his friend.

It would be hard to imagine a sicker racist view than this (although Coates provides many worthy challengers in the course of his writing). In fact, it is hard to imagine how even the ravings of an actual white supremacist could be more demented. And yet Coates is an intellectual icon of the progressive elites at *The Atlantic,* the *New Yorker* and the *New York Times,* once estimable journalistic enterprises that have turned themselves into platforms for racial sewage like this. A recipient of the nation's highest book award and privileges and honors unparalleled among his peers, Coates is a veritable emblem of America's current racial dementia, which is a contagion spawned by the political Left.

Reparations, or Racial Extortion

Coates's first attention-grabbing success was a 2014 cover story for *The Atlantic* called "The Case for Reparations [for Slavery]."[17] A review of the article in the *Washington Post*, described its impact as achieving for Coates "a place of prominence in the stream of American thought, a perch that positions him as an ascendant public intellectual with a voice that stands out in the white noise of a wired and word-flooded era. . . ."[18]

In fact, in his usual tendentious way, Coates was reviving an idea that had been first raised in the 1960s by James Forman and was rejected by all three major civil rights organizations at the time. Black leaders viewed the demand for reparations as divisive and misguided. The slavery power had been defeated by the very government the activists were holding responsible; there were no former slaves still living to receive the reparations. Moreover, the payments would have to be provided by non-black Americans of many colors and ethnicities who had never been slave owners or involved in any way in the slave system. Eighty percent of all Americans, in fact, were descended from immigrants who reached America's shores after the abolition of slavery, while many others were descended from white Americans who had laid down their lives to free the slaves.

Discarded in the sixties for lack of support from the mainstream black community, the reparations claim was revived again by the Left just before the attacks of 9/11. The manifesto of the new reparations movement was a bestselling book written by Randall Robinson called *The Debt: What America Owes to Blacks*. It was informed by the same corrosive racial hatreds that inspired Coates's work. Not surprisingly, when his book was completed, Robinson repudiated his American citizenship and left the country for Jamaica—a move he soon regretted.

The Debt begins with the following declaration: "This book is about the great still-unfolding massive crime of official and unofficial America against Africa, African slaves, and their descendants in America."[19] Robinson explains: "The enslavement of blacks in America lasted 246 years. It was followed by a century of legal racial segregation and discrimination. The two periods, taken together, constitute the longest running crime against humanity in the world over the last 500 years. . . ."[20] No wonder that—according to prominent professor, television personality, and left-wing ideologue, Michael Eric Dyson—"[Americans] can't talk about slavery because it indicts the American soul."[21]

If true, Robinson's statements would make American slavery a more heinous crime than the Nazi atrocities, the Armenian genocide, or the thousand years of black slavery in Africa that took place before a white man ever set foot on the continent. But Robinson's history and statistics are false. North America accounted for less than 1 percent of the global slave trade in black Africans, about 388,000 total out of 10.7 million slaves who landed in the Western hemisphere alone.[22] American slavery lasted for only seventy-six years between the signing of the Constitution and the Emancipation Proclamation. In the Northern states, slavery was abolished within twenty years.

Moreover, America could hardly be guilty of a crime against Africa because of slavery, as Robinson maliciously claims, since it was black Africans who enslaved their brothers and sisters who were sold at auction to slave traders who brought them to America. White Americans began freeing these slaves as soon as their nation was established.

In a more honest time, an African American writer and American patriot Zora Neale Hurston saw the historical reality with great clarity: "The white people held my people in slavery here in America. They bought us, it is true, and exploited us. But the inescapable fact that stuck in my craw was [that] my people had sold me. . . . [M]y own people had butchered and killed, exterminated whole nations and torn families apart, for a profit before the strangers got their chance at a cut. It was a sobering thought. . . . It impressed upon me the universal nature of greed and glory."[23]

When Robinson speaks of 246 years of slavery, he conflates the years before the actual creation of the United States with those after. Running the colonial period, when America was ruled by the British, together with the years after it became an independent nation erases America's revolutionary declaration that all God's children are equal and have an unalienable right to liberty. By ignoring the creation of a sovereign country with revolutionary ideals and an anti-slavery message, this sleight of hand transforms the slavery problem into a problem of "white supremacy" and "whiteness"—something that the subsequent history of America demonstrates is false. Contrary to what racists like Robinson and Coates claim, all white people were not alike. A victorious majority turned out to be anti-slavery and pro-equality.

Every African American alive today owes his or her freedom to Thomas Jefferson and the American Founders and the 350,000 mainly white but also black Union soldiers who gave their lives to end this evil. Opposition to slavery and inequality is a heritage that black Americans share with white Americans, along with the entire multi-racial mosaic that makes up America today. Professor Dyson's malice towards white Americans—and America— notwithstanding, of course we can talk about slavery, and with pride in our role in ending it.

The repellent dismissal of all America's progress towards equality and inclusion—arguably the greatest transformation of race relations ever recorded—is a general theme of the Democrat Party and the racist left.[24] A particularly powerful expression of it can be found in the "Equal Justice Initiative" campaign, which is designed to raise awareness of lynchings, a hateful practice that was put an end to at least sixty years ago. The Initiative is more particularly a campaign to raise awareness of the lynchings of African Americans and *only* African Americans, although about a third of lynching victims were white, and many of the victims had committed criminal acts and were targets of "frontier justice" rather than racism—they were victims of mobs impatient with due process. The most famous lynching, for example, memorialized in the Billie Holiday song "Strange Fruit," was of two young blacks guilty of a brutal murder—witnessed and attested to by their companion, also black, who, though present, refused to participate in the actual murder and was not lynched. He spent seven years in jail as an accomplice and went on to become a noted civil rights leader.[25]

The "Equal Justice Initiative" is funded and promoted by one of America's—and indeed one of the world's—largest corporations: Google. The outrageous theme of Google's campaign is this: "Slavery did not end; it evolved."[26] The insinuation that America, which has elected a black president and had its justice system run by two black attorneys general and its foreign policy by two black secretaries of state, whose popular culture is inconceivable without the major contributions of black Americans, and which has a thriving black middle class, is some kind of slave nation is vile, and insulting to those black Americans who actually were slaves. The fact that this slander is promoted by an organization like Google, which exerts unrivalled control over the information flow of the entire nation, is more than troubling.

Jason Hill, a gay Jamaican philosophy professor at DePaul University, published an "open letter" response to Ta-Nehesi Coates's *Between the World and Me*. The book, he said, "reads like an American horror story and, I'm sorry to say, a declaration of war against my adopted country."[27] This could be said of the writings and agitations of the Left generally. They appear extreme and out of touch with reality because they are, at heart, declarations of war against their authors' own country, which has been a world leader in creating a society that is inclusive and tolerant, and in which all its citizens are equal by law.

PART TWO

Storm Troopers

4

A Poisonous Protest

Ta-Nehesi Coates made this observation about the 9/11 attack on the World Trade Center: "I could see no difference between the officer who killed Prince Jones and the police who died or the firefighters who died. They were not human to me. Black, white, or whatever, they were the menaces of nature; they were the fire, the comet, the storm, which could—with no justification—shatter my body."[1]

This is racist paranoia. The majority of New York police officers are "people of color." While there are—and always will be—instances of abuse, officers are regularly tried for manslaughter or homicide when there appears to be no justification for the use of deadly force. If not enough are, that is something that should be addressed. But human institutions like the justice system will always need to be scrutinized and reformed. It is in the nature of human institutions that they require vigilance to keep them honest. The idea that police officers are racist sociopaths, on the other hand, is malicious hatred, and its fruits are evil.

Yet this is the central thrust of the Black Lives Matter movement, whose protests were reaching a fever pitch as Coates was framing his indictments. In the years 2014 and 2015, "Black Lives Matter" activists were making headlines occupying America's streets, targeting racially integrated and even majority-minority police forces whom they accused of killing blacks merely because they were black. The Black Lives Matter activists fomented riots, burned and looted cities, and incited their followers with chants that ranged from "What do we want? Dead cops! When do we want them? Now!" to "Hands up, don't shoot."[2]

The latter slogan was designed to highlight the movement's false claim that Michael Brown, a nineteen-year-old resident of Ferguson, Missouri, had been singled out because he was black and was shot by a police officer while he was surrendering with his hands up.[3] The protesters demanded that the officer be convicted of murder in advance of any trial—in other words, lynched.

However, the facts as revealed in Grand Jury testimony and subsequent investigations by the Obama Justice Department were quite different. The officer singled out the three-hundred-pound Brown because he had just committed a strong-arm robbery at a convenience store owned by a much smaller Asian shopkeeper, whom he brutalized. When the officer attempted to arrest Brown, the suspect responded by attacking the officer and trying to seize his gun, which was discharged in the scuffle, wounding the attacker. According to the sworn testimony of six black eyewitnesses, Brown was fatally shot while charging the officer, who fired another five rounds in self-defense. The "Hands Up, Don't Shoot" myth was created by Brown's accomplice in the crime. Yet so uninterested in the facts were the Black Lives Matter protesters demanding the officer be convicted of a racial homicide that the chant "Hands up, don't shoot" continued to live on as a battle cry seven years later.[4] And is featured in the Netflix film based on Ta-Nehesi Coates's malicious book.

Black Lives Matter

Black Lives Matter was formed in 2013 in response to the fatal shooting of nineteen-year-old Trayvon Martin by Neighborhood Watch volunteer George Zimmerman, who was Hispanic. Zimmerman phoned his dispatcher and said that he had spotted someone he regarded as a suspicious prowler. But then he violated his instructions and the guidelines of the Neighborhood Watch by leaving his truck and stalking Martin instead of reporting his suspicions to the police and letting qualified officers handle the case. When Martin objected to being stalked, a scuffle ensued, during which Zimmerman shot and killed him with a bullet to the heart. Zimmerman should have been convicted of manslaughter at the very least, but he was acquitted. Even before the trial, though, a lynch mob had formed demanding Zimmerman be convicted of murder.

These passions provided the basis for the formation of "Black Lives Matter" by three self-styled "Marxist-Leninist revolutionaries," who selected as their movement icon convicted cop-killer and Black Liberation Army–member Assata Shakur.[5] Shakur had fled to Cuba after being convicted of the homicide she committed when her car was stopped for a broken tail-light by two New Jersey state troopers. Without any warning, Shakur shot unsuspecting trooper Werner Foerster as he approached her car. The thirty-four-year-old Vietnam veteran was lying wounded on the ground pleading for his life when Shakur walked over and executed him. Officer Foerster left a widow and a three-year-old son.[6]

Black Lives Matter activists refer to the murderer as "our beloved Assata Shakur" and chant her words as a ritual, "at every meeting, every event, every action, every freeway we've shut down, every mall we've shut down."[7] The chant is this: "It is our duty to fight for our freedom. It is our duty to win. We must love and support one another. We have nothing to lose but our chains." The last line is lifted directly from the *Communist Manifesto*, a document, and a war cry, that has led to the murder of millions.[8]

The Black Lives Matter movement is not about particular injustices but about the alleged injustice of the American system, of capitalism, and of so-called "white supremacy." Its mission is not to save black lives. The thousands of deaths from black-on-black homicides draw no attention and inspire no protests, nor do the deaths of black police officers on the integrated police forces Black Lives Matter activists attack. Their ferocious denunciations of slogans like "All Lives Matter" and "Blue Lives Matter" reveal the racist impetus behind their own agenda.[9]

This agenda was on display in November 2015, when a group of 150 Black Lives Matter activists stormed the library at Dartmouth College and screamed at the bewildered students studying for exams: "*F**k you, you filthy white f**ks!*," "*F**k you and your comfort!*" The activists ordered students who supported them to stand up and verbally attacked those who refused, screaming at one of them: "*You filthy white racist piece of sh*t!*" When a female student burst into tears, a Black Lives Matter activist shouted "*F**k your white tears.*" Then: "*If we can't have it, shut it down.*"[10] The only thing missing were black hoods and black sheets to complete the perverse parallel to the KKK racists of the past.

At the July 2015 Netroots Nation convention, a major gathering of the Left, activists shouting "Black Lives Matter" blocked two leftist presidential candidates, Bernie Sanders and Kevin O'Malley, from speaking because they were white. Black Lives Matter founder Patrisse Cullors seized the microphone and said, by way of explanation, "Every single day folks are dying. Not being able to take another breath. We are in a state of emergency. If you don't feel that emergency, you are not human."[11] O'Malley responded, "I know, I know, Let me talk a little bit. . . . Black lives matter, white lives matter, all lives matter."

As the words left O'Malley's mouth, the crowd erupted in boos and catcalls. Then they chanted:

> If I die in police custody, don't believe the hype. I was murdered!
> Protect my family! Indict the system! Shut that sh*t down!
> If I die in police custody, avenge my death!
> By any means necessary!
> If I die in police custody, burn everything down!
> No building is worth more than my life!
> And that's the only way motherf***ers like you listen!

If I die in police custody, make sure I'm the last person to die
in police custody.
By any means necessary!
If I die in police custody, do not hold a moment of silence for
me!
Rise the f*** up!
Because your silence is killing us![12]

"Burn everything down!" is a slogan that mimics Marx's claim that,
"Everything that exists deserves to perish." The nihilistic racism of the
Black Lives Matter message is based on a demonstrably false premise—
that police have declared open season on black men. That premise is false
not only because America's police forces have long been racially integrated: As black talk show host Larry Elder and many conservative
writers have observed, the proportion of blacks killed by police is directly
related to the number of violent crimes committed by black males and
thus likely proportional to the number of blacks involved in violent
encounters with the law.

Despite being almost 65 percent of the population, whites commit disproportionately *fewer* of the nation's violent crimes—10 percent—
and are therefore less likely to have encounters with police. Blacks are
only 13 percent of the population, and black males, who commit the
lion's share of the violent crimes, only 6 percent. Yet black males account
for nearly half the nation's homicides and violent crimes. Since the majority of the black population is law-abiding, the cohort of violent criminals
who are black and perpetrate violent crimes is even smaller.

Notwithstanding this disparity, whites are still 49 percent of the
victims of cop shootings. Criminology professor Peter Moskos looked
at the numbers of people killed by officers from May 2013 to April 2015
and found that while 49 percent were white, 30 percent were black. In
other words, if the statistics are adjusted for the homicide rate (as opposed
to population numbers) whites are 1.7 times *more likely than blacks* to
die at the hands of police."[13] And even this statistic doesn't factor in the

number of blacks killed not by white law enforcement officers, but by black and minority ones.

Despite Black Lives Matter's racist agenda, incitements to violence against police, and disregard for the facts, President Obama invited its leaders to the White House in February 2015 at the height of their protests, riots, and incitements. When the Black Lives Matter leaders arrived at the White House, the president pandered to them, saying, "They are much better organizers than I was when I was at their age, and I am confident that they are going to take America to new heights."[14] Think about that statement for a moment.

In August 2015, the Democratic National Committee passed a resolution endorsing the Black Lives Matter movement and its false narratives: "[T]he DNC joins with Americans across the country in affirming black lives matter and the 'say her name' efforts to make visible the pain of our fellow and sister Americans as they condemn extrajudicial killings of unarmed African American men, women and children."[15] This shameful statement went on to claim that the American Dream "is a nightmare for too many young people stripped of their dignity under the vestiges of slavery, Jim Crow and White Supremacy," to demand the "demilitarization of police, ending racial profiling, criminal justice reform, and investments in young people, families, and communities;" and to assert that "without systemic reform this state of [black] unrest jeopardizes the well-being of our democracy and our nation."[16]

The next month Black Lives Matter activists Brittany Packnett, DeRay McKesson, Johnetta Elzie, Phillip Agnew, and Jamye Wooten were invited to the White House to meet again with President Obama, senior advisor Valerie Jarrett, and other administration officials. It was Packnett's seventh visit to the Obama White House. Afterward, she told reporters that the president personally supported the Black Lives Matter movement. "He offered us a lot of encouragement with his background as a community organizer, and told us that even incremental changes were progress," she stated. "He didn't want us to get discouraged. He said, 'Keep speaking truth to power.'"[17] Evidently it was the police forces in Dallas, Chicago, Baltimore, and other cities, headed by blacks and under siege from the Left, that were the "power" needing to be confronted.

In October, Obama made a public announcement in support of Black Lives Matter, saying, "I think the reason that the organizers used the phrase 'Black Lives Matter' was not because they were suggesting nobody else's lives matter. Rather, what they were suggesting was there is a specific problem that's happening in the African-American community that's not happening in other communities. And that is a legitimate issue that we've got to address."[18]

The president's support for a racist and violent vigilante group, his validation of its false version of reality and hostile attitude towards law enforcement, led predictably to more criminal violence. On July 7, 2016, Black Lives Matter activists staged rallies in numerous cities across the United States to protest the shootings of two African American men by police officers in Minnesota and Louisiana. As was their practice, the demonstrators illegally occupied public thoroughfares and threatened violence, chanting "No justice, no peace." The Minnesota shooting, by a Hispanic policeman, was triggered by panic and should have been prosecuted as manslaughter; the one in Louisiana was the justifiable killing of a career criminal who was reaching for a gun. But like the lynch mobs they despised, Black Live Matters protesters were not interested in seeking remedies through the law. They had convinced themselves there was no such remedy and had been encouraged by the American president to take the battle to the enemy camp—America's racially integrated law enforcement agencies.

The inevitable result was tragedy. At a rally in Dallas on July 8, demonstrators shouted "Enough is enough!" as they held signs bearing slogans like: "If all lives matter, why are black ones taken so easily?"[19] During the demonstration, a black racist army veteran named Micah Johnson assassinated five police officers trying to protect the protesters and wounded nine others. Dallas police chief David Brown, who is black, explained: "The suspect wanted to kill white people, especially white officers."[20]

The rage fueled by the lies of Black Lives Matter reached such a fever point in the wake of the Dallas massacre that to justify the atrocity one Black Lives Matter activist speaking to a CNN reporter shouted: "The less white babies on this planet, the less of you we got! I hope they kill all the white babies! Kill 'em all right now! Kill 'em! Kill your grandkids! Kill yourself! Coffin, bitch! Go lay in a coffin! Kill yourself!"[21]

In the face of this racist hatred, the Obama White House stepped forward to provide still more support for the movement that had supplied the tinder and lit the fuse. At the funeral for the slain Dallas policemen, the president lectured the surviving officers rather than the rioters, schooling them and their grieving family members about the racism of America's police departments: "We also know that centuries of racial discrimination, of slavery, and subjugation, and Jim Crow; they didn't simply vanish with the law against segregation . . . we know that bias remains."[22]

Whose bias, exactly? White Americans played a large and historic role in the civil rights struggles that ended segregation and established the Civil Rights Acts. There is no evidence that the shooter, Micah Johnson, was harassed by or suffered at the hands of white people. But there *was* evidence that he was influenced by Black Lives Matter, the New Black Panthers, and similar black extremists at war with white America and the police. He was deeply affected by the series of false, racist narratives promulgated by these organizations and their allies in the press about the police shootings that had occurred over the previous two years.

The "Ferguson Effect"

The police themselves were also profoundly affected by the anti-police narratives, officer assassinations, anti-cop demonstrations, riots, and threats. According to a Pew Foundation study published in 2017, "More than three-quarters of U.S. law enforcement officers say they are reluctant to use force when necessary, and nearly as many—72%—say they or their colleagues are more reluctant to stop and question people who seem suspicious as a result of increased scrutiny of police. . . ."[23]

This attitude on the part of police in areas that had become the focus of the protest-assaults—Ferguson, Baltimore, Dallas, Chicago—was accompanied by a dramatic spike in homicides, with the perpetrators and victims being overwhelmingly black.[24] As former Baltimore cop and now university criminologist Peter Moskos commented, "Murders and shootings increased literally overnight, and dramatically so. Of course, this took the police-are-the-problem crowd by surprise. By their calculations, police doing less, particularly in black neighborhoods, would result in less harm to blacks. And indeed, arrests went way down. So did stops. So did complaints against policing. Even police-involved shootings are down. Everything is down! Shame about the murders and robberies, though."[25]

The syndrome of police withdrawals' leading to spikes in crime rates was termed the "Ferguson Effect" after the city that was looted and burned following the shooting of Michael Brown and the creation of the myth that he was killed with his hands up. The phrase summed up the unintended, though not unpredictable, consequences of having an extremist organization like Black Lives Matter take over the nation's streets, and—with the help of an American president—shape the national narrative on race.

The power of Black Lives Matter stems from its exploitation of Identity Politics, the ideology of oppression—a ready-made indictment looking for a crime. Black Lives Matter is at the center of a very large network of hundreds of leftist organizations sharing the same vision. Among them: the Freedom Road Socialist Organization, Dream Defenders, Hands Up United, Black Left Unity Network, Black Workers for Justice, Black Alliance for Just Immigration, Right to the City Alliance, School of Unity and Liberation, Dignity and Power Now, Grassroots Global Justice Alliance, Causa Justa/Just Cause, Organization for Black Struggle, Communist Party USA, Showing Up for Racial Justice, and others.

Many of these organizations are funded by America's largest corporations and philanthropies, including the Ben & Jerry's Foundation, the

Ford Foundation, the Rockefeller Foundation, the Margaret Casey Foundation, the Nathan Cummings Foundation, and George Soros's Open Society Institute.

In the summer of 2016, the Ford Foundation and Borealis Philanthropy announced the formation of the Black-Led Movement Fund, a six-year pooled donor campaign whose goal was to raise $100 million for the Movement for Black Lives coalition. This coalition embodies the extremist views, false claims, and racial agenda of the Black Lives Matter radicals. In the official words of the Ford Foundation: "The Movement for Black Lives has forged a new national conversation about *the intractable legacy of racism, state violence, and state neglect of black communities in the United States*" [emphasis added]. According to Borealis, "The Black-Led Movement Fund provides grants, movement building resources, and technical assistance to organizations working to advance the leadership and vision of young, black, queer, feminists and immigrant leaders who are shaping and leading a national conversation about criminalization, policing and race in America."

In a joint statement, Ford and Borealis said that their Fund would "complement the important work" of charities including the Hill-Snowden Foundation, Solidaire, the NoVo Foundation, the Association of Black Foundation Executives, the Neighborhood Funders Group, anonymous donors, and others. In addition to raising $100 million for the Movement for Black Lives, the Black-Led Movement Fund planned to collaborate with Benedict Consulting on "the organizational capacity building needs of a rapidly growing movement."[26]

Black Lives Matter Communism

The fact that Black Lives Matter is now a major national movement funded by America's establishment elites has not prompted its communist founders to reconsider their anti-American agenda or their political infatuation with totalitarians. When Cuba's sadistic dictator Fidel Castro died on November 25, 2016, the Black Lives Matter leadership issued a statement titled, "Lessons from Fidel: Black Lives Matter and the Transition of *El Comandante*."[27] It began,

> We are feeling many things as we awaken to a world without Fidel Castro. There is an overwhelming sense of loss, complicated by fear and anxiety. Although no leader is without their flaws, we must push back against the rhetoric of the right and come to the defense of *El Comandante*. And there are lessons that we must revisit and heed as we pick up the mantle in changing our world, as we aspire to build a world rooted in a vision of freedom and the peace that only comes with justice. It is the lessons that we take from Fidel.[28]

The eulogy then turned to Black Lives Matter's own icon, cop-killer Assata Shakur, who fled to Cuba to avoid paying for her crime:

> As a Black network committed to transformation, we are particularly grateful to Fidel for holding Mama Assata Shakur, who continues to inspire us. We are thankful that he provided a home for Brother Michael Finney, Ralph Goodwin, and Charles Hill [cop-killers and airplane hijackers], asylum to [Black Panther leader, rapist, and murderer] Brother Huey P. Newton, and sanctuary for so many other Black revolutionaries who were being persecuted by the American government during the Black Power era.[29]

The eulogy expressed gratitude to Castro for "attempting to support Black people in New Orleans after Hurricane Katrina when our government left us to die on rooftops and in floodwaters." This was another Black Lives Matter lie, obvious to anyone who watched the rescue efforts on TV, where virtually all the rescuers were white and all the rescued black. Responsibility for the failure to evacuate residents rested squarely on the Democrat mayor of New Orleans, who was black, and who was eventually sent to prison for his crimes. The eulogy lauded a Marxist dictator who put AIDS sufferers, many of whom were black, in concentration camps for having "provided a space where the traditional spiritual work of African people could flourish." In religious language, the tribute closed with these words of fidelity and adoration: "As Fidel ascends to the realm of the ancestors, we summon his guidance, strength, and power as we recommit ourselves to the struggle for universal freedom. Fidel Vive!"

As delusional as these sentiments obviously are, as repellent as they should be to any American, and as troubling coming from an organization endorsed by the Democrat Party and supported by American philanthropy and the Obama White House, they are matched if not exceeded by Black Lives Matter's endorsement and embrace of Islamic terrorists who have sworn the destruction of Jews, Christians, and the United States. In January 2015, Black Lives Matter co-founder Patrisse Cullors joined representatives from Dream Defenders on a ten-day trip to the Palestinian Territories in the West Bank. Their objective was to publicly draw parallels between Israeli "oppression" of Palestinians and police violence against blacks in the United States.[30] The following August, Cullors was one of more than a thousand black activists, artists, scholars, politicians, students, and "political prisoners" who signed a statement of alliance with the Hamas terrorists who ruled the Gaza strip.

Proclaiming their "solidarity with the Palestinian struggle and commitment to the liberation of Palestine's land and people," the Black Lives Matter group demanded an end to Israel's "occupation" of "Palestine," condemned "Israel's brutal war on Gaza and chokehold on the West Bank," and urged the U.S. government to end all aid to Israel. They also exhorted black institutions to support the terrorist-sponsored Boycott, Divestment, and Sanctions movement designed to strangle the Jewish state.[31] On their return to the states, the repulsive call for liberation "from Ferguson to Palestine" quickly became a slogan of the movement.[32]

Black Lives Matter had in fact achieved a kind of transformation. It was the climax of a trend that had begun with the death of Martin Luther King Jr. President Obama had touched on it in his attempts to conflate what he called the "messy" aspects of the Black Lives Matter "protests" with what he regarded as similar rough edges in the Civil Rights and Suffragette movements of the past.[33] But those movements and their leaders were clearly part of the American tradition; their allegiances and beliefs could be traced back to the Founders who had created a Republic based on democracy and individual rights. Black Lives Matter leaders identified with Communist totalitarians and with Islamic imperialists and terrorists who were conducting a seventy-year genocidal aggression against the Jews. They had joined self-proclaimed enemies of the United States and its democratic ally Israel. This was new and disturbing.

Because of its support from the White House and corporate establishment, and because of its size and willingness to incite and commit violence, which was widely excused, and because of the tolerance for anti-white bigotry that Identity Politics and a corrupt school system had created, the racism of Black Lives Matter introduced a new dimension to American politics. The Black Lives Matter riots, which ironically destroyed numerous black communities, showed how the historic mistreatment of black Americans could be used to leverage a hatred of America—the very system that had freed black slaves and made America's black citizenry the freest, richest, most privileged black population in the world.

A Public Hanging

The term "sexism" was coined by sixties radicals in a calculated act of cultural appropriation. It was an effort by radical women to hijack the moral authority of the victims of racism and the sympathy they had earned, and to exploit it for their own gender cause. The political value of the term "sexism" is that it immediately situates women in the hierarchies of oppression central to the radical outlook and instrumental to its wars.

According to the editor of *The Yale Book of Quotations*, the term "sexism" was coined on November 18, 1965, by Pauline M. Leet during a "Student-Faculty Forum" at Franklin & Marshall College. Leet defined "sexism" as a species of racism: "When you argue . . . that since fewer women write good poetry this justifies their total exclusion you are taking a position analogous to that of the racist—I might call you in this case a 'sexist.' . . . Both the racist and the sexist are acting as if all that has happened had never happened, and both of them are making decisions and coming to conclusions about someone's value by referring to factors which are in both cases irrelevant."[1]

This statement is characteristically sweeping, inept, devoid of evidence, intellectually incoherent, and not a little paranoid. It is also insulting to black Americans, whose suffering cannot reasonably be compared to the situation of non-black women in America who were never slaves nor the victims of segregation, lynchings, and other indignities inflicted on blacks. Who exactly proposes that women should be excluded from the field of poetry because they are currently outnumbered? The Greek poet Sappho has been part of the literary canon for thousands of years. Are biological factors *irrelevant* to the differences between men and women, or their interests or their places in society? Does invoking factors unconnected to bigotry as explanations for social disparities really indicate a "sexist" attitude?[2]

The paramount issue for leftists is to secure a place for women at the victim end of the alleged hierarchy of oppression, where they can be identified as objects of malign and criminal practices by predatory males. This is an objectification of women that deprives them of agency—of responsibility for their choices and results. At the same time, it creates the perception that any encounter between women and men involves an inequality, thus providing women with an often-decisive moral advantage in the case of any conflict or dispute.

In America, where the equality of individuals is a right guaranteed to all, how can a hierarchy of oppression be *imposed*? Institutional barriers to advancement on the basis of gender have been outlawed for more than half a century. So they have to be presented as invisible in order to be plausible. This is why leftists invent terms such as "glass ceiling," which is an alleged barrier that doesn't actually appear to be a barrier. But "glass ceiling" is a subterfuge on the same order as "implicit bias," "unintentional racism," and "white skin privilege." In each case the mere fact of difference is said to oppress, and disparities are reflexively taken as proof of manipulation and malice.

Before the invention of "sexism," a wide variety of words were available to describe unwanted behaviors between the sexes: "boorish," "inappropriate," "insensitive," "offensive," "improper," "disrespectful," and so on down a spectrum, until one reached the criminal and prosecutable, such as "molestation," "assault," and "rape." But once all these misbehaviors are subsumed under the rubric "sexism" and thus linked to "racism," committing any of them is easily magnified into an offense associated with discrimination, slavery, and oppression.

On January 21, 2017, the Intersectionalist Left staged a national demonstration against President Trump which they called "The Women's March." The march was endorsed by the Democrat Party's anti-Trump "Resistance," and its organizers claimed to speak in the name of all women, not just the radicals who organized it. The purpose of the march was to protest the inauguration of Trump, whom the Left had framed during the campaign as a symbol of the racist, sexist "matrix of domination" with which they were at war. It was the largest protest in American history, mobilizing between 3 and 5 million individuals, and an estimated 7 million worldwide.[3]

The protest organizers had originally intended to call their event "The Million Woman March" as an homage to the "Million Man March" held in 1995 by the America-hating racist and anti-Semite Louis Farrakhan. The fact that Farrakhan was black gave them a pass in aligning with such a repulsive figure. But the organizers decided to drop the name in favor of "The Women's March" when they realized that a "Million Women March" had taken place in Philadelphia in 1997.[4]

Despite the name change, the self-appointed leaders of the Women's March remained admirers of Farrakhan, a fact that a complicit media helped them to keep in the background for more than a year, until it rose to the surface and produced a split in the movement.[5] The four "co-chairs" running the Women's March were Linda Sarsour, Tamika Mallory, Carmen Perez, and Bob Bland, a white "trans woman" convinced, like Ta-Nehesi Coates, that "white supremacy is what America was founded on."[6] All four were named to *Time*'s "100 Most Influential Women" list for 2017.

Linda Sarsour is a former executive director of the Arab American Association and an outspoken supporter of Hamas terrorists and their goal of obliterating the state of Israel and cleansing it of its Jews. Sarsour and her co-chairs are also vocal fans of Farrakhan and Black Lives Matter icon and convicted cop-killer Assata Shakur.[7] Tamika Mallory is a former executive director of the National Action Network, founded and run by America's second most notorious racist and anti-Semite, Al Sharpton.

Carmen Perez is the executive director of "Gathering for Justice," an organization created by Harry Belafonte, a lifelong supporter of Communist causes and devoted admirer of Fidel Castro, who has long described America as "the Fourth Reich."[8] When the dictator Fidel Castro died in November 2018, Carmen Perez offered this tribute: "R.I.P. *Comandante!* Your legacy lives on!"[9] Perez also identifies with Assata Shakur's Black Liberation Army heroes, paying this tribute to a Black Liberation Army leader in jail for attempting to murder six police officers: "Love learning from and sharing space with Baba Sekou Odinga." Perez accompanied Black Lives Matter leaders on their trip to the West Bank to embrace the Palestinian terrorists and endorse their boycott campaign with its genocidal goal of obliterating the Jewish state.[10]

A fifth radical, Rasmea Odeh—a convicted Palestinian terrorist who set a bomb in a supermarket, killing two students—was also named an official organizer of the Women's March, whose leaders protested when the United States deported her two months later for lying on her visa application.[11]

Of course, the millions of women who responded to social media calls to join the march were mostly unaware of the hypocrisy of the organizers in embracing Farrakhan, a Jew-hating racist, misogynist, and anti-gay bigot. The march succeeded because it was an affirmation of the "Resistance" Democrats had mounted to Trump's presidency and a continuation of the radical war against the so-called hierarchies of oppression.

When Linda Sarsour took the microphone, she launched into a litany of the alleged victims of the oppressive hierarchies the Left had invented to advance their cause: "I ask you to stand and continue to keep your voices loud for black women, for native women, for undocumented women, for our LGBTQIA communities, for people with disabilities. You can count on me, your Palestinian Muslim sister to keep her voice loud. . . ."[12] The radical tenor of the demonstrations was also on display in the often unhinged rhetoric of other speakers, such as the pop star Madonna, who said, to the cheers of the crowd, "Yes, I'm angry. Yes, I'm outraged. Yes, I've thought an awful lot about blowing up the White House."[13]

A Supreme Court Nomination Lights a Fuse

The war waged by the radicals against American principles and institutions and their defenders came to an ugly head six months into the Trump administration when the president announced his nomination to replace retiring Justice Anthony Kennedy. The nominee, Brett Kavanaugh, was a conservative D.C. Circuit Court of Appeals judge and a Roman Catholic. Despite a stellar judicial career and a previous Senate confirmation to the D.C. Court, Trump's choice immediately triggered a confrontation between Senate Democrats and Republicans. This confrontation was characterized by unprecedented venom directed at the candidate himself, along with a disturbing disregard for what had previously been regarded as a fundamental principle of American law: the presumption of innocence until proven guilty. The ensuing drama generated far more heat than light, while also demonstrating how the radical Morality Play had become a controlling theme of the nation's politics.

Immediately upon Trump's announcement of the Kavanaugh nomination, Senate Minority Leader Chuck Schumer held a press conference on the steps of the Supreme Court. Flanked by all ten Democrats on the Senate Judiciary Committee, which would hold the confirmation hearings, Schumer declared, "I'm going to fight this nomination with everything I've got." His statement made the scheduled hearings seem a perfunctory exercise, which Democrats would treat not as an occasion to examine the record and weigh the evidence, but as an opportunity to find excuses to block a nominee they had already made up their minds about.[14]

When the hearings began on September 4, 2018, Republican senator Chuck Grassley, the committee chair, was unable to finish his first words of welcome before Democrat senators led by Kamala Harris and Cory Booker began interrupting him and calling for an adjournment. They did so with such intensity and disregard for committee protocol that Republican Senator John Cornyn was moved to describe their behavior as "mob rule." The two Democrats were protesting that they hadn't had time to read the documents, but the fact that they had already declared their unalterable opposition to the nomination exposed this as a fraudulent pretext.

Abetting the Democrats' obstructionist agenda was an actual mob led by Women's March leader Linda Sarsour, which had filled the hearing gallery and were screaming, "This is a travesty of justice!" "Women rise up!" and other unhinged slogans. The unruly protesters interrupted the proceedings and blocked Kavanaugh from making his opening statements until Capitol Police removed them.[15] The disruptions in the gallery continued throughout the day and throughout the hearings, resulting in hundreds of removals and arrests.

Democrats on the committee defended the mob disruptions as "democracy in action" and an exercise in free speech. They were deferred to by several Republicans, including the chairman, Senator Grassley, who called the mob outbursts a case of "free speech." Grassley was following the Republican Party's general strategy of appeasement in the face of such outrages, attempting to show that Republicans were "reasonable" and not engaged in the war on women of which they were being accused.

In fact, free speech had nothing to do with the disruptions, which were more properly described as fascistic. They were attacks on the committee process and the Congress as an institution, and thus on the very democracy the proceedings were designed to implement. "Free speech" could easily have been exercised outside the hearing chambers and outside the building. This, instead, was a concerted attempt to disrupt and obstruct the hearings. It was a direct attack on the process and, of course, on the Republicans who were being accused of conducting an assault on women by holding the hearing at all.[16]

The disruptions were a strategic effort to create an alternative narrative about the proceedings themselves—to portray them as a radical Morality Play in which the conservative Kavanaugh was cast as an anti-woman predator, guilty before the facts were even examined. As a result of the daily protests by Sarsour and her mob, supported and amplified by a left-wing media and the vocal encouragement of the Democrats on the committee, the presumption of guilt framed the proceedings as an orchestrated attack on women, who were cast as abused, unheeded, and vulnerable victims requiring protection from white men. "These white men, old by the way," offered *The View* host Joy Behar in a typical media comment, "are not protecting women. They're protecting a man who is probably guilty."[17] And how exactly would she know?

Senator Jeff Merkley of Oregon defended the gallery mob calling for a verdict and punishment before the trial. Of the rioters inside the committee chambers, Senator Merkley said, "It was a gutsy thing to do for women treated awfully by powerful white men as if they are the problem instead of an honest presenter of information. And what happened? Well, this crew of white Republican men proceeded to treat these individuals as if they are dishonest, unacceptable, and even as if they're the criminal that needs to be prosecuted. It's a horrific, horrific conduct by my colleagues."[18]

Only in a severely disfigured political environment could these racist (and sexist) attacks on the Republican committee members and these defenses of the mob's attack on congressional proceedings be regarded with anything but outrage and disgust. How could a United States senator describe the disruption of a congressional hearing by protesters shouting "This is a travesty of justice" and "Women rise up!" before it even started, as an "honest" presentation of "information"?

Moreover, the history of previous confirmation hearings showed that the old white males on the Republican side were in fact quite fair to their ideological opponents. Senator Lindsey Graham, one of the conservative

Republicans on the committee, for example, had previously voted to confirm extreme leftist Obama nominee Sonia Sotomayor and liberal Obama nominee Elena Kagan.

In fact, as judges of women candidates, Republican senators on the judiciary committee had proven to be fair to a fault, nowhere more obviously than during the confirmation process for radical activist Ruth Bader Ginsburg. The first woman ever appointed to the Supreme Court, Sandra Day O'Connor, had been nominated by Republican and white male Ronald Reagan. In 1993 Bill Clinton nominated Ginsburg to become the second.

At the time, Ginsburg was general counsel for the left-wing American Civil Liberties Union. She was a radical, a militant feminist who had created the ACLU's Women's Rights Project. Hers was obviously not a resume designed to endear her to Republican senators. But upon her nomination, Republican Senator Orrin Hatch accompanied her through her preliminary interviews with his Republican colleagues, who recognized the importance of including women on the Court. When the vote was finally taken, she was approved by ninety-seven senators—the majority of them white, Christian, and male. Only three votes were cast against her.

A Devious Plot

In contrast to the sexist caricature that the protesting mob and their Democrat abettors used to attack the Republican nominee, in his professional life Kavanaugh had actually been one of the strongest advocates for women jurists. In the words of the *New York Times*, "during his 12 years at the United States Court of Appeals for the District of Columbia Circuit, the majority of Justice Kavanaugh's law clerks were women—25 of 48—and during his confirmation hearings he testified that he had graduated more of them to clerkships at the Supreme Court than any other federal judge."[19]

Kavanaugh had already been confirmed once, for his seat on the D.C. court, and he was the author of over three hundred judicial opinions available for review. He had received the highest rating from the liberal American Bar Association. He was a family man who coached the basketball teams on which his two young daughters played and had an unblemished career during forty years of public service. There was really no prospect of disqualifying him on the basis of his record. But these considerations didn't deter the Sarsour mob or their Democrat abettors on the committee from proceeding with an attempt to destroy his reputation, his family, and his career.

As the hearings drew to a close in late September and Kavanaugh's confirmation appeared inevitable, the ranking Democrat on the committee, Senator Dianne Feinstein, produced a letter which she had been holding since early July, with an explosive charge. The letter was written by a woman who accused Kavanaugh of an assault with sexual overtones, which she alleged had taken place thirty-seven years earlier at a party where only a handful of people were present.[20] Both the accuser and Kavanaugh were high school students at the time the incident was supposed to have taken place, and alcohol was present.

It is hard to imagine another context in which a committee of the United States Senate would even agree to hear such a defamatory complaint. The parties were too young, the incident had never been reported and was too far in the past, and no actual sex had taken place. Moreover, the accuser was exceptionally hazy about the facts, which she attempted to change several times.[21] She could not remember what year the alleged incident had taken place in, whether it was 1980 or 1982—that is, whether she was thirteen or fifteen years old at the time, or, as she also said, "in her late teens," a time when Kavanaugh was already at Yale. She could not remember where the party took place, or who had invited her, how she got there, or how she got home when she left, even though her home, by her own account, was a twenty-minute drive away. Each of the four individuals she named as having been at the scene, including her best friend, Leland Keyser, the only other girl present, denied they had ever attended such a party. When interviewed, Keyser denied she had ever even met Brett Kavanaugh.[22]

In her description of the alleged incident, Ford named a second assailant, claiming that the two boys were so drunk they rolled off her fully clothed body before anything more serious could transpire and began "scrapping with each other," which allowed her to escape. According to her testimony, she had to pass by the three other people who were in the house as she left, including her best friend Leland.[23] But in fleeing the house she did not tell—or warn—her best friend about what thirty-seven years later she was describing as an attempted rape, nor did she report the incident to the authorities. She did not even discuss it later with Keyser, who, if she had actually been there, might have wondered why her friend had left so abruptly. She did not discuss it with her parents. She was worried, she told the *Washington Post*, that she would get in trouble for attending a party where alcohol was present. She told the *Post*: "My biggest fear was, do I look like someone just attacked me?"[24]

She didn't mention the incident to anyone for more than thirty years. But now that Kavanaugh had been nominated by Trump for a Supreme Court seat and was ferociously opposed by the political Left, she was suddenly determined to press her charge, and to do so without any credible corroborating evidence as to whether it had even taken place. Explaining her decision to come forward she wrote: "I felt guilty, and compelled as a citizen about the idea of not saying anything."[25]

Christine Ford could not be unaware of the damage such an accusation would inflict on the Supreme Court nominee and his family, how once aired before a national audience it would blight the Kavanaughs' lives and tarnish an exemplary forty-year career. Yet she went ahead with her charge anyway, spurred on by the Democrat senators on the committee, who were out for blood. Shamefully, the Republicans acquiesced in this reckless and destructive exercise. They were unwilling to risk offending the sensibilities of the hour, or, more likely, they were fearful of how the Democrats would exploit those sensibilities if they took a commonsense stance and refused to allow unsubstantiated accusations to be aired before a national audience.

Kavanaugh's accuser was a Stanford psychology professor. The moment Kavanaugh's nomination became public, Ford had sent letters detailing her allegations to Senator Feinstein and Democrat congresswoman Anna Eshoo and also to the *Washington Post*. She did so with the express intent of keeping her identity hidden and protecting her own privacy. According to her lawyer, a top Democrat operative and campaign donor, Ford was "terrified" of having her identity known. Before launching her campaign, she scrubbed her social media pages to hide the fact that she was a political radical, a Democrat donor, and a fierce opponent of President Trump—along with other clues to her possible motives.[26]

This was perhaps the most revealing aspect of Ford's behavior—her determination to keep her own identity concealed while striking a massive blow at Kavanaugh's reputation, family, career, and life. Few rights are more basic to America's democracy than the right of individuals to confront and cross-examine their accusers. It is the right not to be subjected to character assassination by witnesses who remain faceless and protected from inquiries into their veracity and motives. This right separates us from tyrannies and star chamber proceedings. It is the cornerstone of "due process," the presumption of innocence until—and unless—proven guilty. It is a right enshrined in the "confrontation clause" of the Sixth Amendment to the Constitution. It is considered so fundamental that even child victims of molestation are required to confront their accusers in court.

Ford's effort to remain a faceless accuser was destined to fail. Without consulting her, the Democrats leaked her name to the press, probably realizing that a faceless accuser would lack the credibility necessary to kill the Kavanaugh nomination. This led the committee to summon Ford to testify. She responded by saying she could not make the trip to Washington because she was afraid of flying—a fear she claimed was the result of the trauma she had allegedly suffered thirty-seven years earlier at the hands of the teenager Brett Kavanaugh. In a show of misplaced empathy, the Republican majority offered to interview her in California. But the offer was never communicated to her by the Democrat lawyers who represented her. Perhaps they calculated that her in-person appearance as a witness would best advance their political goals. After causing a week-long delay, she arrived in the nation's capital to testify.

Christine Ford's determination to destroy Kavanaugh and his family while she remained anonymous should have sounded alarm bells about her character to her Democrat sponsors as well as to Kavanaugh's Republican defenders. But no one questioned her about this or so much as mentioned it in the course of the proceedings. To doubt a woman accusing a man of sexual assault—however questionable—was virtually unthinkable in the atmosphere created by the #MeToo feminists and their advocates. "Believe women" was the political slogan of the hour, a tag line on T-shirts, and even the message of a full-page ad in the *New York Times*.[27]

This deference protected Ford from aggressive cross-examination throughout the hearings. That was a privilege denied to Kavanaugh, who was the target of nasty, character-assaulting questions and accusations throughout. This disparity would not have been possible without the Left's success in imposing their ideological views about sexual hierarchies, "toxic masculinity," and oppressive male behavior on the nation's political culture.

To a man, the Republican senators on the Judiciary Committee were so cowed by the prospect of confronting a woman claiming sexual assault and by their vulnerability as "old white males" (a bigoted canard constantly repeated by the Left) that they relinquished their right to cross-examine the accuser altogether. Throughout the entire proceedings, not one Republican senator directly confronted Ford about the multiple inconsistencies, lies, and gaps in her testimony. Instead they joined the Democrats in hypocritically praising her willingness to come forward, while commiserating with her that she had been forced to do so by her Democrat sponsors, and even affirming the "credibility" of her porous memory of the distant past. To insulate themselves from attacks on their alleged "sexism," they yielded all their question time to a prosecutor who specialized in sex crimes and was female.

The prosecutor, Rachel Mitchell, was a seasoned and shrewd interviewer who led Ford through a series of non-confrontational questions about her claims, which had the effect of disarming her. "I just wanted to tell you," Mitchell said at the outset, "the first thing that struck me from your statement this morning was that you are terrified, and I just wanted to let you know I'm very sorry. That's not right."

In the interview with Ford, the prosecutor was hampered by the fact that she was standing in for eleven Republicans and so had to break her questions into five-minute segments. In the intervals, the Democrats on the committee acted as Ford's defense attorneys, providing her with counsel and support. Senator Kamala Harris took her five minutes to tell Ford "I believe you," and to justify the silence the witness had kept for nearly forty years.[28] Others gave Ford useful advice on how to deflect attention from her memory lapses and inconsistencies. But despite these interruptions, the prosecutor was able to maintain her focus and casual tone, with the result that Ford unwittingly revealed how calculating a liar she actually was.

Ford's claim to the committee that she could not testify because of her fear of flying was designed both to protect her anonymity and also to establish that her trauma from the alleged encounter with Kavanaugh had lasted for thirty-seven years and persisted into the present. It was crucial evidence of the damage the young Kavanaugh had allegedly done. The persistence of the trauma also provided a plausible reason for her coming forward only after thirty-seven years of silence. But, as the prosecutor's questioning revealed, it was all made up.

> MITCHELL: I also saw on your C.V. that you list the following interests of surf travel, and you [note], in parentheses "Hawaii, Costa Rica, South Pacific islands and French Polynesia." Have you been to all those places?
> FORD: Correct.
> MITCHELL: By airplane?
> FORD: Yes.

MITCHELL: And your interests also include oceanography, Hawaiian and Tahitian culture. Did you travel by air as a part of those interests?
FORD: Correct.

Realizing that she had exposed her lies and undermined her case, Ford immediately attempted to retrieve the situation. But her defenses had been so lulled by the prosecutor's friendly and seemingly meandering questions that her attempt to "explain" herself came out exceptionally lame:

FORD: Easier for me to travel going that direction when it's a vacation.

At this very point, it was Democrat senator Amy Klobuchar's turn to question the witness. Klobuchar simply ignored the exchange, even though it had exposed the fact that Ford had deceived the Judiciary Committee about not being able to fly to Washington and about the trauma of the purported assault persisting into the present. Klobuchar was uninterested in these revealing details. Instead, in a cringe-worthy gesture, she coached Ford on how to defend her uncorroborated accusations:

KLOBUCHAR: You know, with my memory of things, I remember distinctly things that happened to me in high school, or happened to me in college, but I don't exactly remember the date, I don't exactly remember the time, I sometimes may even not remember the exact place where it occurred. But I remember the interaction. Many people are focused today on what you're not able to remember about that night. I actually think you remember a lot. I'm going to phrase it differently: Can you tell us what you *don't* forget about that night?[29]

The pretended fear of flying was not the only significant lie that Ford had told in an effort to provide credibility for her case. In her letter to Senator Feinstein, she had asserted, without going into any detail, "I have received medical treatment regarding the assault."[30] What this sentence failed to mention was that the medical treatment was a therapy session she had attended with her husband, and that it had taken place in 2012, thirty years after the fact. Moreover, when the therapist's notes were examined, there was no mention of Kavanaugh's name.

The therapy session also provided a pretext for inventing another psychological effect that she claimed had resulted from the alleged trauma. "The reason this came up in counseling," Ford explained to Democrat senator Dianne Feinstein, "is that my husband and I had completed a very extensive, very long remodel of our home and I insisted on a second front door, an idea that he and others disagreed with and could not understand. In explaining why I wanted a second front door, I began to describe the assault in detail." Ford went on, "Anxiety, phobia and PTSD-like symptoms are the types of things that I've been coping with. More specially, claustrophobia, panic and that type of thing."[31]

FEINSTEIN: Is that the reason for the second front door? Claustrophobia?
FORD: Correct.

But this statement by Ford was also a lie. The real estate records showed that the remodel took place in 2008, not at the time of the 2012 therapy session. Moreover, it was designed to create a self-contained rental unit in the house, which required a separate entrance. The records showed that Ford had rented the unit to students.[32]

Inventing two brazen lies designed to make her case against Kavanaugh seem credible was more than just significant and troubling. It was devastating to her credibility and case. But not one of the twenty-one senators on the committee, Republican or Democrat, dared to confront her over them—the Democrats because they were cynical accomplices in her efforts to destroy Kavanaugh, and the Republicans out of fear of being called "sexists."

The questioning of Kavanaugh provided a stark contrast to the committee's treatment of Ford. When it came Senator Richard Blumenthal's turn to question Kavanaugh, his *opening* line was this:

> BLUMENTHAL: You are familiar with *"Falsus in uno, falsus in omnibus,"* are you not?[33]

The Latin phrase—"false in one thing, false in all things"—was a reference to the legal principle that a witness can be regarded as lying about everything if he says one thing that is not true. "The core of why we're here is really, credibility," Blumenthal explained. Such accusatory interrogation was par for the course during Kavanaugh's questioning throughout the hearings. But no one—not one Democrat or Republican—had questioned his female accuser's credibility. Nor, of course, did Blumenthal, even though he claimed to regard "credibility" as "the core of why we're here." Blumenthal was actually the last person who should have questioned anyone's credibility. He had notoriously falsely claimed to have served in Vietnam. In fact, he was never in Vietnam, had sought at least five military deferments, and eventually joined the Marine Reserve where he was effectively guaranteed not to serve in the conflict itself.[34]

The double standard that made it appropriate to attack the accused male's credibility but not the female accuser's, casting the male as guilty before the fact and the female as innocent even after the facts showed she was not, persisted throughout the hearings. It extended even to a last-gasp charade when Democrats trotted out Kavanaugh's high school yearbook and tried to convict him of being a fall-down, violent drunk. No one brought up Ford's high school yearbook which boasted of parties where the agenda was to get so plastered the partier blacked out.[35]

Of course, no one should have brought up either of the high school yearbooks. More important, no one should have provided a public platform for accusations about an alleged incident between two teenagers thirty-seven years in the past, where alcohol was present and the accuser could not remember key facts, had no corroborating witnesses, and did not even claim that a rape took place. But the feminist Morality Play and the Democrats' agenda to destroy Kavanaugh and kill his nomination required it.

What *were* Ford's motives in bringing her charge? "I felt guilty," she had written in her letter to Feinstein, "and compelled as a citizen about the idea of not saying anything." Guilty? Compelled as a *citizen*? What did this have to do with a personal incident that had allegedly happened decades earlier? Ford never went to the authorities, never sought help from medical or psychological facilities set up for that purpose. Whatever did or did not happen on the evening in question, Brett Kavanaugh had lived an exemplary public and family life in the nearly four decades that followed. By all accounts, he had been exceptionally supportive of women. Why would that require a campaign to destroy him? Or make someone feel guilty for deciding not to pursue his and his family's destruction? The only possible reason would be political. But no one interrogated Ford about such a motive—another giant lacuna created by the imperative to protect the presumably fragile female accuser (how sexist is that?) and not to make her feel uncomfortable.

Christine Ford first told her story to the *Washington Post*, whose editors had never endorsed a Republican presidential candidate and whose paper was a leading voice in the attacks on the Trump administration. She then went to two Democrat congresswomen and hired a high-level Democrat political operative and a former Obama official as her lawyers. Although no one thought to ask her, Ford was a regular Democrat Party donor herself, a political activist who had participated in the Women's March and signed a petition with other health professionals to protest Trump's border policies.[36] How deep was her political activism, how extensive her partisanship? These remained unasked and therefore unanswered questions. As a result, her political agenda remains somewhat opaque, but enough is known to provide a reasonable explanation of her attempt to sabotage the Kavanaugh nomination and destroy the man and his family in the process.

For Kavanaugh himself, the hearings were a public crucifixion. As he began his opening statement, his composure was already visibly cracking: "The day after the [Ford] accusation appeared, I told this committee that I wanted a hearing as soon as possible, to clear my name. I demanded a hearing for the very next day. Unfortunately, it took the committee ten days to get to this hearing. In those ten long days, as was predictable, and as I predicted, my family, and my name have been totally and permanently destroyed by vicious and false additional accusations."[37]

Throughout his testimony, Kavanaugh's anguish was transparent. At one point, as he told of his youngest daughter's request that the family pray for his accuser, he was reduced to tears. He denied the allegations "unequivocally and categorically," and said: "The truth is that I have never sexually assaulted anyone—not in high school, not in college, not ever." He warned that, "the consequences extend beyond any one nomination. Such grotesque and obvious character assassination—if allowed to succeed—will dissuade competent and good people of all political persuasions from serving our country."[38] (Actually Democrat candidates hardly need worry, since Republicans have never treated the Democrats' Supreme Court nominees like this.)

The additional damaging accusations to which Kavanaugh referred came from two women who had stepped forward with preposterous character-destroying claims that the Democrats, in their zeal to discredit a political opponent, claimed to find credible. One accused Kavanaugh of attending ten parties where there were gang rapes, which he assisted by spiking the punch with drugs.[39] Kavanaugh had already been subjected to background checks by the FBI six times in conjunction with his high-level appointments. During all those investigations, there was not even a rumor of teen gang-rape parties in the circles he frequented, let alone an accusation that he had attended them.

As the hearings drew to a close and the Democrats continued their assault, one Republican finally had enough and abandoned the decorum that had provided a protective cover for the shameful attacks on the nominee and his family. A furious Lindsey Graham erupted on the dais to accuse Senate Democrats of "the most unethical sham since I've been in politics. . . . What you want to do is destroy this guy's life, hold this seat open, and hope you win in 2020. . . . When you see Sotomayor and Kagan, tell them that Lindsey said hello because I voted for them. I would never do to them what you've done to this guy."

GRAHAM to Kavanaugh: Are you a gang rapist?
KAVANAUGH: No.
GRAHAM: I cannot imagine what you and your family have gone through.
GRAHAM [to the Democrats]: Boy, you all want power. God, I hope you never get it. I hope the American people can see through this sham. That you knew about [Ford's letter] and you held it. You had no intention of protecting Dr. Ford; none.
GRAHAM [to Kavanaugh]: She's as much of a victim as you are. God, I hate to say it because these have been my friends. But let me tell you, when it comes to this, you're looking for a fair process? You came to the wrong town at the wrong time, my friend. . . .
 Your high school yearbook—you have interacted with professional women all your life, not one accusation. . . . Here's my understanding, if you lived a good life people would recognize it, like the American Bar Association has, the gold standard. "His integrity is absolutely unquestioned. He is very circumspect in his personal conduct, harbors no biases or prejudices. He's entirely ethical, is a really decent person. He is warm, friendly, unassuming. He's the nicest person"—the ABA. . . .
GRAHAM [to the Republicans]: To my Republican colleagues, if you vote no [on the Kavanaugh nomination], you're

legitimizing the most despicable thing I have seen in my time in politics.

GRAHAM [to the Democrats]: You want this seat? I hope you never get it.

GRAHAM [to Kavanaugh]: I hope you're on the Supreme Court, that's exactly where you should be. And I hope that the American people will see through this charade.[40]

This was the most—perhaps the only—honest moment of the hearings. The only thing Graham got wrong was calling Ford a victim. She was the aggressor: a cynical liar and character assassin. Graham's misplaced sympathy was a genuflection to the feminist witch hunt that had made the whole travesty possible. It was the gentlemanly thing to do, but it didn't reflect the reality of what this hateful woman had done. Christine Blasey Ford—aided, abetted, and prodded by the Democrats—was the perpetrator of a reprehensible crime against a good and decent man. It was also a crime against her country, as America would not be America without the equal treatment of all, male as well as female, or without the presumption of innocence, the right to cross-examine an accuser, and due process to protect the innocent.

Progressive Character Assassins

The obstructive protests during the Kavanaugh hearings took place inside the Capitol and also at the Supreme Court, leading to three arrests. According to investigative research by a self-described liberal reporter for the *Wall Street Journal*, the demonstrators were organized and funded by a network of organizations created by the leftist anti-American billionaire George Soros: "On Saturday," she wrote, "I also studied the fine print on the signs as protesters waved them defiantly at the Capitol and the high court. They came from a familiar list of Democratic interest groups that have received millions from Mr. Soros: the American Civil Liberties Union, the Leadership Conference on Civil and Human Rights, Planned Parenthood, NARAL Pro-Choice America, the Center for Popular Democracy, Human Rights Campaign and on and on. MoveOn.org, a Democratic organizing and lobbying group founded with Soros money, sent its army of partisan followers regular missives that led them to a Google form to ask for train tickets and places to stay."[1]

The Women's March, which was one of these organizations, tweeted a photo of Susan Collins, the moderate Republican who cast the deciding vote for Kavanaugh, with "Rape Apologist" stamped over her image.[2] "We're being arrested," the Women's March explained, "for protesting the appointment of a sexual predator on our nation's highest court." The protesters chanted "Lock him up," and "A vote for Kavanaugh is saying 'women don't matter.'"[3] As far as the anti-Kavanaugh mob was concerned, guilt by accusation was the new law of the land. Some prominent Democrats concurred, speculating that they might move to impeach Kavanaugh, while the others, without exception, failed to defend his right to be presumed innocent until proven guilty.

It was a powerful irony, since guilt by accusation and dispensing with due process have historically been core elements of the practice of lynching. Progressives' hysteria about hierarchy and oppression has led them to embrace the very mob justice they claim to abhor. The disjunction between the Morality Play that framed Kavanaugh as a rapist and the reality that he was an innocent victim of slanderous, malicious, and unsubstantiated accusations, could not have been greater. Shortly after the hearings ended and Kavanaugh was confirmed, the *New York Times* gave an account of the new justice's first day on the job under this headline: "Justice Kavanaugh's Law Clerks Are All Women, a First for the Supreme Court."

> WASHINGTON — Justice Brett M. Kavanaugh, confirmed to the Supreme Court amid fiery accusations of sexual misconduct against women, arrived Tuesday for his first day on the bench with an unprecedented all-female class of law clerks. As a result, more than half of the Supreme Court's law clerks this year will—for the first time in American history—be women.[4]

Unfortunately, where ideology prevails, facts don't matter, and this real-world consequence of Kavanaugh's confirmation failed to make any impression on his ideological enemies. The ideology prevailed first because belief in hierarchies and the mythology of oppression is essential to the identities of people who call themselves "social justice warriors" and "progressives." But far more important is the utility of these myths as weapons in the wars that leftist politics provoke. Whoever is on the wrong end of the hierarchies, whoever can be stigmatized as a victimizer and oppressor, becomes a ready-made target for public abuse and annihilation. Not only are the epithets "racist" and "sexist" potentially lethal, but so is the ancillary identity—"hater" or "hate-monger." Such defamations by the name-calling Left are now so routine that they have created a "gotcha" culture where a single remark lifted out of context and judged to be politically incorrect, can be a career-ending transgression.

The Academic Lynch Mob

The pioneers of this totalitarian censorship are the faculties of America's liberal arts colleges, which were colonized by radicals of the Vietnam generation who used their student deferments to avoid service in a war they were rooting for the enemy to win. Starting in the seventies they inserted themselves into faculty hiring committees, creating over time a one-party academic faculty and culture throughout the university system. Eventually they reshaped college curricula so successfully that conservative viewpoints have virtually vanished from the institutions of higher learning in America.[5]

Heather Mac Donald is an award-winning journalist and scholar at the Manhattan Institute. She is the author of many articles and two books on the Left's war against police—*Are Cops Racist?* and *The War on Cops*. Her writings demonstrate that the attacks on law enforcement have caused police to be less proactive in inner-city communities and thus have emboldened criminals who prey on the blacks who live there. Mac Donald has explained: "My entire argument about the necessity of lawful, proactive policing is based on the value of black lives. I have decried the loss of black life to drive-by-shootings and other forms of street violence. I have argued that the fact that blacks die of homicide at six times the rate of whites and Hispanics combined is a civil rights abomination. Black children should be able to walk to school with as little risk of a gang attack as white children face."[6]

Mac Donald's criticism of the Left's racist orthodoxies has made her a target of its lynch mobs, which are prominently situated in America's universities. In April 2017, Mac Donald arrived at Claremont McKenna College to give a speech about her book *The War on Cops*. Claremont McKenna is one of the five "Claremont Colleges," also including Pomona, Pitzer, Scripps, and Harvey Mudd, which are among the most elite liberal arts colleges in the nation. Before Mac Donald had even arrived, the leftist students at all five colleges had mobilized to block her speech. Calls went out on Facebook to "shut down [this] notorious white supremacist fascist Heather Mac Donald."[7] A Facebook post signed by "We Students of Color at the Claremont Colleges" proclaimed that "as a community, we CANNOT and WILL NOT allow fascism to have a platform. We stand against all forms of oppression and we refuse to have Mac Donald speak."[8]

Days before the event, the organizers informed Mac Donald that there would be protests and that the venue had been moved by the college administration from the Athanaeum, its originally scheduled site, because there were not enough exits and too much glass in the venue. When she arrived, Mac Donald was shuttled into a safe room where the blinds were drawn and she could not see but only hear the hundred protesters who had gathered outside. One of their leaders shouted "We are here to shut the fucking fascist down," while another led a chant "How do you spell racist?" to which the crowd roared in response, "C-M-C" meaning Claremont McKenna College. Of all the chants, Mac Donald observed, "this was the most absurd" since "racist" Claremont McKenna was so determined to be "diverse" that it had "historically admitted black and Hispanic students with an average 200-point-lower SAT score than white and Asian students."[9]

As the mob swelled to two hundred students, they were able to block the hall where Mac Donald's speech was to take place. The university decided that instead of intervening, they would not have her speak to a live audience, but would stream her talk instead.[10] As was the case in similar incidents across the country, administrators made half-hearted attempts to affirm the value of free speech, and afterwards did impose a handful of suspensions—a rare occurrence. But there were no expulsions, and in their official statements on what had happened, university officials pretended that the student thugs had real grievances against speakers like Mac Donald. Far more significant was the fact that the university had failed to take the necessary steps to see that an invited lecturer would get a fair and civil hearing, and that their students would learn to listen to views they did not agree with.

Some weeks after the Mac Donald fiasco, the president of Pomona College made a bland statement in support of academic freedom. A group of black students responded with a formal "manifesto," whose illiteracy and lack of regard for the most basic principles of American democracy exposed the travesty of what Mac Donald has called the "diversity illusion," which prevails among administrators of American universities and admits select minorities to institutions many of them are not qualified to attend. The manifesto was published in the name of "We, few of the black students here at Pomona College and the Claremont colleges," and went on to other ungrammatical and illogical assertions: "Though this institution as well as many others including this entire country, have been founded upon the oppression and degradation of marginalized bodies, it has a liability [sic] to protect the students that it serves."[11]

The manifesto went on to more depressing illiteracies and contempt for everything that a liberal arts education is supposed to stand for:

> The idea that there is a single truth—The Truth—is a construct of the Euro West. . . . This construction is a myth, and white supremacy, imperialism, colonization, capitalism, and the United States of America are all of its progeny. The idea that the truth is an entity for which we must search, in matters that endanger our ability to exist in open spaces, is an attempt to silence oppressed peoples. . . .

Heather Mac Donald is a fascist, a white supremacist, a warhawk, a transphobe, a queerphobe, a classist, and ignorant of inter-locking systems of domination that produce the lethal conditions under which oppressed peoples are forced to live.[12]

As Mac Donald points out, the real problem—and the real outrage— is that this destructive, absurd, hate-filled outlook is what students at an elite college, with a tuition fee of $47,000 a year, had learned from professors who were devotees of Intersectionalist Marxism. In her book on universities, Mac Donald observes, "Professors in all but the hardest of the hard sciences increasingly indoctrinate students in the belief that to be a non-Asian minority or a female in America today is to be the target of non-stop oppression, even, uproariously, if you are among the privileged few to attend a fantastically well-endowed, resource-rich American college. Those professors also maintain that to challenge that claim of ubiquitous bigotry is to engage in 'hate-speech' and that such speech is tantamount to a physical assault on minorities and females. As such it can rightly be suppressed and punished."[13]

Not surprisingly, a 2018 report by the Foundation for Individual Rights in Education found, "Just over 90 percent of public colleges maintain policies that don't live up to their free speech obligations under the First Amendment. Private institutions are generally not bound by the First Amendment but are responsible for living up to their institutional commitments to free speech. More than 88 percent of private institutions fall short of those promises."[14] If there is anything that sums up the disgraceful state of America's institutions of higher education, it is these statistics.

The Attempt to Cancel Tucker Carlson

Tucker Carlson is a TV anchor with the highest ratings in cable TV news. A feature of his show that attracts these ratings is a set piece where

Carlson confronts guests from the left and puts their hypocrisies to the test. Thus, a guest who indicts white people as a group is asked how he can square this attitude with his professed opposition to denigrating any group on the basis of an unalterable characteristic such as skin color. Another issue Carlson focuses on is illegal immigration. He regularly confronts his guests who support illegal immigration with commonsense questions like, "How much illegal immigration is enough or too much?" and "Why don't Americans have a right to say who gets to enter their country and who doesn't?" His guests routinely avoid answering the questions and move on to their other talking points.

Regular viewers are familiar with Carlson's demeanor and style, which is gracious and reassuring to his guest antagonists. His response when he exposes brazen hypocrisy is good-natured laughter, which is why left-wing guests who are regulars return again and again to his show.

In the spring of 2017, however, the political environment started to change as a result of the election of Donald Trump and the "Resistance" to his presidency. It began with a MoveOn.org guide "How to Bird Dog," which instructed activists on how to "harass officials in public places," in the words of the *Wall Street Journal* reporter who monitored the campaign.[15] The guide was produced in preparation for the town hall meetings held by members of Congress returning to their districts. MoveOn.org made weekly instructional calls to activists on Sunday evenings to "plan the operations and tell their 'troublemakers' how to corner lawmakers."[16]

This use of mob tactics to influence the democratic process quickly escalated, as Trump administration officials found themselves harassed in restaurants where they were dining with their families. One Democrat congresswoman, Maxine Waters, had been calling for impeachment virtually from the day of Trump's inauguration. She incited activists with these words: "God is on our side. If you see a member of Trump's cabinet, push back." And to Trump himself: "Already you have members of your cabinet that are being booed out of restaurants. We have protesters taking up at their house who are saying, 'No peace, no sleep. No peace, no sleep.'"[17] This was a variation on the leftist threat widely deployed in other protests—"No justice, no peace"—a terroristic threat to abandon the process of civil debate on which democratic order depends and resort to violence and anarchy if one's demands aren't met.

While these tactics of intimidation were being deployed around the country, a more radical and violent group—a Marxist militia calling themselves *Antifa*—was getting ready to attack Tucker Carlson and his family in their home. Antifa is an abbreviation for "Anti-Fascist" but no other group—not even the neo-Nazi Right—is more fascistic in its strategies and behavior than Antifa itself.[18] In February 2017, 150 black-clad masked anarchists and Antifa thugs attacked the University of California at Berkeley with Molotov cocktails and commercial grade fireworks and successfully shut down a scheduled speech by conservative Milo Yiannopoulos. The protesters caused $100,000 worth of property damage and injured six people. A second attack in August shut down the university's second attempt to host the speech at a cost of $800,000 in security fees.[19] The attack on the Carlson home was conducted by an Antifa affiliate called "Smash Racism D.C." which posted the Carlson family's address on Twitter along with this threat: "Tucker Carlson, you cannot hide from the people you hurt with your rhetoric, your lies, and your hate."[20]

Carlson and his children were away when the attack took place. The mob trashed the driveway, broke the oak front door and terrified his wife, who was home alone and locked herself in the kitchen where she called the police as the thugs chanted, "Racist scumbag, leave town!" and "Tucker Carlson, we will fight! We know where you sleep at night!" and "No borders! No walls! No USA at all!" which accurately summed up their treasonous commitments and agendas.[21]

Carlson's triggering offense was to have remarked on air: "The Left says we have a moral obligation to admit the world's poor. Even if it makes our own country more like Tijuana is now, which is to say poorer and dirtier and more divided."[22] This reasonable observation was immediately and permanently distorted as an attack on all immigrants, although anyone familiar with Carlson's writings and broadcasts would know that he supports *legal* immigration. His concern was the illegal crossing of America's southern border and the occupation of the country by an estimated 20 million un-vetted and untraceable illegals who were costing Americans more than $100 billion per year in welfare support, education, criminal incarceration, court bills, and the like.[23]

Although some on the left were properly horrified by the attack on Carlson's home, others, like Matthew Yglesias were not. Yglesias, the son of Castro-supporting *Nation* leftists, is the co-founder of Vox, an Internet site in which NBC Universal has a $200 million investment. Yglesias tweeted that he had "no empathy" for Carlson or his wife because "the idea behind terrorizing [Carlson's] family . . . is to make them feel some of the fear that the victims of MAGA-inspired violence feel thanks to the non-stop racial incitement coming from Tucker, Trump, etc."[24] What victims? What violence had they been subjected to? And how, specifically, had that violence been inspired by Tucker Carlson and Donald Trump? Yglesias didn't bother to say. Probably because there were no such connections except in the bigoted imaginations of anti-Trump and anti-American leftists like himself. Yglesias's response was a troubling indication of just how far mainstream progressives might be willing to go if the political environment were to take another dark turn. If a lynch mob can be justified, what cannot?

Fortunately, Carlson's employers stood by him, and the mob attack wasn't repeated. But other zealots immediately took up the cause of driving him off the air. Most prominently, award-winning Hollywood director Judd Apatow, author of social media outbursts calling President Trump an "idiot" and a "sociopath," began tweeting to companies like Subaru, and Pfizer: "Hey @subaru_usa—why would you continue to advertise on @TuckerCarlson's show when he spews so much racism and hate? How does that reflect the values of your company? There must be other shows you can advertise on which are not destructive to our country." Of course, Apatow gave no examples of Carlson's alleged racism or hate, which exist only in the minds of anti-Trump fanatics who confuse reasonable policy differences over America's borders with the non-existent racism they impute to their opponents.

The smear campaign and boycott movement achieved notable success. Within six weeks, nineteen advertisers had withdrawn their support for Carlson's show.[25] But Carlson's employer, Fox News, continued to stand by him and to support democracy in the public square. Enlisting the power of giant corporations to crush a dissenting voice is not the first action one might expect of parties dedicated to overthrowing capitalist patriarchy. But then principled consistency is not a virtue one readily associates with radicals either.

Accordingly, it is hardly surprising that the political Left is not only ready to resort to blacklisting but has created what is without question the largest blacklisting effort in modern times, dwarfing even the notorious antics of the McCarthy era. The blacklist against Communists was confined to a few industries and focused almost exclusively on Communist Party *members* with avowed allegiances to a foreign enemy. It didn't attempt to shut down all Americans with dissenting views on the key issues confronting the nation. But that is precisely what the Left has now mobilized its resources to do.

7

Progressive Blacklists

The chief engine of progressive efforts to blacklist conservatives is a $570 million non-profit misnamed the Southern Poverty Law Center (SPLC).[1] The Southern Poverty Law Center came to national prominence in 1987 when it won a $7 million lawsuit against the United Klans of America, putting them out of business. As it happens, the Ku Klux Klan was already on its last legs, down to 3,000 members nationally from its high in the 1920s of 4 million. The United Klans was already so crippled by lack of support that it was only able to pay $50,000 of the $7 million judgment.

Having slain an already mortally wounded dragon, the SPLC won judgments against other marginal groups like the White Aryan Resistance and the Aryan Nations. SPLC's leaders then hit upon a wildly successful but sinister political and fund-raising strategy—first, exaggerate the threat of marginal neo-Nazi hate groups and, second, conflate them with mainstream conservative groups whom SPLC leftists oppose ideologically.[2] SPLC subsumed these libels under the inclusive term "hate groups" and became the most successful slander machine in American history, comparable to the Nazi smear sheet *Der Stürmer*.

In 1997 the SPLC reported a national surge in "hate groups," a claim it supported by counting all the known branches and chapters of the "hate" organizations it had already listed as separate entities. By 2009, a mere four organizations and their many branches accounted for two hundred twenty-nine separate "hate groups," or one-fourth of the SPLC total.[3] Four years later, using these inflated statistics, the SPLC could claim that over the previous decade the number of hate groups had increased 67 percent and argue that the increase was "fueled by anger and fear over the nation's failing economy, an influx of non-white immigrants, and the diminishing white majority, as symbolized by the election of the nation's first African-American president."[4] In other words, they were slandering the American citizens who had not voted for Obama. On the other hand, the fact that Obama was elected by a majority of white votes was simply ignored. The Trump election in 2016 and the Democrat hysteria surrounding it proved a bonanza for the SPLC. In 2017, the first year of the new administration, the SPLC's direct-mail appeals raised alarm about the alleged rising tide of hate in America and brought in $132 million in donations.[5]

The SPLC's real focus is its political attack on conservatives, Republicans, and patriotic Americans. Its website explains its purpose in these words: "Hate Watch monitors and exposes the activities of the American radical right." The radical Left, represented by such obvious hate groups as Antifa and Black Lives Matter, are conspicuously missing from the purported "hate" groups. The SPLC site even features a report declaring "Black Lives Matter Is Not A Hate Group."[6] As for the "radical right," according to the SPLC this category includes such staid mainstream conservative organizations as the American Enterprise Institute, the Family Research Council, the Federation for American Immigration Reform, and sixty religious organizations whose beliefs on marriage and abortion it finds "hateful."[7] The conservative individuals listed as "hate-mongers" and "extremists" include famed brain surgeon and Trump cabinet member Ben Carson, Somali-born former Dutch Parliament member and human rights crusader Ayaan Hirsi Ali, former Attorney

General Jeff Sessions, and former Ohio Secretary of State Kenneth Black-well who, like Carson, is black.

The sin committed by these conservatives is to disagree with the SPLC's left-wing radicals on affirmative action race preferences, illegal immigration, Islamic terrorism, same-sex marriage, and other policy matters. The SPLC ascribes these policy differences to racism, homophobia, and other demonizing stigmas. Even the liberal magazine *Politico* has noted that the SPLC is "more of a partisan progressive hit operation than a civil rights watchdog."[8] But this is little consolation to those individuals and groups unfairly labeled racist hatemongers, a slander that the mainstream media is happy to spread. Even Fox report-ers too lazy to look into the facts have been known to describe the SPLC as a "civil rights organization."

Politico's conclusion is confirmed by Mark Potok, the SPLC opera-tive responsible for the "Hate Watch" lists. According to Potok, the Center's blacklists "have nothing to do with criminality or violence, or any kind of guess we're making about 'this group could be dangerous.' It's strictly ideological." In another unguarded moment, Potok explained to a *City Journal* reporter, "Our aim in life is to destroy these [conserva-tive] groups. To completely destroy them."[9] It's not too difficult to con-clude that when media like the *Washington Post* and CNN collude with the SPLC in smearing conservatives, it is for the same reason.

In 2016, the SPLC published a *"Field Guide to Anti-Muslim Extrem-ists."* "It is sad but telling," commented Lee Smith, writing for the liberal magazine *Tablet*, "that the SPLC's so-called field guide to Muslim-haters is not a list of violent extremists—who certainly do exist—but is instead a blacklist of prominent writers whose opinions on a range of cultural and political issues are offensive to the SPLC. . . . The SPLC blacklist list con-tains practicing Muslims like Maajid Nawaz, ex-Muslims like Ayaan Hirsi Ali, foreign-policy think-tankers like Frank Gaffney and Daniel Pipes, and right-wing firebrands like David Horowitz—none of whom could be rea-sonably described as anti-Muslim bigots."[10] Maajid Nawaz, the UK resi-dent blacklisted by SPLC's "Hate Watch" as an "anti-Muslim extremist" happens to be a well-known devout Muslim and moderate, "working [in his own words] to push back against extremism."[11] Nawaz sued the SPLC, which voluntarily offered him a $3.4 million settlement.

The swift settlement with Nawaz before the case even went to court could be attributed to stringent British libel laws. In America, libel law is less strict. Since the landmark Supreme Court decision in *New York Times v. Sullivan* there are effectively no libel protections for public figures because the bar was set so high in that case. The law requires a victim to prove malice, to prove that the published statement was known in advance to be false, and to show material damages—things which are normally not easy to establish. It further requires the offending libel to be a factual claim, not an opinion. Calling innocent people "racists" and "hate-mongers" is protected constitutional speech because these are regarded as mere opinions not factual claims. But a willing national media repeats them as facts, without characterizing them as opinions from a biased source.

Weak libel laws may be a good thing for democracy, but they require a level of public integrity that does not exist. If articles appearing in powerful media venues like the *New York Times* or the *Washington Post* refer to a public figure as a "racist" or "white nationalist" or "anti-Muslim extremist," citing the SPLC, even if there is not a shred of evidence to substantiate the claim, the courts will regard it as "opinion," therefore protected by the Constitution. This has relieved media institutions of legal liability for the slanders they publish and promote. Not surprisingly, as law professor Glenn Reynolds observes, "trust in the press has fallen steadily since the *Sullivan* ruling freed media organizations from previously existing legal accountability."[12]

Despite a rash of critical articles appearing in magazines as far left as *The Nation* exposing the SPLC's dishonest standards and questionable agenda, its "Hate Watch" lies are regularly reported in the nation's press and repeated by TV pundits and news anchors. These risk-free slanders are a potent and dangerous force, stigmatizing, suppressing, and marginalizing conservative views.[13]

Indicating just how dangerous, is the fact that among the recent mega-donors to the SPLC, facilitating its defamation crusade, are such titans of the business world as Apple CEO Tim Cook ($1 million) and J.P. Morgan CEO Jamie Dimon ($500,000). The SPLC continues to be cited as a reputable source by mainstream media and student newspapers at virtually every college on whose campuses conservatives attempt to speak. In fact it is the SPLC itself that is a hate group, and its impact can be deadly. In 2012, Floyd Corkins walked into the Washington, D.C., headquarters of the Family Research Council with a handgun and a hundred rounds of ammunition, intending to kill as many people as he could. Fortunately, he was subdued by the building manager before he could carry out his mission. When asked why he had targeted the Family Research Council, Corkins replied, "It was a, uh, Southern Poverty Law lists, uh, anti-gay groups."[14]

The SPLC poison in the nation's political discourse has affected this author personally, despite the fact that I have been a public figure for more than sixty years and my views are well known. For more than a decade I have been at the top of the Southern Poverty Law Center's hate lists, where I am described as an "extremist, " a "hatemonger," and "a driving force of the anti-Muslim, anti-immigrant and anti-black movements."[15] I am further described as an "anti-Muslim fanatic" and "the godfather of the anti-Muslim movement in America," a slander that has put a veritable target on my back.[16]

These are all easily demonstrable lies about my views. In the last eighteen years, I have written and spoken more than half a million words about Islam and the Islamic jihad, including the 2004 book *Unholy Alliance: Radical Islam and the American Left*. My words are readily available in print and on the internet. Yet the SPLC researchers could not turn up a single sentence that a reasonable person would describe as "anti-Muslim." In fact, in speeches and writings available on the Internet I have made it clear that I am not anti-Muslim at all.

In 2009, for example, I gave a speech at the University of Southern California, recorded on YouTube, available online at Frontpagemag.com, and also in my 2014 book, *Islamo-Fascism and the War against the Jews.* I said, "Here are my views concerning Muslims: There are good Muslims and bad Muslims, just as there are good Christians and bad ones, good Jews and bad Jews. Most Muslims are like everybody else; they want peace, and are law-abiding. Probably their religion is very personal to them, and doesn't involve efforts to convert and subordinate or kill others. There is a difference between religious institutions and the religion of individuals. Many Catholics do not follow church doctrine on birth control and abortion, for example. The Ku Klux Klan is a Protestant Christian organization, but virtually all Protestants and their churches condemn the Ku Klux Klan."[17]

In 2012, I spoke at the University of North Carolina, Chapel Hill. There was a demonstration inside my talk by Muslim Students who walked out in protest soon after I began. My comment was this: "It is too bad that all our Muslim friends have left the room and did not stay to hear this; but notwithstanding the evil intentions of Muslim leaders in the Middle East, there are good Muslims and there are bad Muslims, and most are probably good Muslims—decent, law-abiding, desirous of peace."[18]

On virtually every campus I have spoken at in the last ten years, I have repeated these words. Nonetheless, my talks have also been preceded by flyers and handouts filled with the SPLC slanders against me, including the slander that I am "the godfather of the anti-Muslim movement in America." These slanders are featured in college newspaper accounts of my visits, reaching tens of thousands of members of the academic community. This is an experience shared generally by conservatives including Heather Mac Donald, Milo Yiannopoulos, and many, many others.[19]

The charge that I am "anti-immigrant" is also without merit and merely reflects the Left's refusal to distinguish between legal immigration, which conservatives like myself support, and illegal entry into the United States, which we oppose. The SPLC "Hate Watch" report also describes me as "anti-black." This is equally specious but even more personally unpleasant, since I have immediate family who are black. For over sixty years my public life has been dedicated to fighting for the civil rights of black Americans. I have written scores of articles and three books on race—*Uncivil Wars: The Controversy over Reparations for Slavery* (2001), *Hating Whitey and Other Progressive Causes* (1999), and *Progressive Racism* (2016). Each of them is guided by the vision of Martin Luther King—that people should be judged on their merits and not on their skin color.

To call me "anti-black" is a repulsive defamation, but I have no legal recourse to counter this slur or avoid the damage it causes. This is a result of the toothless nature of the nation's libel laws. When my lawyers sent a letter to Common Cause, which had slandered me as a "white supremacist," demanding a retraction, their lawyer, Ballard Spahr—the same who represented Christine Blasey Ford—replied: "Common Cause declines to do so. . . . Common Cause's characterizations of your clients' 'ideas' and 'rhetoric' as 'white supremacist,' 'racist,' 'sexist' and the like, are fully protected expressions of its opinion."

The lawyers—obvious cynics and political leftists—went further, taking the opportunity of the letter to slander me again, a gratuitous and unprofessional act that was driven purely by malice and demonstrated how far politically motivated disrespect for the facts has corrupted our public life: "Even if Common Cause's characterizations of your clients were somehow deemed to be factual in nature [and therefore actionable], there is overwhelming evidence that they are substantially true, as is clear from Mr. Horowitz's many speeches and writings. . . . For example . . . he (a) denigrated the Black Lives Matter movement, calling it a 'racist organization,' (b) referred to 'white skin privilege' as a 'ludicrous doctrine,' . . . (d) called *Roe v. Wade* a 'travesty of justice.' . . . (f) clearly aligned himself with President Trump, who has frequently embraced racist, sexist, homophobic and other bigoted views."[20]

If supporting President Trump, as 63 million other Americans did in 2016, is evidence of racism or calling *Roe v. Wade* a "travesty of justice" along with such prominent pro-abortion liberals as law professor John

Hart Ely, who pronounced it bad law lacking any basis in the Constitution, then we are well along the path to a one-party totalitarian state.[21]

A discredited blacklist like the SPLC's "Hate Watch" is just one example of how the racial politics of the Left labels everyone who opposes their preferred policies—on abortion, affirmative action, immigration, anti-police vigilantism, or due process—"racist," "sexist," and related cancel-culture terms. The vast networks of the Left share the SPLC's political agenda and believe in their own righteousness so passionately that they could hardly be less concerned with the facts, let alone the rights of those who disagree with them. These networks include ancillary smear sites and blacklists such as Right Wing Watch, Source Watch, Media Matters, Think Progress, Bloodmoney.org, Color of Change, and innumerable others that draw extensively on the slanders provided by the SPLC and add some of their own. The slanders are also abetted by journalists too lazy or uninterested to ascertain the facts, and by corporate organizations apprehensive of attacks from the Left should they fail to respect its prejudices.

On March 14, 2019, Morris Dees, the founder of the Southern Poverty Law Center, was fired. His removal was quickly followed by the resignation of the Center's president, Richard Cohen. According to press reports, "Dee's ouster had come amid a staff revolt over the mistreatment of non-white and female staffers, which was sparked by the resignation of the senior attorney Meredith Horton, the highest-ranking African-American woman at the Center. A number of staffers subsequently signed onto two letters of protest to the Center's leadership, alleging that multiple reports of sexual harassment had been ignored or covered up, and sometimes resulted in retaliation against the women making the claims."[22]

The press had a field day reporting the hypocrisy of the SPLC leaders who had proposed themselves as the arbiters of who was and was not a racist, sexist, and hate-monger and should be shunned. But in the end the SPLC was allowed to continue its vigilante crusades and smear campaigns against conservatives, because the demonization of political opponents was so much the chosen strategy of the Democrat Party and progressives generally. Barack Obama's lawyer was entrusted with rescuing the institution—an indication of how central it is to the Democrats and the mainstream Left.

By 2019, the SPLC's slanders were reaffirmed by its new leaders, who resumed its function as the supplier of ideological poison to a vast network of left-wing organizations seeking to shut down the platforms and financial resources of conservatives. One of these organizations, the violent group Antifa is dedicated to the idea that anyone who disagrees with its Marxist agendas is either a racist or a fascist and must be "de-platformed" by any means necessary, including violence.[23]

People who work for organizations or in institutions that they themselves do not run are particularly subject to "cancelling"—being fired and blacklisted for stepping out of line. The platform that enables me to participate in the national debate is one that I created in 1988—the David Horowitz Freedom Center, but even that doesn't protect me from the political censors. In the fall of 2018, one of our donors received the following letter when she tried to get matching funds directed to the Center through a charity set up for that purpose.

> Hi, Anne,
>
> Thank you for reaching out to us about David Horowitz Freedom Center. At this time, the organization that you are interested in supporting is not included in the program because they are on the SPLC watch list. The SPLC is, "Dedicated to reducing prejudice, improving intergroup relations and supporting equitable school experiences for our nation's children." Because David Horowitz Freedom Center is on the SPLC watch list, they have been marked as an ineligible organization. More information on the SPLC can be found on their website (www.splcenter.org/) and if you have any questions for us, please let us know.
>
> Cheers

The letter was signed by the "Goodness Engagement Specialist" of the charity. Orwell could not have named the position more appropriately.

That same fall, Mastercard informed the company that handles the donation website for the Freedom Center that it would no longer honor Mastercard-credited donations. Fortunately, the Center's lawyers were able to get Mastercard to reverse their decision, but not before a considerable amount of money and resources had been expended.

According to Mastercard, their action was taken in response to a complaint from the website Bloodmoney.org, which was created by Color of Change, an organization founded by CNN commentator and Democrat Party leftist Van Jones. A headline at the site reads, "Who's Taking Blood Money from Hate Groups? Financial Service Companies Doing Business with White Supremacists Are Profiting from Hate." According to the Blood Money website, as many as "158 funding sources have been removed from white supremacist sites since the beginning of this campaign."

Breitbart editor Allum Bokhari has called this "financial blacklisting" and declared it, "the most totalitarian form of blacklisting" and a "terrifying new threat to freedom": "Financial blacklisting doesn't just rob you of a chance to spread your message: it robs you of your ability to do business, your livelihood, your very means of functioning in a capitalist society. Thanks to the encroachment of progressive ideology into the financial industry—including major credit card companies like Visa, Discover, and Mastercard—it has now become a reality."[24]

A Chilling Encounter with the Hatemongers

I did not realize the full power of the Left's blacklists until I was invited to address state legislators at an American Legislative Exchange Council (ALEC) conference. ALEC was created in 1973 as a bipartisan organization to draft model legislation promoting limited government, free markets, and federalism. Its annual meeting began on August 10, 2018, in New Orleans. About 1,200 state legislators attended.

I had been invited to speak by a member group hoping to promote their campaign for a "Convention of the States" that would meet to amend the Constitution. The entire thrust of my speech was to berate Republicans for being too timid in advancing conservative agendas and to urge them to seize the opportunities created by President Trump's bold and aggressive example.[25] I pointed out that Republicans had failed to repeal and replace Obamacare though they had pledged and been elected to do just that. I observed that Republicans controlled thirty-three state legislatures but had done nothing to stop Democrat teacher unions and their members from turning the K–12 schools into indoctrination centers for leftist ideas. The result, I said, was that "school curricula have been turned over to racist organizations like Black Lives Matter, and terrorist organizations like the Muslim Brotherhood [through its front group CAIR]." These were the *only* references I made to blacks or Muslims in the entire speech, but they were enough for leftists to use them to attack my hosts and cause massive financial damage to their organization.[26]

In addition to my keynote speech, which received a standing ovation from the assembled legislators, I also spoke on a panel with former senator Tom Coburn. In my remarks I recalled a seminal moment when Trump emerged as a different kind of Republican leader. This took place during the first primary debate, where the first question was to Trump. It came from Fox anchor Megyn Kelly, who accused the novice candidate of calling women "fat pigs, dogs and slobs." Instead of backing away from these charges, as every other Republican would have done, Trump did not miss a beat before answering: "Only Rosie O'Donnell."

O'Donnell was an obese actress with a nasty mouth who had been involved in many ugly public clashes with Trump in the past, handing out insults as good as she got.[27] Trump's response to Kelly's attack won me over. He was the first Republican I had seen who would not be cowed by political correctness, under whose strictures attacking a woman's looks—indeed attacking a woman at all—was off limits. He had made it clear that he would not retreat under fire. Instead he was ready to fight back.

When the panel at the ALEC convention invited questions from the audience, a distraught state legislator from Wisconsin named Chris Taylor rose to attack me. "You can't say that about women," she shouted at me. "You can't call women fat pigs." To which I replied: "Even if they are fat pigs? And with nasty mouths like Rosie O'Donnell? Why do you feel that you are personally implicated by O'Donnell's behavior or Trump's remark—or that women as a whole are? Why doesn't the comment apply the way it was intended, to the individual herself?"[28]

I hadn't realized the questioner was a Democrat, nor did I think much about the incident at the time. Then, three days after I returned home, a report on the convention written by Taylor appeared on PRWatch.org, the website of a leftwing organization called the Center for Media Democracy, which was anything but a center for democracy. Taylor's article was titled "ALEC in Disarray." In it she said, "The biggest disaster I have ever seen at an ALEC conference was on a panel about the Convention of States. . . . One of the key speakers was right-wing provocateur David Horowitz. Horowitz is listed in a Southern Poverty Law Center report published by Alternet with the title: "10 of America's Most Dangerous Hatemongers."[29]

Though there was no evidence to justify it, the SPLC slander proved sufficient to cost ALEC tens of thousands of dollars in donations over the next weeks and months. Two and a half weeks after my speech, PRWatch announced that a coalition of seventy-nine leftist organizations had signed a letter calling on ALEC's corporate donors to withdraw their financial support from the bipartisan organization. At the end of August, the seventy-nine were joined by Common Cause and People for the American Way, once pillars of American liberalism.

In a statement typical of the attacks, Common Cause announced that it had signed on with "more than 70 other government reform, civil rights, labor, environmental, and advocacy organizations urging some of the largest corporate funders of the American Legislative Exchange Council to cut ties with the organization after ALEC gave hatemonger David Horowitz a platform at their recent conference to spread white supremacist, sexist, and racist ideas."[30] Although I had posted my speech on the Internet, no citations from the speech were offered to justify these accusations. Throughout this boycott no example of my alleged white supremacist, sexist, and racist ideas was provided, because there was none.

The letter sent by the blacklist coalition to ALEC's corporate donors began:

> We write to urge that you cease your association with and stop funding the American Legislative Exchange Council (ALEC), which recently provided a platform for white supremacist, sexist, and racist rhetoric at their annual meeting. At its August 2018 convention in New Orleans, ALEC had David Horowitz—a right-wing extremist—as one of its featured speakers at two parts of the conference. Horowitz's Freedom Center has been identified by the Southern Poverty Law Center as a group "giving anti-Muslim voices and radical ideologies a platform to project hate and misinformation."[31]

That was the complete extent of their non-existent case against me. Referring to Black Lives Matter as "racist" and the Muslim Brotherhood as terrorist were sufficient crimes to have me banned as a white supremacist, anti-Muslim "hatemonger." Within a month, Verizon, the largest telecommunications provider in the United States and a sponsor of ALEC for thirty years, told The Intercept that the company was withdrawing its annual $20,000 support: "'Our company has no tolerance for racist, white supremacist or sexist comment or ideals,' Verizon spokesperson Richard Young said."[32] Young did not provide any example of these sins, or give any indication that he had read what I had said, even though it was easily available on the Internet. The imprimatur of the SPLC guttersnipes and Chris Taylor's absurd claim that pugnacious women are above criticism were sufficient to erase who I was and replace me with the political caricature, "extremist, white supremacist, sexist, dangerous hatemonger."

Verizon's withdrawal was followed by AT&T's, whose spokesman, Jim Greer told The Intercept, "We have ended our membership with ALEC and their convention speaker was a key factor in the decision." AT&T also didn't cite anything I actually said that might have prompted their decision. It was just the word of my left-wing defamers and the SPLC. The Intercept also reported that Dow Chemical and Honeywell had withdrawn their financial support.[33]

If the SPLC-inspired witch hunt had been confined to sites like PRWatch and BloodMoney, and to organizations like People for the American Way and Common Cause, it would have been ominous enough. But these organizations reflected the views of constituencies that have become ascendant in the Democrat Party and increasingly shape its political strategies. This was made crystal clear in the 2018 midterm elections, which came hard on the heels of the ALEC fiasco. In these elections, many Democrat candidates played the race card against their Republican opponents, accusing them, without any basis in fact, of being white supremacists and racists.

Thanks to the attacks on my appearance at ALEC, I was dragged into the most dramatic and critical of these races—the gubernatorial contest in Florida. The SPLC's caricature of me was used to tar the Republican candidate, Congressman Ron DeSantis, as a hatemonger too. The outcome of the race in Florida, a critical swing state, was particularly important because of its implications for the 2020 presidential election, since Florida was a battleground state. In September, just weeks after the attacks on ALEC, the Democrat Party and its loyal media were using me—or rather the SPLC's lies about me—as a weapon with which to destroy the character and candidacy of DeSantis simply because he had spoken at events I hosted.

DeSantis is a West Point graduate and Iraq veteran with a stellar legislative record. He was running against the black mayor of Tallahassee, Andrew Gillum, a political leftist who was under federal investigation for corruption—and, as was revealed not long after the election, was a serious drug addict. Gillum regularly fended off his critics by calling them racists. As the campaign began in earnest, the Democrats and the media were already attacking DeSantis as an alleged "racist" for an innocuous remark he had made about Gillum's socialist beliefs.

Noting that Florida's economy was booming, DeSantis had said, "The last thing we need to do is to monkey this up by trying to embrace a socialist agenda with huge tax increases and bankrupting the state."[34] There was nothing remotely racist about this statement. However, the Florida NAACP responded by saying that comparison of blacks to monkeys—a comparison that DeSantis had not made— was "by far the best-known racist reference to African Americans in our national folklore."[35] DeSantis had compared *socialists*, not blacks, to monkeys, but the race-obsessed Democrats and their partisan media simply ignored this fact, knowing the media would not hold them to account. Gillum added fuel to the racial fire, saying, "In the handbook of Donald Trump they no longer do whistle calls [to racists]—they're now using full bullhorns."[36]

Just after Labor Day, as the mid-terms began to heat up, the following headline appeared in the *Washington Post*: "GOP Candidate for Fla. Governor Spoke at Racially Charged Events." The events the *Post* was referring to were ones I had been hosting annually for more than twenty years in Palm Beach as the "Restoration Weekend." There was nothing "racially charged" about these events, whose speakers were from the conservative and Republican Party mainstream. Among the featured speakers we had hosted were three former U.S. attorneys general, along with a raft of congressmen, including Senators John McCain and Lindsey Graham; Senate Majority Leader Mitch McConnell; Congressmen Roy Blount, Mike Pence, Bob Goodlatte, and Devin Nunes; and former Speakers of the House Newt Gingrich and John Boehner. Far from being racist, as the *Post* insinuated—without providing any evidence—the Restoration Weekends also featured prominent black conservatives such as J. C. Watts, Ben Carson, Herman Cain, Jason Reilly, Larry Elder, Allen West, Candace Owens, and Fox Business anchor Charles Payne. We gave an award to Carson and another to Adrian Fenty, former

African-American mayor of Washington, D.C.—and a Democrat—for his advocacy for inner-city black children.[37]

Ignoring these facts, the Post's article began, "Rep. Ron DeSantis (R-Fla.), a gubernatorial nominee who recently was accused [sic!] of using racially tinged language, spoke four times at conferences organized by a conservative activist who has said that African Americans owe their freedom to white people and that the country's 'only serious race war' is against whites." Both statements—which were culled from the Southern Poverty Law Center "Hate Watch" feature—were true. What group in America other than whites could be openly attacked on the basis of their skin color? But in the prevailing political climate these quotes were just dog whistles to progressives geared up for wars against "whiteness" and America, a majority white nation that was indeed responsible for abolishing slavery as immoral after three thousand years in which it had been a socially acceptable institution not only among whites but among black Africans, brown Hispanics, and red-skinned Indians.

The Post's prestige caused the article about my DeSantis connection to ignite a firestorm of attacks on him for his association with me. The Miami Herald, which reprinted the Post article verbatim, was the first of half a dozen major Florida newspapers to run with the slander. In a disgraceful headline that set the tone for many of the attacks that followed nationally, the Huffington Post claimed, "DeSantis Gave Four Paid Speeches for Infamous Racist." Actually, DeSantis had received no compensation for his four speeches—congressional rules forbid members from receiving compensation. His speeches were exclusively about foreign policy. Finally, I was an infamous racist only to hatemongers on the Left, who had lost all touch with reality where race was concerned.

Once a slander is launched, an alarmingly broad cohort of media reporters can be counted on to repeat it without bothering to check the claims. In another typical headline, the website news organization Common Dreams proclaimed, "Newly Revealed Paid Speeches Leave 'No Question Whatsoever' That Republican Ron DeSantis Is a Racist," and then repeated the slanders about me from SPLC's "Hate Watch." Other media outlets joining the attacks included *Esquire, New York Magazine, Politico, Newsweek,* the *Orlando Sentinel,* the *Tampa Bay Post, Naples News,* and the *Sunshine State News.* In blaring headlines, I was called "a hatemonger," "a white supremacist," and a "race war theorist" because of my off-the-cuff comment about whites currently being the only serious targets of a race war.

The entire aim of the malicious distortions of statements and facts—indeed, the whole tenor of the Democrat attacks—was that Republicans were racists, unfit to be taken seriously, and that the country would be better off if there were only one party, a party dedicated to the "socially just" future as seen through the eyes of left-wing zealots. Just before the gubernatorial election, which DeSantis won by a hair, Axios published the results of a poll showing that a majority of Democrats—61 percent—regarded Republicans as "racists," "sexists," and "bigots."[38]

This was entirely predictable for a party that has come to rely on name-calling and hate rather than reason and persuasion, and whose leaders characterize their opponents as "deplorables" and "irredeemables" and "white supremacists." A party that relies on moral indictments to advance its political agendas, and which elevates tribal groups over the individuals who compose them, is a totalitarian party in the making. A party that proposes to "save the planet," or establish a society where "social justice" reigns, is a party that demands intolerance from its adherents and will regard democratic compromise with an imperfect world as a betrayal of its apocalyptic cause.

Such a party's ideological roots and dispositions are the opposite of the liberal principles and values—equal rights, tolerance, and compromise—enshrined in the American Founding. Instead, they are tribal and bellicose. Their origins lie in the nineteenth-century revolts *against* liberal democracy, including fascism, which are the historical antecedents of the modern Left. The clearest and most influential formulations of their doctrines are in the writings of Marx and Lenin.

In Lenin's view, a true revolutionary does not establish the correctness of his beliefs by appealing to evidence or logic, as if there were some standard of truthfulness above social classes. Rather, he engages in "blackening an opponent's mug so well it takes him ages to get it clean again." Nikolay Valentinov, a Bolshevik who got close to Lenin before becoming disillusioned, reports his saying, "There is only one answer to revisionism: smash its face in!"[39] In 1907, [Lenin] characterized his attacks on other Socialists as follows: "That tone, that formulation, is not designed to convince but to break ranks, not to correct a mistake of the opponent but to annihilate him, to wipe him off the face of the earth."[40] In other words, all "truth" is partisan, and all politics is war.

That pretty accurately sums up the goal of the billion-dollar leftist blacklist industry and the Left's general political discourse. Their attitude is reflected in the most popular leftist text of the last fifty years, Saul Alinsky's *Rules for Radicals*: "One acts decisively only in the conviction that all the angels are on one side and all the devils on the other side."[41]

In my ALEC speech I had warned the assembled legislators about the threat posed by Democrats who no longer embrace the principles of American pluralism—individual freedom and individual accountability—but were committed instead to the collectivist and anti-democratic doctrines of group identity, group privilege and group rights: "Why are we raising this prospect of reform to the fundamental law of the land (i.e., the Constitution)?" I had asked. My answer: "It's because we are in the midst of a constitutional crisis the likes of which we have not seen since the Civil War. It's because a political Left that rejects the framework of the Constitution is now in control of the Democrat Party and is pursuing an agenda that has already destroyed key pillars of our democracy and will go on to destroy its very foundations if bold measures are not taken."[42]

8

Orwellian Seditions

At the center of George Orwell's dystopian portrait of a totalitarian future is the dark edifice of the Ministry of Truth. It is an institution that is, in fact, a Ministry of Lies, the central pillar of the despotism that controls every aspect of its citizens' lives. Its slogans—"Freedom Is Slavery," "Ignorance Is Strength," and "War Is Peace"—are designed to destroy independent thinking and to further the ends of the totalitarian state. The first target of the Ministry of Truth is memory, because remembrance of the past is an anchor in reality that will frustrate the state's efforts to control its subjects' minds.

The ultimate purpose of turning truths into their opposites is to turn the enemies of the totalitarian state into objects of hate so their dissent can be suppressed. In Orwell's dystopia, the state organizes "Two Minutes of Hate" sessions and regular "Hate Weeks" as rituals to dehumanize dissenters, to ensure that no one will listen to them or believe a word they say. It is all too reminiscent of the blacklists organized and enforced by the political Left in America today.

In Orwell's dystopia, the mission of the Ministry of Truth is encapsulated in two slogans:

(1) Who controls the past controls the future.

(2) Who controls the present controls the past.

Today the ideological Left already controls a large swathe of the American present. It dominates the intellectual and popular cultures that shape its citizens' perceptions: the universities, the schools, the media, the entertainment industry, and the non-profit world of advocacy institutions which functions as a shadow political universe. Drawing on its prodigious power to affect the nation's consciousness, the Left—led by the *New York Times* and the Pulitzer Foundation—has systematically targeted the American Founding with the intention of burying the American idea and paving the way for a new anti-democratic order.

America is unique among nations in being founded not on an identity rooted in "blood and soil" but on a set of shared universal values. The American Founding in the revolutionary era 1776–1787 was based on what its creators regarded as "self-evident" principles that provided the sinews of a national identity. Commitment to these principles has created a unity among the diverse peoples who have settled and occupied this country ever since. They have been the inspirational force enabling America to abolish slavery, become a universal symbol of freedom, and provide the world's chief bulwark against global tyrannies.

It is this inspirational memory that the political Left has set out to erase and destroy. The most disturbing manifestation of this malevolent aggression is the so-called "1619 Project," the brainchild of a staff writer at the *New York Times* named Nikole Hannah-Jones. It is supported by the Pulitzer Foundation, the Smithsonian Institution, and the nation's cultural elite. Six months after its launch, the "1619 Project" was already a curriculum in thirty-five hundred public high schools spread through all fifty states.[1] Given the extreme left-wing nature of the teachers' unions and the public education establishment, this is hardly surprising.[2]

The "1619 Project" was described by *Times* editorial board member Mara Gay in the following words: "In the days and weeks to come, we will publish essays demonstrating that nearly everything that has made

America exceptional grew out of slavery."[3] In a formal statement, the *Times* editorial board elaborated: "The 1619 Project is a major initiative from *The New York Times* observing the 400th anniversary of the beginning of American slavery. It aims to reframe the country's history, understanding 1619 as our true founding, and placing the consequences of slavery and the contributions of black Americans at the very center of the story we tell ourselves about who we are."[4]

In other words, in its very conception, the 1619 Project is an historically illiterate libel, based on a series of lies, designed to erase the actual Founding of America in 1776 and its revolutionary ideals. That Founding was memorialized by Lincoln at Gettysburg as a "new nation conceived in liberty and dedicated to the proposition that all men are created equal." In its place, the 1619 Project and its progressive supporters propose to substitute a defamation of America's history worthy of its most dedicated enemies.

The creator of the 1619 Project, Nikole Hannah-Jones, an African American, is a pro-Castro leftist. She has written an introduction to the Project titled "America Wasn't a Democracy, Until Black Americans Made It One."[5] The title reveals the racist attitudes of both the author and her Project's sponsors by implying that blacks wrote the Declaration of Independence, created the Abolitionist Movement, drafted and financed the Union Army, sacrificed 350,000 lives to win the Civil War, and wrote the Emancipation Proclamation and the Thirteenth, Fourteenth, and Fifteenth Amendments, which abolished slavery and guaranteed equal rights and full citizenship to freed slaves. To overcome the South's denial of these rights, blacks next unilaterally created and financed the NAACP and other civil rights organizations without major political, monetary, and organizational support from whites, then wrote and passed the Civil Rights Acts. Of course, these are all blatant fictions, and the only reason Hannah-Jones's malicious and ignorant screed is not a subject of ridicule but a curriculum in American schools is because anti-white racism is the fashion among the nation's cultural elites at this troubled moment in our history.

Hannah-Jones explains the Project's decision to make the year 1619 America's Founding in these words: "In August 1619, just 12 years after the English settled Jamestown, Va. . . . the Jamestown colonists bought 20 to 30 enslaved Africans from English pirates. The pirates had stolen them from a Portuguese slave ship that had forcibly taken them from what is now the country of Angola. *Those men and women who came ashore on that August day were the beginning of American slavery.* They were among the 12.5 million Africans who would be *kidnapped* from their homes and brought in chains across the Atlantic Ocean in the largest forced migration in human history until the Second World War" [emphasis added].[6]

So many lies are packed into these few sentences. The statement that 1619 was "the beginning of American slavery" is false. Virginia was not America in 1619. It was an English colony. The shipment of Africans to Virginia was a continuation of English—not American—practice. Moreover, slavery was actually illegal in the Virginia Colony in 1619. The twenty Africans brought to Virginia in 1619 were not slaves but, as the distinguished Princeton historian Nell Painter, herself African American, has pointed out, indentured servants under contracts that would free them in a few years.[7] Nor was indentured servitude exclusive to Africans. The majority of Virginia's labor force was composed of indentured servants who were white.

The casual slander that 12.5 million Africans were "kidnapped" and shipped to America in the Atlantic Slave Trade is misleading, repugnant, and historically false. The Africans who were eventually brought to America as slaves had not been enslaved by whites but by black Africans who sold them to Europeans at slave auctions in Ghana and Benin.[8] Moreover, the proper total of American slaves is 388,000—less than a fraction of 1 *percent* of the slave trade in Africans globally, which exceeded 50 million.[9] This is bad enough, but also a sign that American slavery was a minor part of the global slave trade, and dramatically less than Hannah-Jones and her enablers would like it to be to justify their attack on the country that freed its slaves. The last thing the creators of the 1619 Project would want to do is highlight the far larger, and more brutal and deadly slave systems imposed on Africans by slave masters, including non-white slave masters, in other parts of the world.[10] In Brazil, for example, where the master class was "of color," the slave labor force had to be replaced every year because conditions were so brutal. In America, by contrast, the slave population grew nearly four-fold in the fifty-six years after Americans abolished the slave trade in 1807.[11]

These are not obscure facts. They were readily available to the anti-American ideologues of the 1619 Project should they have cared to look them up. The fact that this vicious attack by the *New York Times* and Pulitzer Foundation on America's creation, its Founders, and its history is based on a series of easily disproved fictions, is a measure of the virulence of the hatred they feel for their own country.

The ideological character of the 1619 Project is manifest in the subtitle of Hannah-Jones's introduction: "Our Democracy's Founding Ideals Were False when They Were Written. Black Americans Have Fought to Make Them True."[12] This racist claim is based first of all on a misunderstanding of the word "ideals," and then on an extravagant distortion of the historical record. "Ideals" are by their very nature aspirations, not facts. The Founders' ideals were actually commitments they made, which—over time and at great human cost—they and their heirs did make good on.

Hannah-Jones's characterization of the Founders as "pro-slavery" is an offensive slander without any basis in fact. In the words of C. Bradley Thompson's scholarly study of the Founders' attitudes, *America's Revolutionary Mind*, "Not a single revolutionary leader ever publicly praised slavery as a positive good. Benjamin Franklin, speaking as president of the Pennsylvania Society of Promoting the Abolition of Slavery, described slavery as 'an atrocious debasement of human nature.' George Washington, a slaveholder, told a friend, 'There is not a man living, who wishes more sincerely than I do to see a plan adopted for the abolition of [slavery].' At the Constitutional Convention in 1787, James Madison told his colleagues, 'We have seen the mere distinction of color made in the most enlightened period of time, a ground of the most oppressive dominion ever exercised by man over man.'"[13]

Hannah-Jones's preposterous claim that the American Revolution was fought to *preserve* slavery is also a transparent lie. The year 1787 saw the passing of the Northwest Ordinance, which established settlement of the region that would become Ohio, Indiana, Illinois, Michigan, and Wisconsin. It was a geographical area as large as the existing thirteen states. Article IV of the Ordinance outlawed slavery in this unsettled land.[14] What rationale would the allegedly pro-slavery Founders have had for doing that?

Inspired by their commitment to equality and liberty, the American Founders immediately began dismantling the institution of slavery in the Northern states, which were soon, when the process of abolition was completed in 1804, referred to as the "Free States."[15] So why didn't they simply abolish slavery throughout all the United States? An obvious, compelling reason was that they feared the catastrophe of a civil war—which eventually did kill more Americans than all of America's other wars to the present day combined. But there was an even worse prospect for them to consider. If the Founders had attempted to abolish slavery in the Slave South in 1787, the South would have joined forces with the British—the greatest empire in the world, whose soldiers managed to burn the White House in the War of 1812. Such an alliance would likely have defeated the free states of the North, and the victorious South might have extended the reign of slavery for generations. So they sought to delay a bloodbath that might result in an extension of slavery, believing it was a backward economic system that was bound to fall of its own weight.

Because of their racist attitudes against whites, neither Hannah-Jones nor the *Times* editors even bother to ask the serious question of why the anti-slavery signers of the Declaration of Independence might have had reason to compromise with the Slave South. For them the only possible answer is white hypocrisy, white perfidy, and white racism.

The real purpose of the 1619 Project is revealed in Nikole Hannah-Jones's baseless claim that "Anti-black racism runs in the very DNA of this country."[16] This is a slander infamously formulated by President Barack Obama some years earlier.[17] James Oakes is one of four major American historians to sign a joint statement challenging the historical distortions of the 1619 Project. Oakes is also a liberal. "These are really dangerous tropes," Oakes warned. "They're not only ahistorical, they're actually anti-historical. The function of those tropes is to deny change over time. . . . They say, 'look at how terribly black people were treated under slavery. And look at the incarceration rate for black people today. It's the same thing. Nothing changes. There has been no industrialization. There has been no Great Migration. We're all in the same boat we were back then. And that's what original sin is. It's passed down. Every single generation is born with the same original sin. . . . There's nothing we can do to get out of it. If it's the DNA, there's nothing you can do."[18]

The obvious point of the DNA metaphor is that racism is America's essence. This is a transparent incitement to destroy America's democracy, which from its inception—and despite setbacks—has been dedicated to liberty and equality and individual freedom.

In the face of withering criticism of the 1619 Project from the nation's historians, the publisher of the *New York Times* and scion of its owning family, A. G. Sulzberger, chose to re-assert the *Times*'s support for the fraudulent project and its racist author in what amounted to a declaration of war. "[The 1619 Project] is a journalistic triumph that changed the way millions of Americans understand our country, its history and its present. Nikole is a brilliant and principled journalist who has deserved every bit of praise that has come her way," Sulzberger wrote. "As I've said many times, 1619 is one of the proudest accomplishments of my tenure as publisher."[19]

The actual history of slavery and its aftermath in America refutes the poisonous claims of America's enemies and tells an opposite story. In *City Journal*, the American historian Allen Guelzo dismissed the *Times* project as a "conspiracy theory" developed from the "chair of ultimate cultural privilege in America, because in no human society has an enslaved people suddenly found itself vaulted into positions of such privilege, and with the consent—even the approbation—of those who were once the enslavers."[20]

Even more powerful scholarly testimony comes from Professor Orlando Patterson, a man of the Left and a renowned Harvard sociologist who has written award-winning books on slavery and race and is an African American. In Patterson's words, "[America] is the least racist white-majority society in the world; has a better record of legal protections of minorities than any other society, white or black; offers more opportunities to greater numbers of black persons than any other society, including those of Africa."[21]

The anti-American hatred embodied in the 1619 Project is not inspired by the history of American slavery and emancipation, but by the anti-capitalist ideology and anti-white racism of the Project's left-wing authors and their patrons on the *Times*'s editorial board. This is evident from the actual articles that make up the Project and its curriculum, which do not examine the facts—complex as they are—of what took place in August 1619, but use slavery as a brush with which to tar every aspect of American life.

The hundred-page special issue of the *New York Times Magazine* that launched the Project reveals all one needs to know about its purpose. The issue includes the following articles (and only these): "America Wasn't a Democracy, Until Black Americans Made It One," "American Capitalism Is Brutal. You Can Trace That to the Plantation," "Why Is Everyone Always Stealing Black Music?" "How Segregation Caused Your Traffic Jam," "How False Beliefs in Physical Racial Difference Still Live in Medicine Today," "The Barbaric History of Sugar in America," "Why Doesn't America Have Universal Healthcare? One Word: Race," "Why American Prisons Owe Their Cruelty to Slavery," "How America's Vast Racial Wealth Gap Grew: By Plunder," and finally one that is entirely transparent in exposing the authors' relentless political agenda—"What the Reactionary Politics of 2019 Owe to the Politics of Slavery."[22] In other words the Trump administration is a legacy of slavery.

The Origins of the 1619 Project

The 1619 Project is a racist falsification of American history, a smear campaign against America's Founding, its achievements, and its present force for good in the world. It is to America what *The Protocols of the Elders of Zion* is to the Jews—a genocidal tract designed to justify their abolition. Already a metastasizing curriculum in America's schools, it is a dagger aimed at America's heart, at its self-esteem, its self-understanding, and its national pride. It aims to destroy America's shield against real-world enemies, who are legion because tyrannies around the world hate democracy in general and American democracy in particular.

As a result of Nikole Hannah-Jones's creation of this repellent and historically illiterate attack on a country that has given her extraordinary freedoms and privileges, she has been showered with awards by the left-wing arbiters of the culture—including a $625,000 MacArthur "Genius Award," and a Pulitzer Prize.[23] What makes the 1619 Project such an ominous portent is precisely that its ignorant bigotry and self-conscious disloyalty are embraced by American elites, including the premier institutions of the Fourth Estate, its top-tier universities and secondary schools, and its "philanthropic" universe.

A sophomoric letter Hannah-Jones wrote to the editor of the *Notre Dame Observer* long before she became a *New York Times* staffer and national celebrity reveals her visceral hatred for America and for white people, despite the fact that her own mother is white. The letter, titled "Modern Savagery," began, "Dear Editor, I was shocked and disgusted when I read Fred Kelly's article in the November 9 issue of the *Observer*. What responsible editor would print an article that applauds and dignifies the white race's rape, plunder and genocide of a whole race of people? . . . The white race is the biggest murderer, rapist, pillager and thief of the modern world. . . . Christopher Columbus and those like him were no different than Hitler. The crimes they committed were unnecessarily cruel and can only be described as acts of the devil."[24]

Perhaps understandable in a college sophomore, this kind of ignorant racism is—or should be—unacceptable in an adult, let alone a reporter for one of the nation's most prestigious media organizations, let alone a recipient of prestigious journalistic awards like the Pulitzer Prize. The ascent of Nikole Hannah-Jones is a cautionary tale in America's precipitous slide down the totalitarian slope.

The anti-American movement legitimized by the Democrat Party and the *New York Times* is not the first narrative to have canceled America's actual heritage and replaced it with a caricature designed to justify its destruction. Following the Bolshevik Revolution of 1917, Communists in America organized a political campaign to replace its liberal democracy with a "Soviet America," modelled on the Stalinist dictatorship that would be responsible for the deaths of more than 40 million Soviet citizens and the creation of a state-induced economic wasteland on a scale unprecedented in all human history.

To advance this destructive cause, a dedicated follower of the Communists named Howard Zinn put together an anti-American narrative that he published as *A People's History of the United States*. This text was designed to justify the seditious agenda of his Marxist mentors. Thanks to the radicals who colonized the faculties of American universities and secondary schools in the 1970s and 1980s and made Zinn required reading for students, *A People's History* is the bestselling history book ever written. Entire university courses in such unrelated fields as "Social Work and Social Welfare" have been designed as week-by-week chapter readings of Zinn's 784-page anti-American diatribe.[25] *A People's History* has sold over 2.6 million copies, while inspiring many parallel indictments of America's heritage, including summaries of his text specifically designed for "young people."[26]

A review of Zinn's book in the *New York Times Sunday Book Review* by Professor Eric Foner, a celebrated leftist historian and scion of a famous Communist family, gave it this establishment imprimatur: "Historians may well view [*A Peoples' History*] as a step toward a coherent new version of American history. . . . [It] should be required reading." But so transparent are Zinn's fictions and deceptions that even some honest leftist historians have been appalled by his zeal in turning history into propaganda.[27] Nonetheless, it took forty years for an academic to produce a book-length study of Zinn's malignant text. This definitive refutation, written by Professor Mary Grabar, is titled *Debunking Howard Zinn: Exposing the Fake History That Turned a Generation against America*. Of course, without support from the nation's teachers and media institutions, Grabar's book was only able to reach a tiny fraction of Zinn's audience.

A true ideologue, Zinn was quite proud of his misrepresentations of the facts, which he regarded as a virtue because they served his only goal: the transformation of America's history into a heritage one can only hate. To take one example: "there is not a country in world history in which racism has been more important, for so long a time, as the United States."[28] Justifying maliciously absurd statements like this, which have no basis in fact, Zinn explains, "Objectivity is impossible, and it is also undesirable. That is, if it were possible it would be undesirable, because if you have any kind of a social aim, if you think history should serve society in some way; should serve the progress of the human race; should serve justice in some way, then it requires that you make your selection on the basis of what you think will advance causes of humanity."[29]

In other words, select the facts and invent the history to support your prejudices. For Zinn, his ideological agenda is more important than the complexities of historical facts. This was exactly the attitude of the Communist totalitarians Zinn admired. It never occurred to him that striving for the most truthful portrait of the past is the only way a real historian can "serve the progress of the human race."

In the service of his perverse enterprise, Zinn describes the Founding of the American Republic, the world's most successful democratic experiment, as an exercise in the tyrannical control of the many by the few for greed and profit. "The American Revolution," he writes with thinly veiled sarcasm, "was a work of genius, and the Founding Fathers deserve the awed tribute they have received over the centuries. They created the most effective system of national control devised in modern times, and showed future generations of leaders the advantages of combining paternalism with command."[30] Coming from an admirer of the mass murderer and "Father of the Peoples," Joseph Stalin, whose gulags were filled with tens of millions of recalcitrant citizens, this caricature of American democracy is simply nauseating.

In Zinn's telling, the Declaration of Independence was not a revolutionary endorsement of equality and liberty. It was a con game designed to manipulate the people into overthrowing their king to benefit rich white men. According to Zinn, the rights it appeared to guarantee were "limited to life, liberty and happiness for white males" even though the word "white" is absent from the Constitution and its Bill of Rights. Zinn condemns the Founders because they "ignored the existing inequalities in property."[31] Attacking inequalities in property was left to Zinn's heroes, Stalin and Mao who, in the name of "social justice," murdered more than 100 million people in order to spread poverty and famine among everyone but the party elites.

Zinn's is an absurdly unhistorical view of the creation of the American republic, but it is the weaponized view embraced by the political Left, for whom Zinn is an icon and his tract a canonical call for America's destruction. Zinn's book was the first comprehensive account of American history from the point of view of its radical enemies. It built on a literature of anti-American hostility that flourished in the 1960s, and it became the dominant theme of university curricula over the next fifty years.[32]

The most prominent and prolific writer shaping these radical narratives was MIT linguist Noam Chomsky. A *Chicago Tribune* profile of Chomsky once described him as "the most often cited living author. Among intellectual luminaries of all eras, Chomsky placed eighth, just behind Plato and Sigmund Freud."[33] According to the *New York Times* Chomsky is "arguably the most important intellectual alive," while to *Rolling Stone*, which otherwise hardly acknowledges the life of the mind, Chomsky is "one of the most respected and influential intellectuals in the world."[34]

In fact, Chomsky is best understood not as intellectual figure, but as the leader of a religious cult—an ayatollah of anti-American hate. This cultic resonance is not unnoticed by his followers themselves. His most important devotee, David Barsamian, is an obscure public radio producer in Boulder, Colorado, who has created a library of Chomskyana on tape from interviews he conducted with the master and converted into pamphlets and books. In the introduction to one such offering, Barsamian describes Chomsky's power over his disciples in these words: "Although decidedly secular, he is for many of us our rabbi, our preacher, our *rinpoche*, our pundit, our *imam*, our *sensei*."[35] Barsamian also quotes this supporting opinion from the *Times Literary Supplement*: "Chomsky's work . . . has some of the qualities of Revelations, the Old Testament prophets and Blake."

According to Chomsky, the unprovoked Islamic terrorist attacks of 9/11 that killed three thousand American civilians because they were "infidels" may have been a great crime, but America's crimes were greater. In Chomsky's view what was striking about 9/11 was that it was the first time America's "victims" had struck back since the War of 1812 when the British (victims?!) burned the White House.

According to Chomsky, Pearl Harbor didn't count because Hawaii was a "colony" at the time and not officially the territory of the United States. "During these years [that is, between 1812 and 1941], the U.S. annihilated the indigenous population (millions of people), conquered half of Mexico, intervened violently in the surrounding region, conquered Hawaii and the Philippines (killing hundreds of thousands of Filipinos), and in the past half century particularly, extended its resort to force throughout much of the world. The number of victims is colossal. For the first time, the guns have been directed the other way. That is a dramatic [and obviously welcome —D. H.] change."[36]

According to Chomsky, America's crusade against communism during the Cold War was actually a crusade "to protect our doctrine that the rich should plunder the poor."[37] According to Chomsky, in the postwar struggle with the Soviet Empire, "the United States was picking up where the Nazis had left off." According to Chomsky, in Latin America, U.S. support by presidents Kennedy and Johnson for legitimate governments against Communist subversion led to U.S. complicity in "the methods of Heinrich Himmler's extermination squads." According to Chomsky, there is "a close correlation worldwide between torture and U.S. aid." According to Chomsky, America "invaded" Vietnam to slaughter its people, and even after America left in 1975, under Jimmy Carter and Ronald Reagan "the major policy goal of the U.S. has been to maximize repression and suffering in the countries that were devastated by our violence. The degree of the cruelty is quite astonishing."[38] Actually, it's the degree of Chomsky's unhinged, lunatic malice and his limitless mendacity that are astonishing.

According to Chomsky, "legally speaking, there's a very solid case for impeaching every American president since the Second World War. They've all been either outright war criminals or involved in serious war crimes."[39] Seen through Chomsky's eyes, what decent, caring human being would not want to see America and its war criminals—who obviously include all its citizens who voted for those presidents—brought to justice, in other words, destroyed?

Bill Ayers, unrepentant sixties terrorist and longtime political ally and confidant of Barack Obama, is one of Chomsky's numerous disciples.[40] In a memoir published on the eve of the 9/11 attacks, Ayers, recorded his joy at striking one of his targets: "Everything was absolutely ideal on the day I bombed the Pentagon. The sky was blue. The birds were singing. And the bastards were finally going to get what was coming to them."[41]

Anti-American Radicals and the Democrat Party

The presence of anti-American radicals on the political fringe in the 1960s was turned into a truly ominous development when activists like Ayers entered the Democrat Party *en masse* during George McGovern's 1972 presidential campaign. Their goal: moving the party to the left and eventually taking it over. The McGovern campaign already reflected their influence in its slogan "America Come Home," as though the principal source of global conflict was not the expanding Communist slave empire but America's efforts to counter its aggressions. When the Democrats gathered in San Francisco for their 1984 presidential convention, U.N. Ambassador Jeane Kirkpatrick characterized them as "The Blame America First Party," because of their reflexive efforts to make America the culprit in the foreign conflicts it was engaged in.[42]

In 1975, the anti-Vietnam radicals succeeded in forcing America's withdrawal and the defeat of the anti-Communist forces in Indo-China. The Communists then proceeded to slaughter two and a half million Indo-Chinese peasants without a single protest from the so-called "Anti-war Left." This was clear evidence—if it was needed—that the cause of the Left had always been hatred of America, not concern for the Vietnamese.

While anti-Communist Republicans mostly held the White House in the two decades following this debacle, the power of the radicals inside the Democrat Party steadily grew from the election of Bill Clinton in 1992 to reaching an epoch-making climax in the party's betrayal of the war in Iraq it had voted to authorize in 2003.[43] The Democrats turned against the war they had voted for only three months into the conflict itself. Their about-face was not prompted by the war itself but by the fact that it was a presidential election year and Howard Dean, a sixties "anti-war" radical, was running away with the party's nomination.[44] The party's eventual nominee, John Kerry, had given an eloquent speech on the floor of the Senate on why the war was a necessity. But he was losing the primary badly to Dean, which caused him to change his view 180 degrees and claim it was "the wrong war, in the wrong place, at the wrong time"—a morale-sapping judgment for the thousands of young men and women he and his Democrat colleagues had sent into harm's way.

It was the first time in American history that a major political party had defected from an American war it had previously supported. The Democrats' opposition to the Vietnam conflict, though an indicator of the direction in which the party was headed, was fundamentally different. By the time the Democrats called for an American withdrawal, both political parties agreed that an American withdrawal was necessary, not least because of the divisions back home. The issue separating them was the terms on which the withdrawal should be made.

Democrats sought to justify their reversal on Iraq by escalating their betrayal, accusing America's commander-in-chief of lying in order to deceive them into supporting the war. This was an impossibility since Democrats sat on the intelligence committees and had access to all the information that the president did. The Democrats' attack on a wartime president while American soldiers were engaged in close combat with a terrorist enemy was as close to treason as an American party had come since the firing on Fort Sumter that began the Civil War.

The false accusation of presidential mendacity that was the focus of the Democrats' attack was designed to distract from the obvious reason for their defection from the war. They betrayed their president and their country for political gain in the 2004 elections and in the face of a shift in their party's political base to the anti-American Left. While Democrats in Congress were denouncing the president as a "liar" and undermining the war effort, the party's radicals were holding massive demonstrations in the streets chanting, "Bush lied, people died!" and calling this moderately conservative president "Hitler"—foreshadowing how they would treat the next Republican president.[45]

Bush was able to withstand the Democrats' sabotage—which included House Speaker Nancy Pelosi's threats to cut off funding for the troops in the field during the "surge" Bush ordered to defeat al-Qaeda in Iraq. But while Bush was able to defeat Saddam's army and the al-Qaeda terrorists, the radical Democrats succeeded in achieving the goal they had been pursuing for more than thirty years. Their propaganda had so damaged the war and its Republican defenders that the Democrats won the 2008 presidential election and saw one of their own enter the Oval Office as the forty-fourth president of the United States.[46]

Barack Obama was raised by Communists, most notably his mentor Frank Marshall Davis, who was a Soviet agent.[47] Before he became a national figure, Obama's entire career was funded, orchestrated, and institutionally supported by the radical Left that had conducted massive protests designed to force America's withdrawal and defeat in the Vietnam War.[48] On the eve of his election, Obama announced his radical intentions, proclaiming, "We are five days away from fundamentally transforming the United States of America."[49] This was an unprecedented departure from the politics of compromise and moderation that the Founders had built into the structures of America's constitutional order. It was also an ominous indication of what Obama thought of the nation that would shortly elect him its commander-in-chief.

Many voters cast their ballots for Obama in hopes of healing America's racial divisions. But his agenda had little to do with healing of any kind, as his eight years in office soon showed. Instead he used his enormous political capital and the control of all three branches of government that he enjoyed in his first two years in office to ram through a socialist transformation of America's healthcare system. He fell short of his true agenda of establishing a "single-payer" system that would eliminate America's private healthcare industry and establish a communist system of full government control of a sixth of the American economy. But his radical intentions to curtail individual freedom and control Americans' healthcare decisions were clear. In stark contrast to the overwhelmingly bipartisan support for previous society-wide programs such as Social Security and Medicare, Obama and his party deliberately passed "Obamacare" without a single Republican vote.

Obama's eight-year administration marked a point of no return in America's division into two irreconcilable political factions, one defending America's traditional freedoms and the other marching towards a totalitarian future. It was a conflict of fundamental values such as had not occurred since America's Civil War. This division came to a head in 2016 with the election of a Republican whom Democrats perceived as a threat to the new progressive America they were creating, beginning with their plans for a socialized healthcare system and the establishment of "social justice" as the race-conscious organizing principle of America's social order.

PART THREE

The Political Future

9

The Anti-Trump Resistance

The Democrats' assault on the basic structures that underpin America's political order was launched in earnest five days after the 2016 election with their formation of a "Resistance" to the Trump presidency and their pledge to obstruct the new administration at every turn. The boycott and sabotage of a new president were direct assaults on the fundamental principle of America's constitutional system—the idea that political conflicts are resolved at the ballot box. Democrats' calls for the impeachment of Donald Trump before he had even been formally inaugurated, and their relentless obstruction of his presidency through the election of 2020 and beyond, constitute the most dangerous sedition in American history since the Civil War itself.[1]

Of course, like their Confederate predecessors, Democrats' conducted their efforts in the name of the Constitution. "The president's actions," declared Speaker Nancy Pelosi, as she launched a partisan effort to impeach him, "have seriously violated the Constitution. Our democracy is what is at stake."[2] But the impeachment proceedings conducted by the Democrat majority in the House of Representatives broke entirely with tradition in denying the president representation, the ability to cross-examine witnesses, and other basic requirements of due process.[3] As a result, there were no Republican votes supporting Pelosi's impeachment.

During the attempt to remove President Clinton more than twenty years earlier, Pelosi's own impeachment manager, Jerrold Nadler, now chairman of the House Judiciary Committee, explained why it had failed: "There must never be a narrowly voted impeachment or an impeachment supported by one of our major political parties and opposed by the other. Such an impeachment will produce the divisiveness and bitterness in our politics for years to come and will call into question the very legitimacy of our political institutions."[4] This obvious and ominous truth didn't stop Nadler from joining Pelosi in pursuing the destructive course he had previously condemned.

The Democrats' impeachment of Trump came during a presidential primary season, prompting critics to question the haste with which the Democrats pressed their case and to ask whether the 63 million voters who had elected the president in 2016 were not being deprived of their right to approve or remove their leader. As head of the House Intelligence Committee, Adam Schiff was assigned by Pelosi to preside over the partisan impeachment hearings. When reporters asked whether democracy and the Constitution would not be better served by waiting for the 2020 election result, which was only months away, Schiff said it was crucial *not* to leave this momentous decision up to the electorate: "As we will discuss, impeachment exists for cases in which the conduct of the president rises beyond mere policy disputes to be decided otherwise and without urgency at the ballot box. Instead, we are here today to consider a much more grave matter, and that is an attempt to use the powers of the presidency to cheat in an election. For precisely this reason, the president's misconduct cannot be decided at the ballot box, for we cannot be assured that the vote will be fairly won."[5]

Schiff's claim that Trump had attempted to cheat in an election was a partisan attack backed by no evidence and not part of the impeachment articles. The idea that Schiff and 231 other House Democrats, rather than the electorate, should decide the fates of 330 million Americans was alien to the American mind and as difficult to fathom as the fact that the entire body of House Democrats—with only two exceptions—found nothing wrong with it.

The seriousness of the Democrats' assault on the very structures of America's political order became evident when Senate Democrats introduced an amendment to abolish the Electoral College, an institution tasked by the Constitution with electing the president. The immediate impetus for this amendment and a similar call to abolish the Senate was the confirmation of Judge Brett Kavanaugh to the Supreme Court.[6] According to its detractors, the Electoral College was racist and—like the Senate—undemocratic.[7] "We should abolish the Electoral College," former Obama cabinet member and 2020 presidential candidate Julian Castro said at a Democrat forum. "It doesn't reflect the will of the people of the country." This was typical of the low level of argument Democrats were satisfied to muster to eliminate an institution central to the American political order and as old as the nation itself.

Both the Electoral College and the United States Senate are institutions the Constitution created to frustrate and thwart a mobocracy, when the electorate becomes swept up in the passions of the moment. Both were designed to prevent a "tyranny of the majority," which the Founders regarded as a clear and present danger that democracies ruled by a popular vote pose to themselves.

During the impeachment process, Speaker Pelosi and the other Democrat leaders of the House continually invoked Benjamin Franklin's answer to a woman whom he encountered as he was leaving the Constitutional Convention. She asked him whether the delegates had created a republic or a monarchy. Franklin replied "A republic, madam, if you can keep it."[8] A republic, not a democracy. The republic created by the Founders featured several crucial anti-democratic institutions, including the Electoral College and the United States Senate, to serve as a check on mass follies and ensure the survival of the constitutional order. The Framers' antipathy for pure democracies was expressed by

John Adams when he wrote, "Democracy never lasts long. It soon wastes, exhausts and murders itself. There was never a democracy that did not commit suicide."[9]

The wisdom behind the Founders' determination not to create a nation ruled simply by popular vote was once part of the civics education of every citizen—a lesson that leftist control of America's schools has all but eliminated. Here is an insightful explanation from the blog of a prominent Philadelphia law firm: "Democracies fail because a majority soon learns that it may legally deprive others of property or liberties. Those 'others' subject to such abuse may be anyone outside the majority who may be of a different race, religion, ethnic background, wealth status or political affiliation. Leaders who use popular prejudices, sloganeering and misleading claims to stir up resentment against the minority and gain power over the majority (demagoguery) become skilled at appealing to the darker emotions of fear, jealousy, xenophobia, avarice, race-baiting and hate. . . . Eventually, such oppression of the minorities and the conflicts that result overwhelm the democracy and cause its collapse."[10]

In March of 2020, a shocking attack on the Supreme Court by the Democrats' leader in the Senate underscored how advanced the Democrats' assault on the fundamental institutions of the republic was, and how dangerous to the republic's future the anti-democratic attitudes of the Left had become.

Senate Minority Leader Chuck Schumer had agreed to address a demonstration in support of *Roe v. Wade*, organized by Planned Parenthood on the steps of the Supreme Court. The purpose of the protest was to pressure the justices to support the Left's demand that abortions should be available without legal restrictions, and in particular to pressure the Court to declare unconstitutional a law that required abortion clinics to employ only doctors who had "admitting rights" to a nearby hospital. Ironically, it had once been a chief argument of the movement to legalize abortion that doing so would prevent "back alley abortions" and make abortion safe. But the ideological passions had advanced so far that this safety measure was now regarded by the protesters as an attack on women's rights.

The Supreme Court is the crown of an independent judiciary, a central feature of the separation of powers instituted by the Constitution for the very purpose of protecting the impartiality of the law. There should never be political protests on the steps of the Court to influence its decisions or, worse, protests featuring leaders of the Senate. Singling out two conservative justices whom he had tried to keep off the Court because they were conservative, the Senate Minority Leader ranted like a mafia don: "I want to tell you, Gorsuch. I want to tell you, Kavanaugh: You have released the whirlwind and you will pay the price! You won't know what hit you if you go forward with these awful decisions."[11]

The backlash to these threats, which included a rebuke from Chief Justice Roberts calling Schumer's rant "irresponsible and dangerous" forced the senator to apologize. "I'm from Brooklyn," he explained lamely on the Senate floor. "We speak in strong language. I shouldn't have used the words I did, but in no way was I making a threat."[12]

While Schumer was rebuked even by Democrats, there was no call from his party to censure or remove him. Nor was there any sense that this was not just a matter of using the wrong language but of attacking the very foundations of the republic he was sworn to serve. In fact, ever since Roosevelt's attempt to pack the Court in the 1930s and the vicious partisan attacks on Supreme Court nominees Robert Bork and Clarence Thomas, members of Schumer's Democrat Party have been working to make the Court an appendage of the political system and to destroy it as an independent, non-political branch of government.

Nor were the Electoral College and the Supreme Court the only fundamental institutions of American democracy under attack by leading Democrats. Another was the United States Senate itself. The attack was led by Democrat congressman John Dingell, who was the longest serving member of the House before he died in February 2019. Not so coincidentally, his attack was launched just as the partisan impeachment of President Trump was about to fail in the Republican-controlled

Senate. Instead of calling for the election of a Democrat majority in the Senate to remedy the situation, Dingell called for the abolition of the Senate. He was supported in this call by Democrat legislators and media anchors. MSNBC-TV host Lawrence O'Donnell, once a Senate staffer himself, presented the following argument for abolition after the Senate acquitted the president in what he referred to as "the Senate's anti-democratic action":

> The Senate is now, always has been, and always will be, an anti-democratic institution. Because the Senate does not represent people. The House of Representatives represents people. That's why it's called the People's House. The U.S. Senate represents land. And because people are not evenly distributed over our land, the 760,000 people of North Dakota get two United States senators, and the 39 million people of California get two United States senators. . . . And so, to the people on Twitter today who found themselves despairing at the Senate's anti-democratic action. . . . American democracy didn't die today. American democracy once again revealed its most serious structural flaw: the United States Senate.[13]

In fact this so-called "flaw" was purposely designed by the Founders to prevent the abuses they feared from an unbridled democracy ruled entirely by the principle of "one person, one vote." O'Donnell's views were shaped by his partisan allegiances to one faction in American politics. He was of the opinion that the previous president, Democrat Barack Obama, was "the most noble man ever to be president." More troubling was his vitriolic hatred for Obama's successor, Donald Trump—a hatred that extended to the American Founders and American presidents generally, and even to Abraham Lincoln, whom O'Donnell described as a genocidal racist:

> There is nothing noble about owning slaves. George Washington became a slave owner when he was 11 years old.

Thomas Jefferson owned slaves. Abraham Lincoln freed the slaves and won the Civil War, but he also played his part in the genocidal war against Native American tribes. That is the forgotten part of the Lincoln presidency. That's the forgotten part of American history. Native American blood on presidents' hands. There is nothing noble about genocide. But our presidential mythology insists that most of the 44 of them have been noble men, despite the fact that most of them tried to exterminate Native American tribes. Most of them were racists. Many, if not most of them, were anti-Semites. Donald Trump will take his place now among the racists who have lived in the White House. . . .[14]

The Democrats' War on America

This anti-American hatred has been a disturbingly prominent trend in the Democrat Party since the Iraq War and the Obama presidency. Consequently, it is hardly surprising that an individual such as O'Donnell, so full of hostility towards his own country and towards the 63 million Americans who voted for Trump, would cavalierly propose abolishing the United States Senate, which has been one of the pillars of America's constitutional republic since its Founding. O'Donnell's views are commonplace among Democrats and in particular the Democrats who contended for the Party's 2020 presidential nomination.

Here is a sample statement riddled with falsehoods, delivered by former presidential nominee aspirant Beto O'Rourke at a Democrat primary debate, where it was left unchallenged by the other Democrat candidates on the stage: "Racism in America is endemic. It is foundational. We can mark the creation of this country not at the 4th of July, 1776, but August 20, 1619, when the first kidnapped African was brought to this country against his will. And in bondage, and as a slave, built the greatness and the success and the wealth that neither he nor his descendants would ever be able to fully participate in and enjoy.[15]

And here is former vice-presidential candidate and U.S. Senator Tim Kaine's cancellation of America's role in ending a slave system it inherited from the British: "The United States didn't inherit slavery from anybody. We created it."[16] So much for America's leading role in the struggle for freedom. Not surprisingly, before he became a senator and vice-presidential candidate, Kaine was a member of the Christic Institute, a Marxist organization supporting the Communist guerrillas in Central America.[17]

The Democrats' assaults on America's political democracy encompass a broad range of destructive proposals. Democrats have waged a multi-year war on the integrity of the ballot by attacking all efforts to verify that voters are living citizens and vote only once. These campaigns typically weaponize racial stereotypes against white people—accusing Republicans of intimidating racial minorities by requiring voter IDs, which are allegedly out of their reach. This is not only false but patronizing to disadvantaged blacks. In fact, photo IDs are readily available to blacks and poor people and are also required for access to a multitude of low-income services including food stamps and welfare. The Democrats' disingenuous claims are also refuted by the fact that minorities have been registering to vote in record numbers, including in states that have introduced ID requirements to prevent voter fraud.[18] The transparent purpose of the "suppression" claims is to make voter fraud easier—a result that long-running Democrat majorities have actually institutionalized, for example, in the state of Minnesota.[19]

The Democrats' anti-American agenda can be seen most clearly in their relentless attacks on America's borders—without which no nation can exist—and their support for illegal immigration and for welfare, free healthcare, and voting rights for unvetted aliens who enter the country by breaking its laws. These are really attacks on the idea of citizenship, and therefore on the nation itself. America is defined by its political culture. In addition to allegiance to the nation, citizenship entails a commitment to the constitutional framework that created America's political order. Democrat support for illegal immigration is manifest contempt for the nation and an ongoing threat to its existence.

Equally disturbing is the Democrats' disdain for the First Amendment, the foundation of all American freedoms. This disdain began as a radical movement in the universities, which spread throughout the educational system and then into the Democrat Party. For fifty years, leftists conducted a long march through the nation's institutions of higher learning, systematically purging conservative professors and conservative ideas. This was accomplished through control of the hiring process and a transformation of curricula into a cornucopia of left-wing ideologies and Marxist prejudices in Women's Studies, Ethnic Studies, Whiteness Studies, Post-Colonial Studies, Gay Studies, and the like.[20]

By 2016 the ratio of registered Democrats to registered Republicans in five ostensibly non-ideological academic fields—economics, history, law, journalism, and psychology—was 10 to 1, according to a study conducted by Mitchell Langbert, Anthony Quain, and Daniel B. Klein. The lowest ratio was 5 to 1, in economics; the highest 33.5 to 1, in history.[21] This ideological purge of conservative faculty and ideas created no problems for self-described "liberal" professors whose silence abetted the purge. By the 2020 election cycle, conservative lecturers merely visiting university campuses became the targets of abusive protests which turned their appearances into circuses rather than intellectual exchanges and even led to outright bans. Today universities are, for all intents and purposes, one-party states hostile to the liberal principles of the American Founding.

In retrospect, it is clear that this was a fifty-year campaign against diversity of ideas and freedom of speech with the clear goal of establishing a left-wing orthodoxy and a one-party state.[22] It would be hard to imagine a goal more inimical to the core principles of a liberal education, or American democracy. The subversion of the nation's universities and destruction of their liberal curricula had a profound social impact, affecting the judiciary, the world of tax-exempt political foundations, the nation's media, and the Democrat Party. In the realm of media, the left-wing television networks and cable channels have become notorious for their monolithic character. Their self-identified "liberal" anchors and commentators seem perfectly at ease with a situation that used to be familiar only in dictatorships and authoritarian regimes.

The new Marxist academic fields have imposed political orthodoxies that are hostile to American principles. Their fruits are a politicized media and judiciary, a race-conscious Democrat Party whose socialist programs aim to redistribute wealth on a political and even racial basis and to create a class of prosecutors and municipal leaders whose sympathies lie with criminals if they happen to be minorities. In the summer of 2020 these municipal officials, corrupted by the academic race industry, demonstrated that they would not defend their citizens or public property in the face of barbarian riots in over six hundred American cities. Nor would they defend the forces of the law, the thin blue line that stands between civil order and barbarism.

Typically, Democrats and their media allies, who are in revolt against America's 243-year-old political system, attribute America's divisions to Republicans and President Trump. Although left-wing channels like CNN and MSNBC are as diverse as Radio Moscow at the height of the Cold War, they point to Fox News as a right-wing monolith and therefore not a real news service. In fact, Fox's main anchor, Chris Wallace, is an anti-Trump leftist and reliable transmitter of Democrat talking points. A second anchor, Juan Williams, is similarly dedicated to delivering the Democrats' anti-Trump party line.

Fox News also features a long roster of paid Democrat operatives who are a daily presence on the channel as paid "Fox contributors." These include former acting DNC chair Donna Brazile; Obama administration spokesperson and apologist for the Benghazi scandal, Marie Harf; top Democrat political consultants Mary Anne Marsh and Jessica Tarlov; and progressive talk show host Leslie Marshall. Fox has also hosted Democrat primary debates and town halls—a gesture not reciprocated by CNN and MSNBC—and daily features Democrat guests such as the fierce partisans Chris Hahn, Robert Wolf, Richard

Goodstein, and Richard Fowler. Despite this diverse reality, Fox is regularly—and contemptuously—dismissed by the Left as Trump's mouthpiece. Some have even referred to Fox News—preposterously—as "Trump's state TV."[23] To admit that Fox is actually relatively and uniquely "fair and balanced" would undermine their smug commitment to a one-party system.

So relentless are the Left's efforts to discredit and silence their opposition that Kamala Harris thought it perfectly natural to ask Twitter to close the president's account so that she—and Trump's 88 million followers—would no longer be exposed to his ideas.[24] This went into the resume that earned her a place with Biden on the Democrat ticket for the White House.

Sympathy for the Devil

Democrats have so intensified the passions of factionalism, making all politics a zero-sum game—and so ramped up their attacks on America's heritage and principles—that they have developed a disturbing sympathy for America's enemies and taken a stance of non-resistance to their threats. They carry water for aggressive foreign dictatorships like China and Iran, support violent criminals on America's streets, and insist on open borders for criminals entering the country from Central and South America. Their support for criminals includes "no bail" reforms that put violent individuals who have been apprehended immediately back on the streets; the release of tens of thousands of convicted felons, allegedly to protect them from the coronavirus; and the creation of sanctuary cities and states for violent criminals who are in the country illegally and have committed hundreds of thousands of crimes.

Democrats have also taken sympathetic positions towards terrorists, both domestic and foreign, who are engaged in a holy war against the West. Barack Obama built his Middle East policy on ending the isolation of Iran—an isolation that had been imposed by America and its allies because of Iran's sponsorship of global terror. In pursuit of this goal,

Obama lifted sanctions on a regime that was—and remains—headed by leaders who chant "Death to America" and are dedicated to an Islamic holy war against "infidels" globally. Obama received no "quid pro quo" for this favor. In the infamous "Iran Deal," Obama and the Democrats provided the anti-American mullahs legitimacy, a path to nuclear weapons, and more than $150 billion in unmarked bills with which they could expand a campaign of terror that had already taken thousands of American lives.

Democrats' reflexive sympathy for America's most aggressive enemy was again on display when Iran launched an attack on the American embassy in Baghdad. In the midst of the attack, Major General Qasem Soleimani, who had headed Iran's terrorist operations throughout the Middle East and was responsible for killing and maiming hundreds of Americans, landed in Baghdad to supervise and escalate the Iranian assault. Even as he arrived, President Trump ordered a drone strike on his vehicle, killing him and ending his reign of terror.

Tony Badran, a research fellow at the Foundation for the Defense of Democracies, summed up the event this way: "At one stroke, the U.S. president has decapitated the Iranian regime's chief terror arm and its most prominent extension in Iraq, where the U.S. Embassy was set on fire last week. In addition to being responsible for killing hundreds of U.S. soldiers during the Iraq War, Soleimani directed a larger state project, which has shaped the geopolitics of the region. . . . Strategically, the killing of Osama bin Laden and, more recently, of ISIS leader Abu Bakr al-Baghdadi, pale by comparison."[25]

Democrats, busy pressing their partisan impeachment of the president, were not about to support their commander-in-chief's bold action, disloyal as opposing it might be. They were also in the midst of a presidential primary. All their candidates, without exception, condemned the president for what they described as the "assassination of a government official of Iran," as though Trump were the terrorist.[26] Writing for the anti-Trump The Intercept Robert Mackey defended these Democrat attacks by calling Trump's action "the killing of a general from a nation the United States has not declared war on, at the express direction of the American president."[27]

While it is true that the United States had not formally declared war on Iran, the United States has not declared war on any country since World War II—not North Korea, not Afghanistan, not Iraq. At the same time, it is an obvious fact that Iran's rulers have declared war on the United States beginning with the regime's creation in 1979. The Islamic fanatics who seized power in Iran that year took America's embassy staff hostage, even as their "Supreme Leader," the Ayatollah Khomeini, pronounced an anathema on America as "The Great Satan."

Four years later, Iran's terrorist proxies, under General Soleimani's command, blew up America's Marine barracks in Lebanon, killing 241 U.S. Marines and 67 others, all of whom were unarmed. In the following decades, the terror regime continued to slaughter Americans, supplying improvised explosive devices (IEDs) to the Iraqis, for example, even as Iran's rulers led Iranian crowds in chants of "Death to America," in case anyone misunderstood their intentions.

The Islamic Republic of Iran is a leader of the holy war that radical Islam has declared on America and the West. Democrats often—as in the case of Soleimani—seem to be in denial that this war even exists. Democrats' animus towards their own country fosters the delusional belief that defending it by confronting "radical Islamic terrorism," is actually anti-Muslim racism or "Islamophobia." On the other hand, Democrats have a warm attitude towards the Chinese Communist dictatorship which has put a million Uighur Muslims in concentration camps. They seem to ignore their own hypocrisy, supporting Islamic hate groups like Hamas, the PLO, and C.A.I.R. and in embracing their own congressional "Squad" of Islamic terrorist supporters.

Their denials blind Democrats to the real threats America faces. The delusion is so powerful that on March 12, 2020, 174 Democrats in the House of Representatives voted *against* an amendment that would have prevented the Transportation Security Administration (TSA) from hiring *convicted* terrorists."[28] Observed Robert Spencer, a scholar of jihadist

Islam, "Yes, you read that right: if these House Democrats had gotten their way, on your next flight, you could have gotten a pat-down from a TSA agent who previously conspired to down the airplane you were planning to fly on. . . . I've been warning for years that it would sooner or later become 'Islamophobic' to offer even the mildest opposition to *jihad* violence, and that the 'Islamophobia' mongers would become increasingly open about their support for *jihad* terrorists, and here we are."[29]

The Democrat Party's seditious commitment to mount a "Resistance" to an elected president has led inexorably to sympathy for America's enemies and the sabotage of American security. This troubling reality was intensified by the Democrats' partisan response to the viral pandemic that spread across America in the winter and spring of 2020.

10

The Invisible War

In September of 2019, an unfamiliar type of coronavirus appeared in a number of patients in Wuhan, China—a city of 11 million people. China's Communist authorities kept this discovery a secret for more than three months, during which time new cases of the virus appeared on a regular basis.[1] During these months the Communists hid the contagious nature of the disease and failed to take measures to stop its spread to other countries. On January 15, the head of China's Center for Disease Control and Prevention declared that "the risk of human-to-human transmission is low."[2] Three days later, Chinese authorities allowed a Lunar New Year banquet to take place in Wuhan where tens of thousands of families shared food.[3]

During the months of December and January, while the rest of the world remained ignorant of the threat, China's Communist dictatorship also concealed the deadly nature of the virus and permitted Wuhan inhabitants to leave the country to celebrate the Lunar New Year and spread the disease around the world. It was not until January 23 that the Chinese government enacted a quarantine.[4] By mid-March when hundreds of thousands had contracted the virus globally, and the disease was spreading rapidly through the United States, government leaders in the White House and Congress were comparing the threat from the virus to a war.[5]

Four months earlier, as the virus began to spread in Wuhan, the Democrat majority in the U.S. House of Representatives was busy passing articles of impeachment against President Trump. The impeachment articles were based on a phone call to the Ukrainian prime minister in which Trump had asked for an investigation into possible Ukrainian interference in the 2016 election at the behest of the Obama administration.[6] Because the Chinese were concealing the danger posed by the virus, it is possible that the grave implications of removing the commander-in-chief responsible for mobilizing Americans to fight external threats may not have been obvious. But when the threat began to manifest itself in cases within the United States, Speaker Pelosi and the Democrats doubled down on their seditious agenda and showed they regarded their anti-Trump crusade as more important than any viral contagion. They had failed to impeach Trump over the Russia collusion hoax. Now they would seek to blame Trump for the virus and use it in their attempt to defeat him in the elections scheduled for November 2020.

On December 18, 2019, House Democrats impeached the president without a single Republican vote.[7] Despite the urgency with which she had conducted the impeachment process, Pelosi then refused to send the articles to the Senate for trial.[8] It was not until January 15, 2020, that she changed her mind and submitted them.[9] This was only six days before the Chinese acknowledged the first death from the virus, and before the first U.S. case was detected in a man who had traveled to Wuhan.[10] On January 23rd, the Chinese government sealed off Wuhan to stop the virus's spread, even as the House prosecutors opened their case for removal of the president who had been elected to defend the nation as its commander-in-chief.[11]

Trump's War on the Virus

On January 30, the World Health Organization declared a "global health emergency" because of the dangers posed by the virus.[12] The next day President Trump declared a state of emergency and imposed a ban on all travel from China—a measure that had never before been taken in the nation's history.[13] For three years Democrats had been attacking Trump's efforts to secure the borders as "racist." Now they applied the same charge to his China ban. The accusation came in the form of a statement by former vice president Joe Biden, the leading Democrat contender for the party's presidential nomination and soon to be its choice. Biden attacked Trump's precautionary travel restriction as "hysterical xenophobia . . . and fear-mongering."[14]

Five days later, Trump delivered his annual State of the Union message to a joint session of Congress. In it he said, "Protecting Americans' health also means fighting infectious diseases. We are coordinating with the Chinese government and working closely together on the coronavirus outbreak in China. My Administration will take all necessary steps to safeguard our citizens from this threat."[15] At the end of the speech, Speaker Pelosi, who was standing on the podium behind the president, tore up the official copy of his remarks in front of the television cameras in an unprecedented gesture of contempt for the president of the United States.[16]

The next day the Republican Senate voted to acquit Trump of the Democrats' impeachment charges. It was only then that Pelosi's party finally took up the subject of the virus, doing so in a sub-panel on Asia of the House Foreign Affairs Committee.[17]

Dealing with a viral epidemic is a complex business for any leader. It requires sorting out conflicting recommendations from the scientific community, and a balancing act between reassurance and caution. Avoiding panic is one priority, and sounding sufficient alarm so that potential victims will take precautions is another. The two can obviously be in conflict. Trump sounded the alarm but also attempted as the nation's leader to provide Americans with the reassurance that the national team fighting the epidemic had it "under control."[18] This contradiction was immediately exploited by Trump's Democrat enemies, who ignored the steps he took to fight the epidemic and claimed that he wasn't taking it seriously, didn't know what he was talking about, and was reckless and "not up to the job."[19]

Trump's task in leading the country in the face of the pandemic was made immeasurably more difficult by the Democrats' reckless caricature of him as a "pathological liar," "incompetent," "bigoted," "unfit for the office," and therefore a threat to national security.[20] As Biden put it, in response to Trump's life-saving ban on travel from China: "This is no time for Donald Trump's record of hysteria and xenophobia."[21]

The Democrats' War on Trump

In mid-March Trump declared himself "a wartime president," fighting "an invisible enemy," which he described as the most dangerous enemy of all.[22] But anyone paying attention to the political battlefield knew that there were actually two wars engulfing the country and posing dire threats to its future.

The second was the visible war Democrats had launched four years earlier with their resolve first to prevent Trump from being elected by falsely accusing him of treason, then to sabotage his presidency through a vaunted "Resistance," and finally to remove him from office through several rigged impeachment attempts that failed.

The first principle of psychological warfare is to attack the moral character and credibility of the adversary's commander-in-chief. If a leader is convincingly portrayed as being driven by ulterior motives that have nothing to do with the common good or winning the war, or worse as being a compulsive liar, he is effectively crippled in the task of mobilizing a united front to prosecute the war. Most people understand this, which is why there were so many calls for "unity" and "working together" in America's war on the virus, which the Democrats mainly disregarded. That is why in wartime if the nation's leader misspeaks or makes mistakes in assessing the battlefield, his countrymen who are dependent on his leadership for their survival normally rally around him and hope he will do better. The last thing they do is exaggerate his errors, or invent them, or do everything in their power to undermine his effectiveness as their leader.

But that is exactly what the Democrats did. The visible war to destroy Trump's presidency by destroying the man continued unabated throughout the coronavirus crisis. Biden's first presidential campaign ad appeared in March, featuring this message: "Crisis comes to every presidency. We don't blame them for that. What matters is how they handle it. Donald Trump didn't create the coronavirus, but he is the one who called it a 'hoax,' who eliminated the pandemic response team, and who let the virus spread unchecked across America. He should stop talking and start listening to the medical experts."[23]

Every one of these statements was a lie, including the canard that the president wasn't listening to the medical experts. Trump had shut down travel from China, declared a state of emergency, and held daily televised hour-and-a-half briefings at the White House flanked by officials from the Centers for Disease Control and Prevention to reassure, caution, and guide the public in dealing with the virus and its spread.

Trump campaign communications director Tim Murtaugh responded to Biden's ad by pointing out the political disaster that was taking place. Americans had traditionally come together to face adversities like the pandemic, which made no distinctions between its citizens: "It used to be that Americans faced national adversity with unity," Murtaugh observed, "but Joe Biden and his allies have abandoned that principle in favor of rank, despicable politics."[24]

Nor was it just the Biden campaign that was cynically sabotaging the president's efforts to turn the tide of the contagion. The leadership of the Democrat Party and its media allies spread the false charges that Trump had dismissed the virus as a "hoax," cut the budget of the Centers for Disease Control and Prevention, and failed to provide an adequate number of surgical masks and ventilators to hospitals and their staffs.[25]

The "hoax" charge was particularly absurd, since Trump had closed the border with China in the face of Democrat slanders that the measure was unneeded and "racist," and had declared a state of emergency, making the pandemic the top priority of his presidency. The "hoax" comment his enemies were referring to was a reference to the attacks on him, which claimed he was doing nothing to fight the epidemic or fighting it incompetently.[26] Those responsible for these slanders were the same people who had peddled (and were still peddling) the discredited "Russia hoax" designed to undermine and destroy him. The analogy was exact. Trump's reference to a virus hoax was a reference to the phony accusations they had used to obstruct and attack him over alleged Russia collusion in the past and were now using to undermine his efforts to lead the country's defense against the pandemic.

Nor did Trump shut down, disband, or fire the White House pandemic team, as Biden's ad (and many Democrat officials and media allies) falsely claimed. The team had been reorganized within the National Security Council by its leaders to make it more efficient.[27] Similarly, the scarcity of masks for which Democrats blamed Trump was actually the result of the Obama administration's failure to replenish the nation's mask stockpiles after depleting them in the course of the H1N1 and Ebola epidemics.[28]

The same dishonesty was evident in the claim that Trump had sought to cut the budget of the Centers for Disease Control and Prevention. It was the Obama administration that had sought multi-million-dollar cuts in the CDC budget, which were blocked by the Republican Congress. Trump had actually increased its funding.[29] Ventilator shortages were a system-wide problem that included derelictions by the Obama administration but also by the governors in charge of the health systems of their respective states—a problem that Trump quickly remedied, turning America into the chief ventilator producer in the world.[30] The Democrats' baseless and seditious attacks on Trump were made possible by a corrupt media, which uncritically repeated Democrat slanders while suppressing the evidence that refuted them.

Despite Trump's deference to CDC scientists, an army of Democrat and media saboteurs relentlessly attacked him as "anti-science," as in denial about the seriousness of the virus, and as failing to listen to his medical experts.[31] These charges were explicitly refuted when Dr. Anthony Fauci, the epidemiologist who headed his medical team, stated that he had never been overruled by the president when they disagreed. After his defense of the White House, Fauci—a Democrat—had to be assigned special security because of the death threats he received. Dr. Deborah Birx, who coordinated the virus task force, was viciously attacked as a "Stepford Doc" and medical "hack" by former Clinton press secretary Joe Lockhart because she, too, had defended the president's handling of the virus and testified to his respect for the views expressed by his scientific advisers.[32]

In the war against the virus, Democrats had a laser focus. But it was not on the virus. It was on Trump. The malice of the blame-Trump chorus was crystallized in a statement by Democrat Senator Chris Murphy: "The reason that we're in the crisis that we are today is not because of anything that China did. It's not because of anything the World Health Organization did. It's because of what this president did."[33]

The Divisive War over the Virus

Given the right parameters, it would be possible to take a critical view of everyone who was involved in the fight against the virus and made decisions about it, including Trump and his Democrat scientific advisers Fauci and Birx. Conflicting estimates of casualties and conflicting advice on masks, lockdowns, and social distancing were still not resolved even six months into the epidemic. The one indisputable lesson of the war against the virus was that everyone was wrong at some point and had to reverse himself at another. That included not only the nation's political leaders but the scientific experts who were essential players in the battle against the virus, and who produced models based on erroneous assumptions that resulted in costly misreadings of the crisis.

But Democrats were not in the mood to take a reasonable position on the virus response or to temper their criticisms to come together to deal with the danger in a bipartisan way. While they attacked Trump for holding rallies where masks were not worn and social distancing was not observed, they refused to make similar judgments about Black Lives Matter demonstrations that involved tens of thousands of individuals. Hypocrisy was no obstacle to their relentless war against Trump.

Whenever Trump made a decision or drew a conclusion, Democrats were quick to pounce on it and make it seem as though Trump were incompetent, irresponsible, or both. Pelosi's repeated claims that Trump was to blame for the unemployment that resulted from the orders to shut down the economy was a prime example of the Democrats' vindictive disregard for the facts. The shut-down orders came from governors. Initially, the most consequential were from Democrat governors in New York, California, Pennsylvania, Illinois, Michigan, Louisiana, and New Jersey.

But the most revealing case of the Democrats' cynical determination to use the war against the virus to destroy Trump was their response to his decision to withhold funding from the World Health Organization (WHO) for its role in helping China create the global pandemic. China denounced Trump's withdrawal from the organization as a "genocide"—a ludicrous charge typical of the Communist dictatorship that was responsible for the pandemic, but one that Democrats did their best to promote.[34]

Pelosi called Trump's threat to defund the WHO "dangerous" and "illegal," and said it would cost lives and be "swiftly challenged."[35] Then she called it a "betrayal," recalling the bogus charge she had used to impeach Trump, in case anyone had missed her intentions. Democrat donor Bill Gates piled on: "Halting funding for the World Health Organization during a world health crisis is as dangerous as it sounds."[36] Actually not. Trump was just withdrawing one nation's financial support. Senator Ted Cruz immediately calculated that Gates's $107 billion personal fortune would make up the deficit caused by the United States' withdrawal for twenty-seven years, if it was that important. The U.S. was contributing $400 million annually to the WHO, about ten times what the Chinese gave.[37] So if it really amounted to a genocide, China could stop that by simply paying its fair share of the WHO budget.

Betrayals

In assessing the decision to stop supporting the WHO, consider the reasons for the action. The evidence suggests that China developed the novel coronavirus in its Wuhan virology laboratory, setting off a contagion in Wuhan itself. This breakout occurred in December. Although China knew the disease was intensely contagious and deadly, Chinese officials assured the world that it was not transmittable from human to human. China was backed in this lie by the WHO through its director, Tedros Adhanom Ghebreyesus, who owed his U.N. position to the Chinese dictator Xi.[38]

China then permitted the citizens of Wuhan to hold a Lunar New Year celebration involving crowds that were numbered in the tens of thousands. It also allowed 5 million citizens of Wuhan to leave the city and travel outside of China and around the world to celebrate the Lunar New Year abroad.

At that point, what may have originated as a lab accident became a calculated biological war against the rest of the world. Tedros and the World Health Organization, whose alleged purpose is to keep the international community safe from deadly viruses, covered for the Chinese Communists, enabling the spread of the virus, which resulted in millions of cases and more than a million deaths globally.

Who is Director Tedros? According to *The Hill*, he is not a medical doctor, and he had no global health management experience before China shoe-horned him into the director's seat at the WHO. According to *The Hill*—a publication with which Nancy Pelosi is surely familiar—Tedros is a communist and terrorist who served in the infamous Marxist dictatorship in Ethiopia known as the Derg, which slaughtered thousands of its subjects. He went on to serve as an executive member of the Tigray People's Liberation Front, an organization listed in the Global Terrorism database, and as Ethiopia's foreign minister; that is, he represented a country known as "Little China," because the Chinese Communists have invested in it so heavily and made it a strategic bridge in their imperialist designs on the African continent, just as they have made the World Health Organization a strategic bridge in their designs on the rest of the world.[39]

The treacherous lengths to which leaders of the Democrat Party were willing to go to support China's attacks on America's president were highlighted by their efforts to tar him as a white supremacist because he insisted on referring to the infection as a "Chinese virus." For using that descriptor, Hillary Clinton accused Trump of "turning to racist rhetoric."[40] Her attack was framed in the language that had become the creed of the Democrat Party. Calling the term "Chinese virus" a racist epithet was an absurdity to anyone not sharing the ideological assumptions of Identity Politics and Cultural Marxism.

The names of other troublesome diseases—such as "German measles," "Lyme disease," and "Spanish flu"—were also derived from their geographical points of origin. Not only had the virus originated in China, but by concealing its appearance and allowing millions of Wuhan's citizens to leave the infected city and travel to unsuspecting countries abroad, the Chinese Communist dictatorship had cynically and deliberately exposed the global population to its deadly effects.

The president was, in fact, playing defense against Chinese Communist propaganda. To cover up its war crimes, the Chinese Communists had launched a global propaganda campaign accusing the U.S. military of deliberately creating the virus and maliciously spreading it. As Trump explained, "China was putting out information, which was false, that our military gave this to them. That was false, and rather than having an argument, I said I have to call it where it came from."[41] So seriously did the Chinese Communist rulers take the psychological war that, on the basis of their lies, they launched a $2 trillion lawsuit against the United States for allegedly creating and spreading the virus.[42]

In this Cold War, the Democrat Party presented itself as appeasers of—or outright collaborators with—an enemy assault on their own country. Not only was Clinton abetting a disinformation campaign against her own country, she was actively undermining her commander-in-chief's efforts to combat a virus that threatened all American citizens.

Clinton's disturbing willingness to support China's psychological warfare was immediately praised by China's ambassador to the United States who said: "Justice speaks loudly."[43] What was resonating loudly and clearly, however, was self-evidently not justice, but a fault line in America's body politic so deep and volatile as to pose an existential threat to the nation itself.

Pelosi's Viral Impeachment Gambit

Personifying this threat were Speaker of the House Nancy Pelosi and her impeachment point man Representative Adam Schiff, who as head of the House Intelligence Committee had led the failed partisan attempt to remove Trump. In the midst of this new controversy, Pelosi and Schiff proposed a new congressional oversight committee and a "9/11 Commission" to investigate what they regarded as the president's criminal mishandling of the anti-virus effort.[44] Pelosi's call for the oversight committee bristled with hatred for Trump: "As the president fiddles, people are dying," she told CNN's Jake Tapper. "The president, his denial at the beginning was deadly," she said, ignoring the fact that Trump had banned travel from China in January, while she and her party were focused on impeaching him and denouncing his ban as racist and xenophobic.[45]

"I don't know what the scientists said to him," Pelosi added. "When did this president know about this, and what did he know? What did he know and when did he know it? That's for an after-action review."[46] Her word-for-word invocation of the central question in the impeachment of Richard Nixon made it quite clear that her war to remove the president from his office was her all-consuming purpose, and that she viewed the pandemic as the latest means to accomplish this—the country and its citizens be damned.

Pelosi's attempt to convict the president of criminal behavior had no basis in fact. And her hypocrisy knew no limits. In late February, after the virus had reached America's shores, the World Health Organization had declared it a global health emergency, and President Trump had declared it a national health emergency, Pelosi was making a publicized tour of Chinatown and its restaurants, urging her San Francisco constituents not to stay home but to join the crowds celebrating the Chinese New Year. "It's exciting to be here, especially at this time," said Pelosi as she walked around Chinatown surrounded by media and onlookers. "We want to be careful how we deal with [the coronavirus]. But we do want to say to people, come to Chinatown. Here we are, again, careful, safe, and come join us."[47]

At every turn of the crisis, the Democrats and their media allies attempted to twist statistics about the spread of the disease into indictments of Trump's alleged derelictions, adding up to an alleged failure to manage the fight against the virus. A typically slanted report in the *Washington Post* made it seem as though Trump were incompetent compared to every other world leader, and in effect responsible for all the coronavirus deaths. "While most developed countries have managed to control the coronavirus crisis, the United States under Trump continues to spiral out of control, according to public health experts, with 3.3 million Americans infected and more than 133,000 dead."[48]

This comparison turned out to be premature, as a new surge of the virus overwhelmed many of those other countries and placed America somewhere in the middle. And like all the attacks on Trump, the *Post* article overlooked the fact that Trump had no control over the healthcare systems of the fifty states. America's federal system vests that authority in the state governments. The president's role is to back up the policies the governors put in place—in this case by supplying ventilators and masks that the Obama administration had failed to stock, by providing tests to discover and track cases, and by putting federal resources behind the search for viral antidotes and vaccines.

In fact, Trump performed admirably on all these tasks, making the U.S. the number one producer and exporter of ventilators, supplying the needed masks, and speeding up the development of vaccines to a record pace. Moreover, he supplied them to all parties, Democrat-run states as well as Republican. The worst death rate, not just in the country but in the world, belonged to New York, whose Democrat governor, Andrew Cuomo, ordered nursing homes which housed the most vulnerable citizens to accept coronavirus patients, even though Trump had sent a hospital ship to New York to handle virus cases and provided other facilities expressly for the purpose—which remained empty. The result was more than 6,000 unnecessary deaths of elderly citizens who had an average of 8–10 years of life expectancy ahead of them.[49]

The Politics of the Pandemic

In the nation as a whole, in the first six months of the pandemic, Democrat-run congressional districts had more than three times the number of cases and over 90 percent more deaths than Republican-run states. According to a Pew report, as of May 20, 2020, "Of the more than 92,000 Americans who had died of COVID-19 as of May 20 (the date that the data in this analysis was collected), nearly 75,000 were in Democratic congressional districts. In terms of the 50 states, those that were Democrat-run states had 3 times the cases and 3 times the deaths of Republican-run states.[50] Despite these facts, Democrat presidential nominee Joe Biden claimed in stump speeches that no one would have died "if Trump had done his job."[51]

Democrats picked isolated, sometimes contradictory comments by Trump to use as evidence that his handling of the epidemic was incompetent and irresponsible. But they themselves were flexible when it came to such matters. They readily flipped their views 180 degrees on policies they claimed were basic to controlling the virus. After governor-ordered business shutdowns left 41 million Americans unemployed, Trump tried to re-open the country in April. He argued that business depressions and shutterings had health consequences too and the country could not afford an economic collapse. Democrats countered by accusing him of advocating a policy that would kill Americans. They argued that "social distancing" was the cornerstone of any effort to end the epidemic. Democrat governors banned strolling in parks and sitting on beaches, going to hair salons, and attending church services. But when hundreds of thousands of Black Lives Matter protesters poured into the nation's streets two months later, they insisted that the protests took precedence over health measures.

The bottom line was that Trump did not control the response to the virus. Pelosi's attempt to name it the "Trump virus" and the almost daily accusations by Democrats that the president was responsible for more than 200,000 coronavirus deaths was just politics at its most seditious and irresponsible worst. Democrats' hatred of Trump was so irrational and intense, and also so cynical, that they made this accusation the centerpiece of their election campaign in the fall. In the final presidential election debate, Joe Biden opened his remarks this way:

> BIDEN: 220,000 Americans dead. You hear nothing else I say tonight, hear this. Anyone who is responsible for not taking control. In fact, not saying I take no responsibility initially. Anyone who is responsible for that many deaths should not remain as president of the United States of America.[52]

As if this were not low enough, Biden made the following indictment a staple of his speeches in the final days of his campaign: "The first step in beating the virus is beating Trump." And then: "Trump is the virus."[53]

A Totalitarian Insurrection

America's political order is built on the principles of individual identity, individual accountability, and individual freedom. These are a reflection of the Christian idea that human beings are endowed by their Creator with immortal souls and free will. This perspective makes each individual unique, and therefore accountable for what they do and who they are. This is also the foundation of the American principle of equality, which insists that by law, citizens are to be judged on their individual merits—not their gender, ethnicity, or skin color. It took nearly two hundred years to approach this ideal, but only fifty years for Democrats to resurrect race politics and make them the center of political discourse. From the moment the Civil Rights Acts were passed, Democrats worked tirelessly to reintroduce race and other collectivities into every aspect of public life. Now there are few public transactions, and almost no public discourse, without them.

This reversal of American values began with the campaign for racial preferences in school admissions and employment opportunities, which were advanced as attempts to redress the injustices of the past. In the process the new "reforms" committed injustices in the present—not only against Asian and European Americans, whose access to university admissions and jobs was restricted, but the supposed beneficiaries "of color" as well. Studies soon showed that affirmative action policies did not close the education gaps; in fact, they increased the dropout and failure rates of those they were supposed to benefit.[1] But actual results didn't matter to the reformers; what mattered was the ideology and the virtue-signaling opportunities of "social justice."

The racial agitation of the Left was formalized in the doctrines of Identity Politics and Intersectionality by radicals who had taken control of the universities.[2] This Cultural Marxism, practiced by the Democrat Party and progressives generally, developed into a racial politics that is the very antithesis of the American idea. In the last few years it has become so much a part of the Democrat mindset that Senator Elizabeth Warren could say unselfconsciously at a presidential primary debate, without any challenge from her colleagues: "We cannot just say that criminal justice is the only time we want to talk about race. We need race-conscious laws."[3] A white supremacist like David Duke could not have put it more clearly.

Race-conscious laws are the aspiration of slave owners, segregationists, and racists. It would be difficult to express a more anti-American sentiment. Not surprisingly, Warren is also the Senate leader in the campaign to eliminate the Electoral College, to suppress free speech, and to shut down entire industries by executive *diktat*. She is also one of the two or three most popular leaders of the Democrat Party.

Democrats' rejection of America's constitutional framework is the root source of their antipathy to Trump. At its core is hatred of Trump's "America First" patriotism, which Democrats deride as "white nationalism"—fitting it into the racist narrative they have adopted. This hatred is reflected in the Democrat Party's attacks on the idea of citizenship and on America's borders. It lies behind Democrats' enthusiasm for Bernie Sanders and other lifelong supporters of Communist dictators and Communist causes. It inspires their attacks on American corporations and billionaires, their disregard for Americans' security at home and abroad, and their readiness to embrace America-hating, terrorist-supporting anti-Semites like Congresswomen Ilhan Omar, Rashida Tlaib, Ayanna Pressley, and Alexandria Ocasio-Cortez. It is manifest in Democrats' eagerness for communist schemes to nationalize or destroy whole industries, and to establish total government control of healthcare, putting every American under Washington's bureaucratic heel.

The Danger of Political Factions

Even more telling than their destructive policy proposals, rejection of a national election result, readiness to undermine and obstruct a duly elected president, and support for hate-America radicals like Sanders, O'Rourke, Harris, Booker, Kaine, Warren, and the "Squad" is the Democrats' assault on the constitutional pillars of American democracy. America's Founders feared most of all the division of the country into party factions that might prey on the emotions and illusions of the electorate in order to divide the country and set it against itself.

James Madison, the principal architect of the Constitution, began *Federalist* 10, with this observation: "Among the numerous advantages promised by a well-constructed Union, none deserves to be more accurately developed than its tendency to break and control the violence of faction. The friend of popular governments never finds himself so much alarmed for their character and fate, as when he contemplates their propensity to this dangerous vice. . . . The instability, injustice, and confusion introduced into the public councils have, in truth, been the mortal diseases under which popular governments have everywhere perished. . . ."[4]

The Founders feared that factions would lead to a tyranny of the majority that would run roughshod over the minority. This is a pretty accurate summary of the Democrats' three-year campaign to resist, obstruct, and remove Trump, a president elected by 63 million Americans and 304 votes in the Electoral College. The Democrats are utterly unwilling to accord their Republican opponents basic respect. Democrat proposals to pack the Supreme Court with leftists and to abolish the Electoral

College and the Senate because they are "undemocratic" and "racist," are red flags Americans ignore at their peril.[5] Along with the Democrats' efforts to stamp out voter ID laws, blur the distinction between citizens and non-citizens, and commit the nation to a collectivist, racial ideology, these are direct attacks on the constitutional foundations the Framers created to protect American freedoms.

So it is with their socialist ambitions. In *Federalist* 10, Madison warned about the dangers of radical factions and explained the Founders' plan to protect the new nation from "a rage for paper money, for an abolition of debts, for an equal division of property, or for any other improper or wicked project." These wicked projects are the core agendas of today's Democrat Party.

By the spring of 2020 the legal foundations of a totalitarian state were already in place. At that point forty-seven of the fifty states had passed "hate crimes" legislation. A "hate crime" is a thought crime. Every totalitarian regime in history from the Spanish Inquisition to the Stalinist show trials has outlawed unwanted thought. In Stalin's Russia, being "anti-Soviet"—a critic of the socialist dictatorship—was a thought crime for which tens of millions were dispatched to concentration camps and firing squads.

The First Amendment, guaranteeing freedom of religion, speech, assembly, and expression, is the foundation of all American freedoms. If citizens cannot form and express opinions freely, they lose the ability to defend their other freedoms. To go from prosecuting "hate crimes" to banning "hate speech" is a small step—and an inevitable one toward the establishment of a totalitarian order. A "cancel culture" that destroys the reputations of dissenting individuals, deprives them access to public platforms, and causes them to be fired from their jobs is the express program of vigilante organizations like Black Lives Matter and Antifa, but also of the academic Left and progressives generally. Worse, it has the support of the leadership of the Democrat Party, whose presidential candidates have even called for the de-platforming and censorship of the president of the United States.[6]

At present, the political Left lacks the power to enforce a cancel culture throughout society; it is only effective through the institutions the Left administers or can influence. Unfortunately, these include the most powerful institutions of American culture—universities, K–12 schools, and the "media," which are already virtually one-party states. The totalitarian ethos is already being deployed to suppress the opinions of defenders of America's traditional constitutional framework and to advance radical agendas.

Consider Wikipedia's explanation of the "hate crime" concept: "A hate crime . . . is a prejudice-motivated crime which occurs when a perpetrator targets a victim because of their membership (or perceived membership) in a certain social group or race. . . . A major part of defining crimes as hate crimes is determining that they have been committed against *members of historically oppressed groups*" [emphasis added].[7]

Built into this definition of hate crimes is a political perspective central to the Left's view of societies as hierarchies of "oppression." What exactly constitutes "oppression" in a society like America, where every citizen is guaranteed equal rights with every other citizen, a society in which discrimination by race or social group is expressly forbidden? Moreover, what ethnic or racial group in America has *not* been historically oppressed? White people—the alleged oppressors— are Irish, Italian, Jewish, Catholic, Protestant, and so forth, all groups that have suffered discrimination and persecution in America. "Identity Politics" ignores these crucial components of their identities in favor of a racial category—"white"—that stigmatizes them as "oppressors," and therefore as guilty and deserving of having their rights taken away.

The goal of "hate crime" and "hate speech" legislation is to outlaw distasteful thoughts. Purging forbidden thoughts has been the goal of witch-hunters since the beginning of time. The category "hate" is so vague and so malleable that it can be wielded by the unscrupulous as a weapon against any critic or dissenter. And so it increasingly is, in America today.

The "Anti-Racist" Party Line and the Totalitarian Future

In the spring of 2020, two runaway bestsellers provided the theoretical framework for the anti-white racism that lay behind the Black Lives Matter riots, which began that May. One of them, *White Fragility*, explains that white people are racists by birth, regardless of anything they say, do, or intend.[8] If they deny they are racists, they are just manifesting their inability to admit that they are—hence their "fragility."

The other bestseller, *How to Be an Antiracist*, by a National Book Award recipient named Ibram X. Kendi, was hailed by the *New York Times* as "the most courageous book to date on the problem of race in the Western mind." *How to Be an Antiracist*—already a required text in college courses across the nation—is a manual on how to use flexible definitions of "hate" to demonize and destroy political opponents. *How to Be an Antiracist* provides a rationale for the efforts of left-wing activists to redefine racism to cover any viewpoint that doesn't conform to theirs. In short, it is a handbook of totalitarian ideology.

The intellectual levels and factual bases of both these highly praised books are appallingly low. Kendi's inspired this ribald observation from liberal *Rolling Stone* writer Matt Taibbi: "antiracism, a quack subtheology that in a self-clowning trick straight out of *Catch-22*, seeks to raise awareness about ignorant race stereotypes by reviving and amplifying them."[9]

The success of these books (and a rash of others such as the Oprah-sponsored *Caste*, which compares America's treatment of blacks to Hitler's treatment of Jews) is explicable only in terms of the anti-American, anti-white hysteria that has swept the constituencies of the political Left—including its high culture—since the 2016 election. This hysteria has led to preposterous claims, such as this statement from Kendi:

> Racist ideas have defined our society since its beginning and
> can feel so natural and obvious as to be banal, but antiracist

ideas remain difficult to comprehend, in part because they go against the flow of this country's history.[10]

Kendi's absurd assertion inverts the historical reality, which begins with the revolutionary declaration in America's birth certificate that "all men are created equal," and extends through the Emancipation Proclamation and Lincoln's Gettysburg Address to a nation "conceived in liberty" to the Thirteenth and Fourteenth Amendments, which abolished slavery and asserted equal rights for all Americans, to the Civil Rights Acts of 1964 and 1965, which extended these rights to black citizens in the segregated South.

From America's beginnings, anti-racist ideas have defined the nation's aspirations and self-understanding and inspired its contributions to the progress of freedom all over the world. Kendi's twisted view is the product of a virulently anti-white and anti-American university system and its faculty Marxists and the elite political culture it has produced.[11] Consequently, he doesn't see the need to actually argue his case, which leads to ludicrous and illiterate statements like this binary absurdity: "There is no such thing as a not-racist idea, only racist ideas and antiracist ideas."[12]

Thus, according to Kendi, there are only racists and anti-racists. There is no third alternative, no group that is not racist and opposes racism but doesn't subscribe to the radical policies that Kendi and his leftist friends consider "anti-racist."

In other words, there is only Us and Them. Disagree with Us on policies that affect blacks and you're a racist. And because you're a racist uttering hate speech, you and your views should be cancelled and suppressed. This, as previously noted, is the main theme of Antifa's *Anti-Fascist Handbook*, an official justification for suppressing by any means necessary—including murder—anyone who disagrees politically with the Antifa radicals and, according to Antifa, is therefore a racist or a fascist.[13]

In Kendi's telling, opponents of affirmative action, who are against institutional racism and believe that college admissions and job-hires should be race neutral, are actually anti-black racists.[14] This includes people who draw on statistics to show that affirmative action preferences actually hurt blacks. Calling everyone who disagrees with you on policy a racist, even if they disagree because of their concern for blacks' wellbeing, is nonsense—and dangerous. But this is the sum and substance of the bestselling *How To Be An Antiracist*, which was named "one of the best books of the year by the *New York Times Book Review, Time*, NPR, the *Washington Post, Library Journal, Publishers Weekly*, and *Kirkus Reviews*."[15]

According to Kendi, racism is not about regarding another race as inferior, or lumping all members of a race together without regard to their individuality or character. According to Kendi, "racism is a powerful collection of racist *policies* that lead to racial inequity and are substantiated by racist ideas" [emphasis added]. This is a tautology that makes no sense. You can't define "racism" by repeating the word three times. But the bottom line for Kendi and his admirers is clear. Anyone who disagrees with them is a racist.

Kendi assumes without evidence that racist *policies*—whatever he decides they are—*cause* racial inequities. This is a fallacy that is virtually universal in the way so-called liberals think about race. Thus, if blacks are adversely affected more than other groups by the coronavirus, then "systemic racism" must be to blame. The more obvious explanation is cultural differences that create unhealthy conditions such as obesity, which is the source of several co-morbidity factors for the disease, including diabetes and high blood pressure. African Americans have the highest rates of obesity of any group in the United States.[16]

Kendi defines his own position as an "anti-racist" with the same tautological nonsense he used to define racism: "Antiracism is a powerful collection of antiracist policies that lead to racial equity and are substantiated by antiracist ideas." As in his previous definition of racism, Kendi posits an apparent standard: promoting racial equity. But he doesn't take this standard seriously. While he condemns critics of affirmative action as "racists" and proponents as "anti-racists," affirmative action policies have not closed the academic performance gap between blacks and other groups or led to "racial equity."[17] Naturally, the actual results are of no concern to Kendi and the race crowd. To them the accusation of racism does not need to be justified by serious analysis and argument. It is a ready-to-hand weapon to stigmatize and defeat their political adversaries.

A more perfect rationale for a one-party state would be hard to come by. Unfortunately, Kendi's indefensible position is the party line of the Left generally, and of the Democrats in particular, as the absurd praise for Kendi's tract shows. Throughout the Trump presidency, Democrats attacked support for secure borders, opposition to immigration from terrorist states, and opposition to government-controlled health care as "racist"—as motivated by bigotry and hate. For Kendi and the Left generally, such views are "hate" because they allegedly support racial inequity and "oppression." Therefore, in the name of social justice, those views should be suppressed. This silencing of legitimate views is the end of democracy as we know it.

How far is Kendi ready to take his illogic? As far as he needs to. According to Kendi, "Do-nothing climate policy is racist policy, since the predominantly non-White global south is being victimized by climate change more than the Whiter global north, even as the Whiter global north is contributing more to its acceleration."[18] This fact-challenged statement (and why the caps for "Whiter?") is intellectual garbage. While the United States has dramatically reduced its carbon footprint, India and China, two non-White nations representing nearly 3 billion people, are the chief polluters on the planet. So theirs is the greater responsibility for any damage or inconvenience their populations suffer from global warming. Worse, both of these countries have refused to implement any of the anti-pollution goals of the Paris Climate Accord (which is why Trump withdrew the United States from the pact); they are participants in the Accord only to get subsidies from the United States and other wealthy "White" countries. Kendi's anti-racism turns out to be merely another form of racial extortion.

Moreover, why exactly is America a "White" country? Do its large populations of blacks, Hispanics, and Asians count for nothing? Are they not part of the national conversation? Was America an anti-racist country when Obama signed the Paris Climate Accord, and did America become a racist country when Trump withdrew from the Accord? Climate change was extremely low among the concerns of voters in the 2016 election. Was it high on the lists of African Americans or Hispanics? If not, should we regard them as racists? Silly question. By definition, according to leftist ideologues like Kendi "people of color" can't be racist.

As we have seen, the unfounded presumption underlying Kendi's poor excuse for an argument is the assumption that racial disparities, referred to by Kendi's followers as "racial inequities," are actually *indications* of racism—*caused* by racist policies. Confusing disparities with discrimination is a leftist leap of faith that has little or no basis in reality in a country governed by the Civil Rights Acts.[19] So-called "racial inequities" are generally caused by cultural and behavioral factors, as in the disproportionate cases of coronavirus. If the black poor are poor because of "systemic racism," how did the majority of black Americans manage to get into the middle class?

Income inequalities affect blacks in large part because of off-the-charts out-of-wedlock births among poor black communities and the absence of fathers in the home. Statistical evidence shows that a child raised by a single-parent mother is four to five *times* more likely to be poor than the child of a two-parent family, regardless of race or any other factor.[20] Close to 70 percent of black children are born out of wedlock, the highest percentage of any group in America.[21] For the Kendis of this world, pointing to realities like this is "blaming the victim," therefore racist, therefore not to be discussed.

Kendi was recently appointed head of Boston University's newly created "Center for Antiracist Research." The Center was launched with a $10 million donation from Twitter CEO Jack Dorsey.[22]

A Racial Hoax and a Totalitarian Uprising

The same contempt for the facts was behind the racial hoax spread by Black Lives Matter following the death of a black felon in police custody in Minneapolis on May 25, 2020. The misrepresentation of George Floyd's arrest and death was expanded by Black Lives Matter radicals into a monstrous political lie—that racist police were systematically singling out blacks and murdering them across the country. This baseless slander, refuted by every statistic on police-inflicted deaths, triggered an epidemic of violence that rapidly spread to hundreds of American cities and resulted in thousands of injuries, scores of deaths, billions in destruction, a call to defund and dismantle police departments, and a dramatic spike in violent crime—all justified as advancing social justice.

As in the case of the 1992 Los Angeles riots triggered by the arrest of Rodney King, a bystander video provided the pretext for the "uprising" and became a symbol of the "systemic" racial injustices and brutalities allegedly committed by police against the black population. The protests and riots that followed Floyd's death were so large and destructive, involved so many Americans, and included such powerful elements of the nation's culture that it reshaped its political alignments, affecting a presidential election and inspiring one of the largest internal migrations from America's cities ever recorded. It was, in sum, an earthquake in the nation's landscape that altered its political and social fault lines for good.

Studies by Princeton University and the Armed Conflict Location and Event Data Project found that in the first 102 days of the unrest, there were 633 violent protests in 220 locations across the United States. Riots had taken place in 48 of the 50 largest American cities, and 74 of the top 100. Black Lives Matter activists were involved in 95 percent of those violent and destructive incidents.[23] According to the studies, there were also 2,400 "peaceful protests" that advanced the same Black Lives Matter message: America and its law enforcement agencies are systemically racist.

During the riots, Black Lives Matter leaders issued no condemna-
tions of the violence, which was a direct contrast to the Civil Rights
Movement leaders of the 1960s, who insisted on the principle of non-
violence and whose demonstrations were accompanied by no attacks on
police or destructions of local businesses. The peaceful protests associated with Black Lives Matter were staged during the daytime but regularly morphed into riots under cover of night.[24] These facts make it
difficult to regard them as distinct and separate from the violence rather
than as fraternal accessories to it.

The revolutionary nature of the Black Lives Matter protests was
captured in the principal slogan used by both demonstrators and rioters:
"No justice, no peace!" This is a thinly veiled terrorist threat: *Accept
our views and meet our demands or face destructive chaos.* The chant
"No justice, no peace!" accompanied by such large-scale violence implied
that the remedy to the alleged problems was not—and could not be—a
reform within existing institutions. To secure justice, the system first had
to be "dismantled and then "re-imagined," to use a favorite radical verb.
The message was clear: Only extreme measures could make a just solution possible. Only a revolutionary force outside the system and disregarding its laws and values could fix it. Ironically, Minneapolis and other
major centers of the Black Lives Matter violence were entirely run by
liberals who had endorsed the Black Lives Matter movement.

The bystander video that triggered these events showed Minneapolis
police officer Derek Chauvin applying a knee to the right side of George
Floyd's neck until he expired. To the uneducated observer Chauvin's knee
was the cause of Floyd's death. But the "Wisconsin Knee," as it is called, is
an approved police procedure precisely because pressure applied to one side
of the neck cannot cause death by strangulation.[25] In order to choke a person, one would have to apply similar pressure to the subject's windpipe. The
procedure is designed to render a recalcitrant prisoner, such as one high on
drugs—and therefore a danger to himself and others—unconscious. As
the toxicology report showed, Floyd's death was not caused by strangulation but by the lethal level of the drug Fentanyl in his system.[26]

The video the public saw seemed to prove otherwise. It showed a handcuffed Floyd prone on the pavement, pleading for his life, saying "I can't breathe," while a white police officer applied his knee to Floyd's neck and held it there for eight minutes and forty-six seconds, after which Floyd expired. The image provided by the video was chilling—a prone black man who seemed to be posing no threat as a white cop apparently squeezed the life out of him, all for the alleged crime of passing a phony twenty-dollar-bill. It seemed injustice personified.

To the Left this was an emblem of the alleged "systemic racism" of the American system their propaganda had been attacking for years. As Black Lives Matter followers began the siege of Minneapolis and other cities, they invoked this false narrative to justify their violence. In the manner of a lynch mob, they called for a pre-investigation and pre-trial verdict of murder against the officers involved in Floyd's arrest, threatening to continue their destruction if they didn't get it: "No justice, no peace!"—a slogan that sums up the attitude of all the lynch mobs they claim to abhor.

The Minnesota criminal justice system was headed at the time by Attorney General Keith Ellison, who openly supported the rioters. Ellison immediately obliged the lynch mob by charging all four arresting officers with third degree murder—without the investigation that normally precedes such charges. Not only was it telling that the murder charges were filed in advance of the investigation; the charges also made it clear that the claim that Floyd was the victim of a racist killing—which was used to justify the riots—was false. One of the officers charged with murder was African American, another was Asian American. But in the lynch mob atmosphere that prevailed, no one seemed to notice.

As weeks passed and major cities went up in flames, it became clear that the image provided by the original video was not an accurate rendering of George Floyd's arrest or death. Crucial to understanding the reality of what had taken place were the video-cams worn by the arresting officers, not to mention the coroner's toxicology report, which identified the actual cause of Floyd's demise.

The video cams showing George Floyd's behavior on his arrest—as well as that of the arresting officers—had been deliberately suppressed by Attorney General Keith Ellison, who was a former spokesman for Louis Farrakhan and, worse, a current supporter of the Antifa radicals who were spearheading the violence and arsons.[27] In response to the pressures of the Black Lives Matter coalition, Ellison now elevated the charges against the four arresting officers to second degree murder, even though there had still been no investigation of the actual facts.

Also suppressed—this time by the nation's media—were facts that might have provided an accurate picture of Floyd himself, who was portrayed as "a gentle giant," an innocent victim of outrageous police brutality and racism. In reality, Floyd was a career criminal who had served eight different jail sentences for various crimes, including a fairly recent five-year sentence for the armed robbery of a pregnant black woman whom he terrorized by pointing a gun at her womb while his accomplices looted her home.[28]

Also withheld from the public was the fact that Floyd was a drug addict. As the toxicology report eventually showed, Floyd had a lethal level of the opioid Fentanyl in his system when the officers attempted to arrest him. Both Fentanyl and COVID-19 suppress lung functions. Floyd also had ingested the drug Methamphetamine. In addition, he had arteriosclerotic and hypertensive heart disease. The arresting officers were unaware of his condition.[29] Given these underlying circumstances, it is clear that his attempt to resist arrest led directly to his death—and to the riots.

Nearly three months after Floyd's demise, a British newspaper, the *Daily Mail*, obtained the video-cam footage taken by the two officers who made the initial arrest, one of whom was African American. Floyd was six foot three and over two hundred muscular pounds—potentially difficult to handle even in the absence of drugs. The video showed Floyd to be disoriented, delirious, paranoid, and unable to follow the commands they gave him for more than a few seconds. It showed him unwilling to be put in the police vehicle and saying that he was "claustrophobic" although he had been arrested while sitting in his own vehicle. It showed him crying "I can't breathe" seven times, while he was in standing and sitting positions, well before he was prone with Officer Chauvin's knee on his neck.

More important, it showed that the officers charged with second degree murder for a racial crime were solicitous, polite, and worried about Floyd's state, asking him if he was on drugs. The video cams not only showed no hostility—racial or otherwise—on the part of the officers; it showed their obvious concern for the man they were arresting. When Floyd complained he was not able to breathe, they immediately called an ambulance.

In other words, prior to the video scene of him cuffed and prone with officer Chauvin's knee on his neck, George Floyd was already near death from the drugs he had ingested—a fact confirmed by the autopsy report, which showed that he was not strangled, as he could not have been by a single knee applied to one side of his neck.

But in the hands of the Black Lives Matter radicals the death of George Floyd became a justification for condemning—without any credible evidence—the entire criminal justice system, not only in Minneapolis but throughout America. It was an incitement to launch the terrifying violence and destruction that followed. The lie that launched the rioting was made even more incendiary with the help of a media eager to support the rampages by not questioning any of the outrageous charges against the officers in the case, or law enforcement generally. Instead they gave credence to violent and destructive radicals who were bent on blowing up "the system" and the country that had created it.

Supported by a vast array of left-wing organizations that had been peddling these false accusations for years, the insurrectionists claimed that black Americans were the victims of rampant police brutality and "systemic racism." The term "systemic" soon became a buzzword for the politically correct, signifying that they condemned the entire criminal justice system. This blanket charge led to the greatest outbreak of violence since the Civil War, a tragedy made possible by the support that Democrat mayors, city council members, and governors provided to the rioters.

This support took the form of refusing to respond to civil disorders, ordering police to "stand down," and instructing them to allow looting, arson, and destruction, while releasing those arrested immediately when they were taken into custody. When radicals occupied the center of Seattle, calling it an "autonomous zone," the mayor portrayed their lawlessness as a block party and a "summer of love"—permitting a lawless situation to develop in which a black youth was murdered by the radicals' security forces, who prevented the Seattle police and medics from entering the zone to save him.[30]

Dissenters from the Black Lives Matter methods and agenda were faced with public shaming, loss of jobs, and ruined reputations by the "cancel culture" the Left had created to silence its critics. The statement that "All Lives Matter" was regarded as an unacceptable attack on blacks, who were singled out for injury and death by a "white supremacist" criminal justice system. In one of many such cases, the dean of the nursing school at the University of Massachusetts was forced to resign during the Black Lives Matter riots in Boston because she committed the thought crime of saying "Everyone's Life Matters."[31] In another, a twenty-four-year-old Navy wife and mother was shot and killed for telling a Black Lives Matter crowd that "All lives matter."[32]

Minneapolis set the pattern repeated by Democrat authorities in all the major cities subjected to violent attacks, including Chicago, Philadelphia, New York, Portland, Atlanta, Seattle, and Washington, D.C. The mayor and city council members in all these cities were sympathetic to the rioters and looters, and to their transparently empty claims of being "peaceful protesters" for "social justice." Consequently, the authorities refused to deploy sufficient force to discourage the mobs, allowing them to own the streets.

When local authorities did dispatch a token police force, they were so outnumbered that the criminal mobs turned on them, injuring thousands. Law enforcement on the run—or absent—was a green light to urban street gangs to conduct their own rampages and turf wars without fear of reprisal. And in Washington, D.C., the Democrat mayor even marched with the Black Lives Matter demonstrators and ordered Pennsylvania Avenue in front of the White House defaced with the slogan "Black Lives Matter" in gigantic yellow letters.

The majority of the ravaged cities were run by Democrats, and had been for fifty to a hundred years. In Minneapolis, which was typical, the mayor, the city council members, the police chief, the attorney general, and even the officer who applied the knee to George Floyd's neck were Democrats. The police union, usually a culprit in protecting bad officers, was Democrat as well. The police chief was also black. If there was a "systemic" race problem to blame for what had happened to George Floyd in Minneapolis, Democrats were 100 percent responsible. And the same thing was true of every major city the Black Lives Matter mobs targeted. The posture of the Democrats was explicable only in terms of their racial ideology, which caused them to defend and applaud, as a protest for social justice, the movement responsible for the mayhem. To a man and woman, Democrat officials described the violent riots as "peaceful protests." Their vice-presidential candidate Kamala Harris called the mobs "A Coalition of Conscience."[33]

Six weeks after the Democrat establishment surrendered Minnesota to the insurrection, the property damages in that state alone had already reached $500 million.[34] According to Fox anchor Tucker Carlson, prominent Democrats who raised money to fund the insurrectionists and vandals through a BlackVisionsmn.org website included vice presidential candidate Kamala Harris, radical congresswoman Alexandria Ocasio-Cortez, and staff members of Joe Biden's presidential campaign.[35]

From the outset of the destruction, President Trump had pled with Democrat governors and mayors to deploy sufficient police and National Guard forces to quell the riots and had been ignored. In a move that proved typical, Minnesota's Democrat governor promptly submitted the damage bill to Trump and the federal government, although it was obviously incurred by his own refusal to call in the

National Guard. Trump rejected the governor's request.[36] House Speaker Nancy Pelosi then inserted a trillion dollars into a proposed "stimulus" package—an add-on to a bill designed to deal with the deprivations caused by the coronavirus pandemic—to bail out the Democrat states that had mismanaged their budgets and the riots. Trump rejected her proposal as well.

The excuse that was ritualistically given by the Democrat mayors of the stricken cities for enabling the destruction and refusing to arrest the rioters and stop the mayhem was the myth that the rioters were actually "peaceful protesters" against police brutality and racism. But every available statistic of police shootings and arrests showed that the Black Lives Matter cause was a transparent hoax, and miles of video footage showed that the so-called protests were anything but peaceful.

Statistics Show the Black Lives Matter Campaign Is a Racial Hoax

According to Black Lives Matter propaganda, Americans live under a "white supremacist system" in which black Americans are routinely targeted for "extrajudicial killings . . . by police and vigilantes."[37] In the malicious words of the Black Lives Matter website, "Black Lives Matter is an ideological and political intervention in a world where Black lives are systematically and intentionally targeted for demise."[38]

There is no evidence to back up such an incendiary racist slander. A 2001 Bureau of Justice Statistics report examined incidents where police used deadly force to kill criminal suspects between 1976 and 1998. It found that blacks were killed by police in exact proportion to the number of violent crimes blacks commit, which is what one would expect from a race-neutral system.[39] If an individual is a violent criminal—as George Floyd was—that individual is likely to be involved in armed encounters with the law, and to get killed in the process. The latter is particularly likely to be true if the individual resists arrest, as have virtually all the individuals BLM claims were "murdered" by police, including George Floyd, Michael Brown, Eric Garner, and Rayshard Brooks.

Even Breonna Taylor, whose death was a cause célèbre not only for the rioters but for celebrities like Oprah Winfrey, was killed in a crossfire initiated by her boyfriend, a low-grade drug dealer, who shot an officer entering her house with a search warrant. Her previous boyfriend had been a high-level drug dealer, whom she had assisted in his criminal trade, which is what prompted the police to obtain the warrant to search her house. She was complicit in the crimes that led police to her house and at best collateral damage in the war on drugs, not a "murder" victim, as Oprah and Black Lives Matter shamefully claim.

There are a few tragic exceptions on the Black Lives Matter martyr list—Tamir Rice and Philando Castile, to name two. The armed Castile was killed by an Hispanic cop who panicked during a traffic stop. But such exceptions are rare, and they were undoubtedly influenced by the fact that while black males constitute 6 percent of the population, they commit more than 50 percent of armed robberies and murders—a statistic that goes generally unreported in the politically correct media, but that explains a lot of the suspicions and stops of innocent blacks who are bystander victims of the black crime wave—and also the occasional tragedy in which an innocent suspect is killed.[40] Tamir Rice, for example, was a youth killed while brandishing a toy replica of a real gun.

The central accusation, and the biggest lie, spread by Black Lives Matter radicals and encouraged by a credulous media is that the police killings of blacks are racially motivated. As we have seen in the case of George Floyd, this accusation is false, and demonstrably so. The 2001 Bureau of Justice Statistics report found that in nearly two-thirds of all justifiable homicides by police from 1976 to 1998, the officer's race and the suspect's race *were the same*. When a black officer killed a suspect, that suspect was black 81 percent of the time. The rate at which black officers killed black felons was more than double the rate at which white officers killed black felons.

Another Bureau study shows that of all suspects killed by police from 2003 to 2009, 41.7 percent were white, and 31.7 percent were black. But blacks accounted for 38.5 percent of all arrests for violent crimes. As John

Perazzo, author of *Exposing the Lies of Black Lives Matter* has written, "These numbers do not in any way suggest a lack of restraint by police in their dealings with black suspects. On the contrary, they *strongly* suggest *exactly the opposite*."[41]

Roland Fryer is an African American economist at Harvard. In a 2018 study titled "An Empirical Analysis of Racial Differences in Police Use of Force," Fryer concluded that Houston police officers were nearly 24 percent less likely to shoot black suspects than white suspects. In studies of three Texas cities, six Florida counties, and the city of Los Angeles, Fryer found that (a) officers were 47 percent less likely to discharge their weapon without first being attacked if the suspect was black than if the suspect was white; (b) black and white individuals shot by police were equally likely to have been armed at the time of the shootings; (c) white officers were no more likely to shoot unarmed blacks than unarmed whites; (d) black officers were more likely to shoot unarmed whites than unarmed blacks; and (e) black officers were more likely than white officers to shoot unarmed whites.[42]

A 2019 study published in *Proceedings of the National Academy of Sciences* shows that white officers are no more likely than black or Hispanic officers to shoot black civilians. "In fact," observes Manhattan Institute scholar Heather Mac Donald, the study found that "if there is a bias in police shootings after crime rates are taken into account, it is against white civilians." The authors compiled a database of 917 officer-involved fatal shootings in 2015 and found that 55 percent of the victims were white, 27 percent were black, and 19 percent were Hispanic.[43]

If there is a disproportion in the fatal encounters between black criminals and cops, it is the reverse of what Black Lives Matter claims: "The per capita rate of officers being feloniously killed is 45 times higher than the rate at which unarmed black males are killed by cops. And an officer's chance of getting killed by a *black* assailant is 18.5 times higher than the chance of an unarmed black getting killed by a cop."[44] Naturally, this makes officers jittery when they face armed individuals who are black, and it can lead to fateful misjudgments in their reactions.

There is no "open season" on blacks. Quite the reverse: in 2012 and 2013, blacks in the U.S. committed an annual average of 560,600 violent crimes (excluding homicide) against whites, while whites committed a yearly average of 99,403 violent crimes against blacks. According to Perrazo, "In other words, blacks were the attackers in about 85 percent of all violent crimes involving blacks and whites, while whites were the attackers in 15 percent."[45] Perazzo explains, "In more recent years, the disproportionate prevalence of black-on-white crime has only gotten worse. According to the Bureau of Justice Statistics, in 2018 there were 593,598 interracial violent victimizations (excluding homicide) between blacks and whites in the United States. Blacks committed 537,204 of those interracial felonies, or 90.4 percent, while whites committed 56,394 of them, or about 9.5 percent."[46]

The facts show that blacks are far more likely to commit racist crimes against whites than vice versa. According to Mac Donald, based on Justice Department data in 2018, blacks were overrepresented among the perpetrators of offenses classified as "hate crimes" by a whopping 50 percent—while whites were underrepresented by 24 percent.[47]

These statistics are quoted at length because they reveal beyond a reasonable doubt that the violence that swept through American cities, involving billions of dollars in damage, costing scores of mainly black lives, and supported by hundreds of millions of dollars in donations from major corporations, celebrities, Democrat donors, and the political Left—this entire destructive movement was based on demonstrable lies. Systemic victimization of blacks was a lie, and so was the ludicrous and sinister attack on "white supremacy," a creed that is in reality confined to the fringes of American society, unlike the black supremacy of Louis Farrakhan, the Nation of Islam, and Black Lives Matter, which is supported by leaders of the Congressional Black Caucus and the Democrat Party.[48]

A Reprehensible Sermon and a Trashed Holiday

A summary moment in the life of the racial hoax took place at George Floyd's memorial service, where convicted liar and racial arsonist Al Sharpton was selected to deliver the eulogy. The memorial audience included Hollywood celebrities and captains of industry who had provided bail money for the criminals arrested for looting, arson, and various crimes of destructive violence. As his tribute, Sharpton, one of the nation's most notorious racial demagogues, delivered one of the most offensive racist attacks on record.

Portraying career criminal George Floyd as a stand-in for all black Americans, Sharpton attacked white America as the source of black America's plight: "George Floyd's story has been the story of black folks because ever since 401 years ago, the reason we could never be who we wanted and dreamed of being is you kept your knee on our neck. . . . The reason why we are marching all over the world is we were like George, we couldn't breathe, not because there was something wrong with our lungs, but that you wouldn't take your knee off our neck. We don't want no favors, just get up off of us and we can be and do whatever we can be."[49] In other words white Americans are racists whose bigotry has systematically blocked the aspirations of black Americans for 401 years.

This is a reprehensible, racist lie—actually several lies. Sharpton's "401 years" is a reference to 1619, the year the first Africans were shipped to the Jamestown Colony in Virginia. But in 1619 there was no "America," white or otherwise, to put a knee on black people's necks. The creation of America was 168 years in the future. But why quibble over arithmetic when you are intent on indicting a whole race of people so you can blame them for your problems and extort reparations in return?

The phony figure of "four-hundred years of slavery" has long been a battle cry of the racial demagogues who corrupted the Civil Rights Movement after the death of Martin Luther King and turned it into a racial shakedown operation. In point of historical fact, black Americans have more rights, more power, more wealth, more privilege, and more opportunity than blacks anywhere on earth, including all the black nations of Africa which have been independent for sixty years, and all the black nations of the West Indies, which in the case of Haiti have been self-ruled for over two hundred years.

Sharpton's demagoguery as spiritual leader of the protests over George Floyd's alleged murder exposed the real nature of the insurrections in American cities. The real target of the Black Lives Matter Marxists, the anarchists, the arsonists, and looters is not only white Americans. Their target is America, the nation that gave blacks opportunities they have been denied everywhere else, which these "protesters" take for granted and are fighting to despoil. Sharpton personifies the way in which the civil rights struggle has degenerated over the last sixty years into a racial extortion racket. Indeed, a Black Lives Matter leader defended the criminal looting that followed George Floyd's death as "reparations."[50]

The anti-American agenda of Black Lives Matter was manifest in the violent mobs that gathered in Lafayette Square in front of the White House during the riots and set fire to St. John's—"the church of presidents"—knocking over police barriers and threatening the White House itself. Democrats, eager to protect and enable the vandals in the streets, claimed they were "peaceful protesters," but every honest observer understood that if the Secret Service and National Guardsmen had not been present, the mob would have climbed the fence and attempted to burn the White House too.[51]

Why was the White House a target for the protesters? The president had repeatedly called for "law and order" and urged Washington's Democrat mayor, who marched with the demonstrators, to deploy the force necessary to defend the church and clear the street. The president himself had no authority over the local police forces the rioters were protesting against. If the so-called protests were actually about systemic racism in police departments, their target should have been the Democrat Party, whose elected officials were in charge of those departments and thus had made such injustices possible. But the Democrat overlords of America's major cities were not the focus of their rage. It was the Trump

White House. The targets were the president and White House as symbols of America itself.

The anti-American agenda of the Black Lives Matter coalition was clear from the statements of its Marxist leaders and was manifest across the country in the weeks leading up to the nation's holiday, the Fourth of July. Leftist mobs proceeded to tear down, deface, and destroy the nation's monuments under the pretense of fighting "racism." The destruction began with statues of Confederate generals like Robert E. Lee but quickly spread to American Founders George Washington and Thomas Jefferson; to Ulysses S. Grant, who won the war that freed the slaves; to the abolitionist Matthias Baldwin, an outspoken opponent of slavery for decades before the Civil War; and even to the Emancipation Memorial in Lincoln Park.

The Emancipation Memorial portrays Abraham Lincoln freeing a slave rising from his knees. The monument was paid for and donated by emancipated slaves.[52] This meant nothing to the protesters, because their passion was not to defend black Americans but to destroy the nation that gave them unparalleled opportunity and freedom.

The vandals burned a statue of the Virgin Mary and called for the destruction of statues and paintings of the "white Jesus," showing that their hatred was directed at America's founding by Christians, and the values—family, faith, the sanctity of individual life—that they had bequeathed to their heirs. This destruction was encouraged by Democrats and only ended when President Trump signed an executive order that made a ten-year prison sentence the minimum for attacking public monuments.

The agenda of the rioters was reflected in a statement by one of their icons, former NFL quarterback Colin Kaepernick, who had created a widely displayed gesture of contempt for his country and flag by "taking a knee" when the national anthem was being played before games. Kaepernick called the nation's holiday "A celebration of white supremacy."[53] This was particularly offensive coming from the son of an interracial couple who had been adopted and raised by a white couple after he was abandoned by his black father. At the time of his protest, Kaepernick was a multi-millionaire thanks to the opportunities provided him by a nation that was the opposite of what he claimed, but which he despised like a spoiled brat.

President Trump chose to celebrate the nation's birthday with a speech at the base of Mount Rushmore, a monument to America's greatest presidents—Washington, Jefferson, Lincoln, and Roosevelt. His speech celebrated America's racial and ethnic diversity and its historic contributions to freedom. The anti-Trump media, led by the *New York Times*, which had had nothing negative to say when Barack Obama visited the site, now described Mount Rushmore as "racist," linked the monument to slavery and the Ku Klux Klan, compared America to Nazi Germany, and ignored what Trump actually said in his remarks. In place of the uplifting paean to America and its racial and ethnic diversity that Trump had actually given, the media made the false claim that he had used the occasion to defend Confederate generals. In fact, he never mentioned the Confederacy or its generals, which didn't prevent the *Times* from describing his celebration of the heritage of all Americans as "dark and divisive."[54]

Leading up to the July 4 commemoration, the lawlessness in America's streets had already caused violent crime rates to soar. The support for the violence by the Black Lives Matter coalition and Democrat officials now escalated into a demand to "defund the police," who continued to be slandered without reason or restraint by the nation's left-wing media. Disarming the police and abolishing the border patrol, ICE, were now specific goals of the Left's protests.

One week before the Fourth of July holiday, the Democrat city council in Minneapolis voted unanimously to "dismantle" the police department and replace it with social workers. In New York the Democrat city council abolished the plainclothes anti-crime unit tasked with disarming criminals carrying illegal weapons. The New York City council slashed the police budget by a billion dollars. In Los Angeles Democrats cut $100 million from the police department budget while other Democrat cities like Seattle and Washington, D.C., announced plans to follow suit.[55]

When Seattle's police chief, a courageous African American named Carmen Best, criticized the plan to drastically cut the police budget, which meant cutting mainly minority officers, the left-wing city council retaliated by reducing her salary. When she saw the hypocrisy of the council leaders who were prepared to gut the programs that protected Seattle citizens and promoted racial equality, Best resigned. At the same time, the Democrats' presidential candidate Joe Biden, along with other Democrat leaders, voiced his support for "redirecting" police funds, which was a euphemism for defunding the police. He also went out of his way to attack the police for using military vehicles for mob control and to stem the chaos, saying they had "become the enemy."[56]

From the infamous sixties' slogan "Off the Pigs" to the Black Lives Matter chant "What do we want? Dead cops," disarming law enforcement has been as central a goal of the revolutionary Left as unilaterally disarming America's military. Even the Democrats' "Green New Deal" calls for a 50 percent cut in defense spending, a demand not readily connected to "saving the environment." It is more accurately seen as rendering the "Great Satan" defenseless before its Marxist and Islamic enemies.

The results of these attacks on civil order were as predictable as they were catastrophic. During the week of the July 4 holiday, 101 people were shot in New York City, an increase of 300 percent over the same period a year before. In Democrat-run Chicago over the same weekend, ninety people were shot and eighteen killed. All the victims were black. A dozen of them were minors, including a seven-year-old named Natalia Wallace. In Atlanta, another Democrat city, thirty-one people were shot and five killed.

Nowhere were the battle lines of the insurrection more clearly drawn than in the siege of Portland, Oregon, where the attacks had been a nightly occurrence for more than seven straight weeks and showed no signs of abating. The city government, led by radical mayor Ted Wheeler, was firmly on the side of the rioters and in open defiance of appeals from President Trump to seek federal help to halt the destruction. On July 16, the acting secretary of the Department of Homeland Security, Chad Wolf, issued the following official statement:

> The city of Portland has been under siege for 47 straight days by a violent mob while local political leaders refuse to restore order to protect their city. Each night, lawless anarchists destroy and desecrate property, including the federal courthouse, and attack the brave law enforcement officers protecting it.
>
> A federal courthouse is a symbol of justice to attack it is to attack America. Instead of addressing violent criminals in their communities, local and state leaders are instead focusing on placing blame on law enforcement and requesting fewer officers in their community. This failed response has only emboldened the violent mob as it escalates violence day after day.
>
> This siege can end if state and local officials decide to take appropriate action instead of refusing to enforce the law. DHS will not abdicate its solemn duty to protect federal facilities and those within them. Again, I reiterate the Department's offer to assist local and state leaders to bring an end to the violence perpetuated by anarchists.[57]

The secretary's appeal was rebuffed by the Portland authorities, who had obviously joined the insurrection.[58] In response the federal government sent in the promised security forces to restore law and order. No leader of the Democrat Party had condemned the rioters or called on the Portland administration to uphold the law. But when agents of the federal government entered the city to protect its citizens and property, national Democrats led by House Speaker Nancy Pelosi went on the attack, comparing the defenders of Portland's civic life to Nazis. This was Pelosi's unhinged statement: "Trump & his storm troopers must be stopped. Unidentified storm troopers. Unmarked cars. Kidnapping protesters and causing severe injuries in response to graffiti. These are not the actions of a democratic republic."[59]

The federal agents were not unidentified; the cars they used were not "unmarked," the rioters they arrested were not kidnapped. The injuries suffered by police who were attacked with explosive devices, bricks, and lasers (which went unmentioned by Pelosi) were not less or more infrequent than those sustained by the rioters, whose illegal occupation of the streets, arsons, and assaults were what provoked the confrontation in the first place. The propaganda of dictatorships was not more blatantly mendacious or offensive than Pelosi's slanders against her own government.

Pelosi went on to describe the riots as an exercise of "First Amendment speech," which had been attacked by "Trump's secret police": "First Amendment speech should never be met with one-sided violence from federal agents acting as Trump's secret police, especially when unidentified. This is disgraceful behavior we would expect from a banana republic—not the government of the United States.[60]

These were all brazen lies that originated as propaganda claims by Antifa and the criminals in the streets. To take just one of her preposterous allegations—that the crimes being committed were a matter of "graffiti," a reporter on the scene, Andy Ngo, commented: "Graffiti? How about explosives, hammers, knives, sledgehammers, slingshots w/ metal ball bearings, blinding lasers, pipe bombs and more? You have no clue what is going on here."[61]

The insurrection had been launched and justified by the charge of "systemic racism" against the nation's police departments triggered by the still uninvestigated death of George Floyd. But no statistics or actual facts backed up this charge, which remained a baseless accusation by an organization dedicated to anti-American violence and Marxist revolution. Was there a police officer, or a politician from the president on down, who in the week of George Floyd's death stepped forward to defend the alleged perpetrator? There wasn't. So how is this fact compatible with the claim of systemic racism? Is there a single statistic that would establish that systemic racism directed against black people characterizes the criminal justice system? There is no such statistic, and there is no evidence that the American people are racists.

What is striking about this tragedy is the lengths to which Democrat leaders were prepared to go to support the defamation of their own country and the violence against it. Because President Trump attempted to restore law and order, Speaker of the House and architect of the partisan impeachment Nancy Pelosi called him a Nazi, while Communist apologist Bernie Sanders accused him of "advocating armed violence" against black communities across the country.[62] What is more racist than conflating the black community with its criminal element? In fact, the overwhelming majority of black Americans support the police and a tough stance against criminals, not least because they are the chief victims of the violence the Left has unleashed.[63] America's minorities are patriots, and no amount of malicious propaganda will dissuade them from supporting their flag and country.

What is troubling for America's future is the fact that the leaders of the Democrat Party and the so-called "liberal" establishment have shown that they will support treasonous efforts to overthrow the elected president of the United States on the basis of demonstrably false accusations; that they will promote racist lies against their own country; and support racist anti-American violence from paramilitary vigilantes like Antifa and Black Lives Matter; that they will suppress free speech in the name of "equality"; and that they will propose communist "solutions" like the Green New Deal that would bankrupt the country and eliminate its freedoms.[64]

Heading towards the Abyss

On the rotunda of the Jefferson Memorial in Washington are inscribed these words: "I have sworn upon the altar of God eternal hostility against every form of tyranny over the mind of man." This statement by Jefferson is the heart of the democracy in whose Founding he played so central a role. It is why the First Amendment of the Bill of Rights is the *First* Amendment, and not the Second, or Fourth, or Fifth. It keeps the mind free, which is the chief bulwark against the establishment of a totalitarian state.

Today America is facing the most serious threat of the establishment of such tyranny in its history. This threat comes from a political faction that calls its reactionary creed "progressive." Its goals are advanced under the Orwellian names "Critical Race Theory" and "Anti-Racism." These doctrines have already been embraced by American universities and public schools, tax-exempt advocacy foundations, the corporate culture, and the Democrat Party. They are racist ideologies that indict every white person as a participant in an imaginary system of "white supremacy" allegedly oppressing every "person of color." In this twisted perspective, any deviation from the political perspective of the Left—for example, on the need to maintain enforceable borders or to secure civil law and order, or to afford due process to the accused—is racist and potentially makes the person who holds that view a hate criminal worthy of suppression.

As our nation enters the third decade of the twenty-first century, it is divided not by race—no society has ever been more diverse and inclusive—but by race *politics*, by an ideology that is totalitarian in nature. A dramatic illustration of the chasm splitting America occurred in the first presidential debate of the 2020 campaign, when the supposedly neutral moderator Chris Wallace directed a ferociously partisan question to President Trump, regarding Trump's recent executive order banning diversity training sessions in federal agencies on the grounds that they were indoctrination sessions in radical Identity Politics and "Critical Race Theory."

> WALLACE: President Trump. . . . Your administration directed federal agencies to end racial sensitivity training that addresses white privilege or critical race theory. Why did you decide to do that, end . . . sensitivity training? And do you believe that there is systemic racism in this country, sir?[1]

The fact that Wallace, who is an anchor on Fox, a channel routinely derided by anti-Trump media outlets as a pro-Trump platform, would direct so hostile and factually false a question to the president is an eloquent testament to just how pervasive this left-wing ideology has become.

The purpose of Trump's executive order, in its own words (which were available to Wallace) was "to combat offensive and anti-American race and sex stereotyping and scapegoating."[2] Its preamble invoked the long arc of America's struggle for civil rights for all its citizens, and described the Founders' belief in equal rights as "the electric cord [that] links the hearts of patriotic and liberty loving [people]. . . . It is the belief that inspired the heroic black soldiers of the 54th Massachusetts Infantry regiment to defend that same Union. . . . And it is what inspired Dr. Martin

Luther King, Jr., to dream that his children would one day 'not be judged by the color of their skin but by the content of their character.'"[3]

Trump's order singled out the adversaries of this American creed in these memorable words:

> Today, however, many people are pushing a different vision of America that is grounded in hierarchies based on collective social and political identities rather than in the inherent and equal dignity of every person as an individual. This ideology is rooted in the pernicious and false belief that America is an irredeemably racist and sexist country; that some people, simply on account of their race or sex, are oppressors; and that racial and sexual identities are more important than our common status as human beings and Americans.
>
> This destructive ideology is grounded in misrepresentations of our country's history and its role in the world. Although presented as new and revolutionary, they resurrect the discredited notions of the nineteenth century's apologists for slavery who, like President Lincoln's rival Stephen A. Douglas, maintained that our government "was made on the white basis by white men, for the benefit of white men." Our Founding documents rejected these racialized views of America, which were soundly defeated on the blood-stained battlefields of the Civil War. Yet they are now being repackaged and sold as cutting-edge insights. They are designed to divide us and to prevent us from uniting as one people in pursuit of one common destiny for our great country.[4]

Chris Wallace's accusatory question to the president about this model defense of the American creed must rank as one of the most disgraceful interventions by a presidential debate moderator on record. Wallace had done his best to make a presidential order designed to defend what has been the unifying inspirational creed of Americans from Thomas Jefferson to Martin Luther King sound like a racist policy.

Wallace's question ignored the clear statement of Trump's executive order and essentially asked why the administration was ending training designed to make white people less racist. But the president had an answer for that:

TRUMP: I ended it because it's racist. I ended it because a lot of people were complaining that they were asked to do things that were absolutely insane. That it was a radical revolution that was taking place in our military, in our schools, all over the place. And you know it and so does everybody else. And he [Biden] would know it.[5]

Unfazed by his own dishonesty and malice, and disregarding the president's clear words, Wallace adopted a *faux* innocence and asked this question:

WALLACE: What is radical—what is radical about racial sensitivity training?
TRUMP: . . . we would pay people hundreds of thousands of dollars to teach very bad ideas and frankly very sick ideas. And really, they were teaching people to hate our country. And I'm not going to do that. I'm not going to allow that to happen. We have to go back to the core values of this country. They were teaching people that our country is a horrible place, it's a racist place, and they were teaching people to hate our country. And I'm not gonna allow that to happen.
WALLACE: Vice President Biden?
BIDEN: Nobody's doing that. He's just, he's just racist.[6]

Few exchanges could demonstrate more conclusively how a racist ideology that goes under the names Identity Politics, Cultural Marxism,

Critical Race Theory, Intersectionality, and "Anti-Racism" has been embraced by the leaders of the Democrat Party and by progressives generally, and how this ideology is the basis of the brazen attacks on Trump and his patriotic supporters as white supremacists, white nationalists, and racists.

"Diversity training" programs are not about racial sensitivity. They are about demonizing white people and the constitutional order of individual freedom, equality, and accountability that the American Founders created. Trump's executive order was based on an investigation of actual diversity training sessions by journalist Christopher Rufo. "These training sessions had nothing to do with developing 'racial sensitivity,'" Rufo commented after the debate exchange. "As I document in detailed reports for *City Journal* and the *New York Post*, critical race theory training sessions in public agencies have pushed a deeply ideological agenda that includes reducing people to a racial essence, segregating them, and judging them by their group identity rather than individual character, behavior and merit."[7]

The examples are instructive. Here is what Rufo found when he looked into a training program for Treasury Department employees run by an African American named Howard Ross, whose company the government had paid $5 million for the sessions: "At a series of events at the Treasury Department and federal financial agencies, diversity trainer Howard Ross taught employees that America was 'built on the backs of people who were enslaved,'" and that all white Americans are complicit in a system of white supremacy "by automatic response to the ways we're taught." The claim that America's wealth is based on the slave system is a common line among ideologues who use it to justify reparations, but it has no basis in fact. A main reason the South lost the Civil War was because its reactionary plantation system was inferior to the free market industrial capitalism of the North.[8]

"Mr. Ross argues that whites share an inborn oppressive streak. 'Whiteness,' employees are told, 'includes white privilege and white supremacy.' Consequently, whites 'struggle to own their racism.'" In other words, if you are white and deny that you are a racist, that just proves that you are one. "Ross instructs managers to conduct 'listening sessions' in which black employees can speak about their experience and be 'seen in their pain,' while white employees are instructed to 'sit in the discomfort' and not 'fill the silence with your own thoughts and feelings.' Members of "the group you're allying with are not 'obligated to like you, thank you, feel sorry for you, or forgive you.'" You, on the other hand, are obligated to shut up and accept their judgments. If you don't, you are a non-cooperating racist and, therefore, your job and professional career are at stake.

Rufo reported on a "racially segregated training session" for white male employees at the Sandia National Laboratories, "which develop technology for America's nuclear arsenal executives." The three-day event was led by a company called "White Men as Full Diversity Partners." Its goal was "examining 'white male culture' and making the employees take responsibility for their 'white privilege,' 'male privilege' and 'heterosexual privilege.' In one of the opening exercises, the instructors wrote on a whiteboard that 'white male culture' can be associated with 'white supremacists,' 'KKK,' 'Aryan Nation,' 'MAGA hat' and 'mass killings.' On the final day, the trainers asked employees to write letters to women and people of color. One participant apologized for his privilege and another pledged to 'be a better ally.'"

Rufo also reported, "At the Department of Homeland Security, diversity trainers held a session on 'microaggressions,' based on the work of psychologist Derald Sue. In his academic work, Mr. Sue argues that white Americans have been 'fed a racial curriculum based on falsehoods, unwarranted fears, and the belief in their own superiority,' and thus have been 'socialized into oppressor roles.' Trainers taught Homeland Security employees that the 'myth of meritocracy' and 'color blindness' is a foundation of racist microaggressions and 'microinequities.' The trainers insisted that statements such as 'America is the land of opportunity' and 'the most qualified person should get the job' are racist and harmful—merely code for 'People of color are lazy and/or incompetent and need to work harder.' If a white employee disagrees, his point of view is dismissed as a 'denial of individual racism'—another type of microaggression."[9]

In other words, if you're white you are a racist, and if you deny that you are a racist, you are an unrepentant racist.

To any fair-minded observer, Rufo concluded, "these are not 'racial sensitivity trainings,' as Chris Wallace described them at the [presidential] debate. They are political indoctrination sessions."[10] Moreover, they are political indoctrination in anti-white racism, and across-the-board hostility to the individual freedoms on which America's democracy is built. All paid for by the government.

The demagogue Huey Long once famously quipped, "Sure, we'll have fascism in this country, and we'll call it anti-fascism."[11] Figures are hard to come by, but as of 2003, U.S. companies were already spending an estimated $8 billion a year on "diversity" trainers and programs.[12] A 2009 study found that Fortune 1000 companies were spending an average of $1.5 million per company, and other studies show that universities where these racist indoctrination programs first took root often spend over $100 million per university on racist indoctrination programs, adding up to untold billions nationally as well.[13] Over decades, these investments have created an infrastructure of political indoctrination and control that is the antithesis of America's democratic system and its values.

It is a replica of the system of "people's commissars" created by the Bolsheviks to shape a society and political order in which they were a tiny minority. People's commissars were dedicated members of the Communist Party. In 1917, this was a group on the fringes of Russian society, numbering only 23,000 members in a country of 91 million. The Bolsheviks had staged a coup in 1917, rather than a revolution. Consequently, the first problem they faced was controlling a general population that did not share their ideology.

The first institution they had to tackle was the military. There was no organic loyalty on the part of a sufficient number of military commanders to ensure that they would carry out the Party's will. To rectify this situation, the Party placed a "people's commissar" at every level of command in the Soviet military. The commissars had to sign off on military orders. Trotsky summarized this solution to the problem of control: "We took a military specialist and we put on his right hand and on his left a commissar. . . ."[14] The commissars overrode the existing professional structure of the military. Obeying the political expert was necessary to career success. Opposing him was "anti-Soviet" and could be career- or life-ending.

How effective might such a system be in America without the support of a police state? The diversity apparatus in American universities is a multi-million and often a centimillion-dollar operation on every campus. Over the last forty years, thanks in part to the efforts of these trainers and overseers, conservatives have become as rare as unicorns on university faculties, which in effect are now one-party states where conservatives and their views are either absent or suppressed.[15]

The diversity networks in America do not operate in the name of a party, but of a radical ideology that is the antithesis of America's constitutional framework. Yet they have the backing of America's major corporate and educational institutions, which gives them the power to infiltrate every nook and cranny of the body politic. As a common business slogan puts it, "Diversity is good for business."

This potential for control is greatly magnified, moreover, by the seductive packaging of an anti-democratic ideology as a democratic enhancement. Dressing up a racial attack and demand for conformity as racial sensitivity towards minorities is perhaps the only way such an anti-democratic set of ideas could be imposed on the American mind. Connecting a racist indoctrination to the Civil Rights struggles so central to the American narrative is the final seduction. In this way, and without much resistance, an extremist ideology has been inserted into the cultures of the existing institutions of American society, and a political minority has been put in a position to reshape the whole of American society and its political order.

The disturbing effectiveness of this strategy is evident in the way it has overwhelmed the thought processes of otherwise intelligent human beings—Chris Wallace would be an obvious example—blinding them to the polar opposition between real racial sensitivity and racist indoctrination, between respecting the feelings of racial minorities and racist attacks on a racial majority.

Otherwise, how is it possible that the three top political bestsellers for 2020, embraced by America's elite cultures, can advance the propositions that white people are racists because of their skin color (*White Fragility*), that America's treatment of blacks is akin to Hitler's treatment of Jews (*Caste*), and that supporting meritocracy is racist (*How to Be an Antiracist*)?

How can a major political party—the Democrats—propose to jettison overnight such fundamental American values and institutions as individual freedom and accountability, innocence until proven guilty, and the system of checks and balances provided by the Electoral College, the Senate, and the nine-justice Supreme Court, or the establishment of identity and citizenship as prerequisites for voting, along with the Founders' skepticism about the judgment of the electorate, as embodied in the separation and division of powers?

If you are guilty because of your skin color, and if a statement as innocuous and factually correct as "America is a land of opportunity" constitutes a racist "micro-aggression," then in asserting this obvious truth you are skirting the edge of a hate crime. All that is lacking is a malicious antagonist to file a complaint, as former Google engineer James Damore discovered when he was cancelled for expressing the politically incorrect idea that women may be choosing *not* to pursue STEM field careers.

Another high-tech company jumping into this breach to signal its "wokeness" is Yelp, a company that provides a consumer guide to a wide variety of businesses and has the power to benefit or damage them. Acting in the wake of the George Floyd incident, Yelp decided to launch an "anti-racism" program. According to Yelp's announcement, "In the last few months, we've seen that there is a clear need to warn consumers about businesses associated with egregious, racially-charged actions to help people make more informed spending decisions. . . . Now, when a business gains attention for reports of racist conduct, Yelp will place a new 'Business Accused of Racist Behavior Alert' on their Yelp page to inform users, along with a link to a news article where they can learn more."[16]

Yelp is a billion-dollar company reviewing businesses for more than 130 million customers a month. Its "anti-racism" program dispenses with due process and institutionalizes the principle of "guilt by accusation (and punishment to follow)." How could this happen in America?

A handful of Internet platforms—among them Google, Facebook, and Twitter— effectively control the public discourse of 330 million Americans, and the information that is available to them.[17] All these platforms have established censorship boards whose arbiters are drawn mainly from the ranks of Democrat operatives and the political Left. These individuals are accountable to no one but the tech giants. Yet they are able to ban and block users and sources of information at will. They are protected by the privacy that shields business from the kind of scrutiny that government agencies operate under. Their bans employ a variety of pretexts to justify their censorship decisions. These pretexts fall into such vague categories as "abusive," "dangerous," "harmful," "fake news," "misinformation," and "hate speech."[18]

As Allum Bokhari, a reporter and critic writing about the Internet for Breitbart, frames the problem posed by such an unregulated system of censorship: "What do these words mean? Where did the words come from and who decides what is 'fake'? Is there an agreed definition? More important, which definition is Google or Facebook or Twitter using?" There are no answers to these questions because the companies are private and for obvious reasons don't want to open their actions to outside scrutiny. In other words, there is no publicly available standard they have for cancelling individuals, destroying entire news organizations and shaping the universe of information and opinion to which Americans have access.[19]

There are 190 million Americans on Facebook. Recently, Facebook instituted a "Hate Agent Policy," which describes a series of signals Facebook uses to categorize someone or some publication as a "hate agent," and ban them from the platform, effectively defunding them and shutting down their operation if they are a business. As Bokhari writes, the signals that trigger this censorship "include a wide range of on- and off-platform behavior. If you praise the wrong individual, interview them, or appear at events alongside them, Facebook may categorize you as a 'hate agent.' Facebook may also categorize you as a hate agent if you self-identify with or advocate for a 'Designated Hateful Ideology,' if you associate with a 'Designated Hate Entity' (one of the examples cited by Facebook as a 'hate entity' includes Islam critic Tommy Robinson), or if you have 'tattoos of hate symbols or hate slogans.' (The document cites no examples of these, but the media and 'anti-racism' advocacy groups increasingly label innocuous items as 'hate symbols,' including a cartoon frog and the 'OK' hand sign.)"[20]

According to Bokhari, who obtained a copy of the Facebook document called *Hate Agent Policy Review*, "Facebook will categorize you as a hate agent for 'statements made in private but later made public.' Of course, Facebook holds vast amounts of information on what you say in public *and* in private [and has used its access] to publicize private information on their users to assist left-wing media in hit-jobs on regular American citizens."[21]

What makes these networks even more sinister is the symbiotic relationship between the Silicon Valley tech giants and the Democrat Party. As Bokhari reported, "The back-and-forth links between Silicon Valley and senior Democrat politicians is shocking—one investigation by the online news publication The Intercept found that 55 Google employees left the tech giant to take positions in the Obama administration, and 197 government employees moved from the federal bureaucracy to Google or to other companies and organizations owned by Eric Schmidt, who was then executive chairman of the company. To get a sense of how extraordinary those numbers are, there are currently only 377 people employed in the West Wing."[22]

According to The Intercept, "Google [alumni] work in the departments of State, Defense, Commerce, Education, Justice, and Veterans Affairs. One works at the Federal Reserve, another at the U.S. Agency for International Development. The highest number—29—moved from Google into the White House."[23] The links are distinctly political. Using LinkedIn's database of Facebook employees for 2018, Bokhari "found forty-five Facebook employees who had previously worked for Hillary Clinton's election campaigns, Barack Obama's election campaigns, or Barack Obama's White House. By way of comparison, I found just seven Facebook staffers who had previously worked for Mitt Romney's 2012 campaign."[24]

In sum, the apparatus of a totalitarian tyranny already exists for a party willing to use it to acquire and keep the reins of power. That party, too, already exists and is fully mobilized behind a platform to dismantle the American political order; its principles of individual accountability, equality, and freedom; its system of checks and balances for encouraging compromise and restraining government; and its protections for minorities against a tyranny of the majority.

CODA

Love against Hate

The 2020 presidential election perfectly reflected the crossroads to which the nation had come. Despite rigged pre-election polls that purported to predict a Democrat landslide and were designed to discourage pro-Trump voters; despite a dishonest media suppressing information favorable to the president and refusing to report information detrimental to his opponent; despite relentless Democrat and media attacks on Trump as an incompetent impostor, a traitor, a mass murderer of COVID-19 patients, and the worst human being ever to occupy the Oval Office; despite Democrat and media slanders smearing his supporters as white nationalists and racist yahoos; despite a wall of unprecedented libels and character-defaming lies, the Trump campaign won 74 million votes, 10 million more than Barack Obama's 2012 total, and 5 million more than the total of any previous candidate for the presidency in American history.[1]

In a column titled "An Election between Love and Hate," which appeared five days before the election, noted commentator Daniel Greenfield posed a pivotal question about the two campaigns for president.[2] His question was inspired by the series of rallies Trump held in the weeks before the election, which attracted tens of thousands of supporters, as many as fifty thousand in cities as small as Butler, Pennsylvania; and, by contrast, the minimalist campaign of his opponent, whose crowds were confined to handfuls of staffers and supporters in the range of thirty to a hundred people.

In view of this disparity, which reflected a gaping lack of enthusiasm for the Democrat candidate, Greenfield asked: "Why are President Trump's rallies packed while Biden's rallies are deserted? Where were all the Democrats who joined in the Black Lives Matter riots, who packed the streets of D.C. for the Women's March, who wailed in front of the Supreme Court and burned Portland for months on end?"

His answer: "The Biden-Harris ticket is a placeholder, two candidates picked by Wall Street and Hollywood, by corporate donors looking for the best angle, bringing together a friend of segregationists and the woman who accused him of racism, and then negotiated with the party's socialist wing to split the difference between the prospective administration's crony capitalism and socialism. Nobody's going to a rally for that."

His conclusion, obvious to every honest observer: "The Democrats aren't campaigning for Joe Biden, but against Donald J. Trump."

At bottom, the 2020 presidential campaigns weren't about personalities; they were about the deep divisions in the nation at large. As Greenfield summed up, "The 2020 election can be boiled down to love against hate. It pits 'Make America Great Again' against the 1619 Project, those who love this country against those who want to destroy it. At Republican rallies, American flags are waved, at Democrat riots flags, churches, and shops are burned. The active part of the Democrat base won't show up to a Biden rally because they won't be allowed to destroy things, and because they're not animated by the positive, but by the negative."[3]

The effort to rig the 2020 election was launched in earnest in July when Joe Biden and the Democrat Party dispatched six hundred lawyers and ten thousand volunteers "to make voting safe and accessible for citizens, especially the most vulnerable, or call out local rules that don't adequately ensure access to vote."[4] In fact, all the "reforms" the

Democrat legal teams were able to put in place, some within weeks of the actual election, were efforts to loosen existing regulations that had been designed to protect the integrity of the vote and thwart potential fraud. In the service of making voting more "accessible," many of the new laws extended voting and counting deadlines to weeks and even months before and after Election Day. The result was the effective elimination of Election Day and the creation of many new opportunities to rig the results.

The *prima facie* evidence that there were problems with the results is overwhelming. To believe that fraud did not take place on a significant scale, as the anti-Trump political universe claimed, one would have to believe that while Trump outperformed every incumbent president before him and won 94 percent of Republican votes, Biden got 16 million *more* votes than Obama did in 2008 and 12.5 million more than he did in 2012. Or one would have to explain how Biden under-performed Hillary Clinton in every major city but not in four key Democrat-controlled cities in battleground states—Detroit, Milwaukee, Atlanta, and Philadelphia— all of which experienced unprecedented stops in vote counting and then massive mail-in ballot dumps in the middle of the night while Republican observers were barred from the counting rooms.[5]

Or one would have to explain how, except for the top of the ballot, where Trump outperformed his 2016 victory by a record margin, the only wave in the election was decidedly red. Republicans cut the Democrats' lead in the House of Representatives from thirty-six seats to ten.[6] As summarized by the *Washington Examiner*: "Republicans won all 27 House races the *Cook Political Report* rated as 'toss-ups' in its 2020 election analysis, in addition to picking up seven of the 36 seats the outlet rated as 'likely Democrat' or 'lean Democrat.'"[7] Is it plausible that in the middle of this red tide Biden legitimately won a record 81 million votes—nearly 16 million more than Barack Obama did in his 2008 performance?

Pollster Patrick Basham, the founding director of the Democracy Institute, has drawn attention to other unexplained anomalies in the official results, basing his doubts on metrics that have "a 100% accuracy rate in terms of predicting the winner of the presidential election." Those metrics include "party registration trends, how the candidates did in their respective presidential primaries, the number of individual donations, [and] how much enthusiasm each candidate generated in the opinion polls. In 2016, they all indicated strongly that Donald Trump would win against most of the public polling. That was again the case in 2020. So, if we are to accept that Biden won against the trend of all these non-polling metrics, it not only means that one of these metrics was inaccurate . . . for the first time ever, it means that each one of these metrics was wrong for the first time and at the same time as all of the others."[8]

Yet another telling anomaly was registered in the nineteen "bell-wether counties" that have correctly predicted every presidential election since 1980. Some have accurately predicted the results since the 1920s. In 2020, Trump won all of these counties but one.[9]

Many of the fraud-encouraging reforms that Democrat lawyers were able to put in place were unconstitutional and therefore illegal. The U.S. Constitution specifies that election laws are the purview of the state legislatures. But in the key battleground state of Pennsylvania, for example, the election laws were (illegally) changed by the Democrat-controlled State Supreme Court. According to Pennsylvania's secretary of state, Trump won Election Day votes, 2.7 million to 1.4 million. But after a massive mail-in ballot dump in the middle of the night, which Republican poll watchers were (illegally) barred from observing, the official count reported that Biden had won 76 percent of the votes.[10]

In addition to the middle-of-the-night ballot dump, election officials in Pennsylvania's heavily Democrat counties provided voters in those locales with the ability to "cure" defective ballots, while denying the same privilege to voters in Republican precincts—a clear violation of the equal protection clause of the Fourteenth Amendment.

The Democrats' assault on the electoral system was so transparent that on August 23, months before the actual vote, President Trump warned on Twitter: "The greatest Election Fraud in our history is about to happen."[11] He was referring specifically to the 92 million mail-in ballots that were about to be sent out by thirty-seven states.[12] Under pressure from the Democrats' legal squad these states had already changed key aspects of their mail-in voting procedures on the pretext that such changes were necessitated by the dangers posed by the coronavirus pandemic.[13] Mail-in ballots are banned in most countries.[14]

As a result of the decisions of the Democrat-allied tech industry to suppress information unfavorable to the anti-Trump forces, facts like these were not easily accessible to the American public. One had to dive deep into the Google search index to find an entry supporting Trump's concern. Five index pages in, one might come across Justice Department official John R. Lott's article "Why Do Most Countries Ban Mail-In Ballots?"[15] Or to bump into the fact that the 2005 bipartisan Commission on Election Reform, co-chaired by former president Jimmy Carter concluded: "Absentee ballots remain the largest potential source of voter fraud."[16]

The fraud potential of *unsolicited* mail-in ballots is many times greater, still. They are sent out to registered-voter lists, which may contain the names of the dead, people who have moved out of state and voted at their new address, and people here illegally, as in sanctuary states like California, where voting is so unrestricted that this kind of fraud is common. In a major 2012 study, the Pew Research Center reported that "approximately 24 million voter registrations in the United States—one of every eight—are no longer valid or have significant inaccuracies."[17] Harvesting mail-in ballots, removing their identifying envelopes and voting the anonymous ballot inside is relatively easy and made easier when hundreds of thousands of votes are counted by partisan poll workers in the middle of the night while Republican observers are physically barred from overseeing the process by Democrat thugs, as happened frequently during the 2020 election according to hundreds of sworn affidavits.

On top of this, voting machines and associated software used in over twenty states were designed to change votes from one candidate to another. How these machines were used to switch votes from Trump to Biden was explained by MIT scientist and inventor of email, Dr. Shiva Ayyadurai.

Testifying before the Arizona state legislature on November 30, 2020, Dr. Ayyadurai reported that of the 2,036,563 Maricopa County, Arizona, residents who voted in the 2020 presidential election, 35.3 percent were Republicans, 31.3 percent were Democrats, 32.3 percent were Independents, and 1.1 percent were Libertarians. Using sophisticated computer technology, Dr. Ayyadurai showed that Republican voter turnout in majority-Republican precincts was extremely high, whereas Democrat and Independent voter turnout in majority-Democrat-and-Independent precincts tended to be quite low.[18]

But despite the Republican advantage and Trump's record numbers nationally, the official vote tally across the county's 743 separate precincts provided Biden with the margin of victory. The Democrat was credited with capturing 49.8 percent of all ballots, while Trump was allotted only 47.6 percent.

Given these facts, Dr. Ayyadurai observed, Biden's victory in Maricopa County was "highly implausible." The only way it could have occurred is if every vote for Biden had been statistically "weighted" to count as 1.3 votes, and every vote for Trump had been statistically manipulated to count as just seven-tenths of a vote. Dr. Ayyadurai then stated that the Dominion voting machines used in Maricopa County "do have this [weighting] feature" where "votes are stored not as whole integer numbers, but as decimal fractions, which means . . . you could have external programs intersect, communicate with those programs, and alter them using external software programs which could also do weighted race features." This "fractional voting" amounts to "vote swapping," he elaborated, for the sole purpose of "enabling cheating."[19] For Biden to win the election in Maricopa County, every vote cast for him would have had to count as 1.3 votes, while every Trump ballot would have had to count as only 0.7 of a vote.

No court, including the Supreme Court, deigned to hear or examine the evidence that the White House amassed to show that in six battleground states the election was decided on the basis of illegal and/ or suspect ballots. The courts' refusals to hear the evidence were based on procedural objections, but partisan politics and, in the case of the Supreme Court, fear of violence played significant roles in what was an epic dereliction of duty by the nation's judiciary.

The White House dealt with this dereliction by summarizing the evidence in a thirty-six-page document compiled by Peter Navarro and titled "Immaculate Deception."[20] In the words of the report, "Evidence used to conduct this assessment includes more than 50 lawsuits and judicial rulings, thousands of affidavits and declarations, testimony in a variety of state venues, published analyses by think tanks and legal centers, videos and photos, public comments, and extensive press coverage." The report summarized its findings by noting that in five of the six key battleground states that decided the election, Biden's margins of victory were a total of 158,114 votes, but legally questionable votes in those same states exceeded 1.4 million—enough to decide the outcome.[21]

The Democrats' attack on the voting process was transparent to any independent observer. It was evident in the Democrats' zeal in barring Republican poll watchers from observing the vote counts. This was brazenly illegal, and also inexplicable if the Democrats had nothing to hide. It was also obvious in their post-election claims that questions about the integrity of the election were "baseless" and "conspiratorial," and their denial that *any* voter fraud had taken place or needed to be investigated. It was also transparent in their hypocritical indictments of Republicans as "insurrectionists" for questioning an election result after they themselves had challenged both Republican election victories in 2000 and 2004 and refused to accept the results of the 2016 election for four destructive years.

But it was the aftermath of the election result, when Joe Biden had been declared the "president-elect" and the Democrats had "won" all three branches of government, that showed the Democrats' true colors and long-range agenda. January 6 was the date designated for the Congress to certify the electors and therefore the vote. President Trump, who had just had the presidency stolen from under him and was faced with an opposition that denied him the recourses provided by the Constitution, called on his followers to gather at the Ellipse—the oval-shaped field between the Mall and the White House—for a last stand to protest the greatest political crime in the history of the country.

The president spoke for over an hour to hundreds of thousands of supporters. In the course of his remarks, he said: "I know that everyone here will soon be marching over to the Capitol Building to peacefully and patriotically make your voices heard." Unfortunately, the anger a small minority of the crowd felt at the destruction of so fundamental a freedom as the freedom to vote—and no doubt the spectacle of a summer of mainly unpunished left-wing riots—led to an attack on the Capitol itself. The attack turned violent, and five people died.

The victorious Democrats responded by blaming Trump falsely for inciting the attack, calling it an insurrection. The same Democrats, including the president-elect and his vice president, had applauded and abetted the 633 violent insurrections in 220 American cities by Black Lies Matter radicals during the summer of 2020. They had described the mob obstruction of the Kavanaugh hearings by leftists who had to be removed from the chambers by Capitol police as "democracy in action."

Democrats went further. They called the mob incident the worst attack on the Capitol since the British burned the White House in 1812 and then compared it to 9/11 and the Holocaust. A more apt comparison would be to the Reichstag fire, which the Nazis exploited to destroy the Weimar Republic and establish the Third Reich. Immediately Democrats and their partners in tech did exploit the incident, setting out to criminalize and silence anyone or any party that questioned the election result as though that were an insurrectionary act in itself.

President-elect Biden, who had declared "healing" and "unity" his "highest objective," singled out Senators Josh Hawley and Ted Cruz and compared them to Nazi propagandist Joseph Goebbels. Their crime? Supporting the challenge to the election result. Several Democrat members of

Congress then called for their removal from Congress for their offense, which was in fact the exercise of a frequently invoked American right.

Twitter, Google, Amazon, and Facebook then announced a series of bans barring from their platforms the defeated Republicans, beginning with the president, whose 88.6 million Twitter followers were denied access to his thoughts. The idea that two Silicon billionaires, Jack Dorsey and Mark Zuckerberg, could censor the president of the United States who had just received in excess of 75 million votes was troubling enough. But then the same companies extended the ban to the social media platform Parler which was created by conservatives to provide them with a voice after being censored on Facebook and Twitter.

The vindictive Nancy Pelosi announced plans to impeach Trump for "inciting insurrection" even though he had only two weeks left to serve out his term, while Democrats in Congress drafted legislation to ban "Make America Great Again" rallies, which had created the first conservative mass movement in the modern era.

In sum, everything Democrats and their allies did with the power they had won showed that their ultimate goal was not to replace or destroy one man in office, or to win one election, but to establish a one-party state.

Acknowledgements

An author's occupation is in all cases a lonely one. For weeks and months on end, an author inhabits a world in which he is the sole traveler and to whose trials and tribulations he is the only witness. When the terrain is as dark and despairing as the subject of the present volume, the pressures on a human soul can be overwhelming. I bring this up not to seek sympathy—this is after all the life I have chosen—but to indicate the great debt I owe to my friends and family for their love and support. Because of the animosity that my political adversaries have directed towards me, I hesitate to name them, but they know who they are. What they may not know is what a powerful shield their affection has provided to make possible my work. The love of my family members—and also my extended family members—is ultimately what keeps me going.

I do need to mention one person near and dear to me whom I couldn't hide in any case: my wife, April, my companion and support in the most productive years of my life and the greatest blessing in age that anyone could wish for.

My publisher Tom Spence is an unsung hero among conservative publishers. In 1999, when I was kicked out of the New York publishing world for proposing a book titled *Hating Whitey and Other Progressive Causes,* Tom came to my rescue and published it as the head of a small eponymous publishing house in Texas. Now as the head of Regnery, Tom has put the power of a major conservative publisher behind three of my recent books including *The Enemy Within.* I am greatly in his debt for being my enabler and my friend.

I am indebted to two of Tom's excellent editors, Elizabeth Kantor and Laura Spence Swain, for making this text the best that it could be. Thank you both.

The redoubtable Sandy Frazier has handled media relations—radio and TV—for me for years, and played an important role in the success of my last three books—*Big Agenda, Dark Agenda*, and *Blitz*—which collectively sold over 400,000 copies and were 21 weeks on the *New York Times* bestseller list, although otherwise ignored by the mainstream press.

My friends and colleagues at the David Horowitz Freedom Center have stood by me throughout the personal attacks that have been directed at me by people who have never read a word I have written and have no idea who I actually am. My coworkers and board members at the Center and the courageous individuals who are our financial sponsors have been a bulwark against the many forces who have tried to destroy me and suppress our work. I am deeply grateful to you all. Mike, Elizabeth, Sandy, and Lonny have helped to bring my work before larger audiences and have provided me the technical support necessary to do what I do. Sara and Sean have spearheaded our fight against indoctrination in the schools. Jamie, Daniel, Robert, Caroline, Bruce, Mark, Raymond, Katie, Bosch, Jason, Lloyd, Joseph, Danusha, and many others have made our webzine Frontpagemag.com a flagship in the battle we are all engaged in to save our magnificent country from the ignorant and totalitarian Left.

Finally, I must mention John Perazzo, the supplier and verifier of many of the sources drawn on in this text. John and I have co-authored many articles and pamphlets on these and related subjects. More important, John is the driving force behind an idea I had fifteen years ago to create an encyclopedia of the Left called DiscovertheNetworks.org. Discover the Networks is particularly indispensable because the Left is so committed to flying under false flags like "peace," "justice," and "anti-racism," whereas their true agendas are exactly the opposite. How Orwellian is that? Thank you, John, for making my work more accurate and informed than it otherwise would have been.

Notes

Chapter 1: White Male Christians

1. "Identity Politics," Wikipedia, note 7, https://en.wikipedia.org/wiki/Identity_politics#cite_note-7.

2. Combahee River Collective, "The Combahee River Collective Statement," April 1977, http://circuitous.org/scraps/combahee.html.

3. Ibid. "As Angela Davis points out in 'Reflections on the Black Woman's Role in the Community of Slaves,' Black women have always embodied, if only in their physical manifestation, an adversary stance to white male rule and have actively resisted its inroads upon them and their communities in both dramatic and subtle ways."

4. Thomas Sowell, "Economic Mobility," Creators.com, March 5, 2013, https://www.creators.com/read/thomas-sowell/03/13/economic-mobility; Thomas Sowell, *Economic Facts and Fallacies* (New York: Basic Books, 2011).

5. Matthew Dowd, "Us White Male Christians Need to Step Back and Give Others Room to Lead," ABC News, September 30, 2018, https://abcnews.go.com/US/leadership-means-making-oneself-dispensable-opinion/story?id=58193412. When I published an article on Dowd's column, his response was to ban me from his Twitter feed. This is characteristic of the Left, which rarely chooses to engage an actual argument, responding either with defamatory name-calling or with silence.

6. A classic instance of this is the French Revolution. See Simon Schama's classic *Citizens: A Chronicle of the French Revolution* (New York: Alfred A. Knopf, 1991).

Chapter 2: An Anti-American Creed

1. On the anti-Christian agendas of the progressive Left, see David Horowitz, *Dark Agenda: The War to Destroy Christian America* (New York: Humanix Books, 2019).
2. David Horowitz, "The Communist Manifesto—100 Years of Evil," Orthodox.net, https://www.orthodoxnet.com/news/150YearsOfEvil.html.
3. In the course of writing five books on American universities, I have examined ethnic and gender studies courses at scores of universities. As academic professions they are organized at the national level and subscribe to common principles. See, e.g., David Horowitz, *The Professors* (Washington, D.C.: Regnery, 2006) and David Horowitz and Jacob Laksin, *One-Party Classroom* (New York: Crown Forum, 2009).
4. A Google search for "abolition of whiteness" yields over one million results: https://www.google.com/search?client=firefox-b-1-d&q=abolition+of+whiteness.
5. John Perrazo, "The Ugly Racism of 'Whiteness Studies' Programs," FrontPageMag, https://www.frontpagemag.com/fpm/263671/ugly-racism-whiteness-studies-programs-john-perazzo.
6. "Noel Ignatiev," Wikipedia, https://en.wikipedia.org/wiki/Noel_Ignatiev.
7. Tom Rosentiel, "Inside Obama's Sweeping Victory," Pew Research, November 5, 2008, https://www.pewresearch.org/2008/11/05/inside-obamas-sweeping-victory/.
8. "Just Communities Central Coast (JCCC)," Discover the Networks, https://www.discoverthenetworks.org/organizations/just-communities-central-coast-jccc/; "The National Federation for Just Communities. . . .," National Federation for Just Communities, http://federationforjustcommunities.org/; http://www.faireducation.org/wp-content/uploads/2019/02/frontpage-mag.pdf. For more information on the political use of K–12 classrooms, see "Code of Ethics for K–12 Teachers," Stop K–12 Indoctrination, www.stopk12indoctrination.org.
9. Matthew Vadum, "Parents Sue to Fight Anti-White, Anti-Male, Anti-Christian, Communist Indoctrination in California: Leftist Group 'Just Communities' Is in the Legal Crosshairs," FrontPageMag, February 22, 2019, https://www.frontpagemag.com/fpm/272954/parents-sue-fight-anti-white-anti-male-anti-matthew-vadum. Created in 2001, the organization co-founded the National Federation of Just Communities

and changed its own name to Just Communities Central Coast. This is a partial list. I have left out alleged "forms of oppression" such as "ableism" and "ageism" because, in addition to being ludicrous, they are marginal even in the litanies of the Left.

10. Cory Collins, "What Is White Privilege Really?," *Teaching Tolerance*, fall 2018, https://www.tolerance.org/magazine/fall-2018/what-is-white-privilege-really.

11. Just Communities, *Forms of Oppression* (curriculum), no page numbers.

12. "White Privilege," Wikipedia, https://en.wikipedia.org/wiki/White_privilege.

13. "Stop-and-Frisk Data," New York Civil Liberties Union, https://www.nyclu.org/en/stop-and-frisk-data; Collins, "What Is White Privilege?" The ugly neologism "Latinx" is a term invented by leftists to erase gender differences.

14. Heather Mac Donald, "Distorting the Truth about Crime and Race," *City Journal*, May 14, 2010, https://www.city-journal.org/html/distorting-truth-about-crime-and-race-10730.html.

15. Heather Mac Donald, *The War on Cops: How the Attack on Law and Order Makes Everyone Less Safe* (New York: Encounter, 2017), Kindle edition, loc. 479.

16. James P. O'Neill, "Crime and Enforcement Activity in New York City (January 1–December 31, 2018)," https://www1.nyc.gov/assets/nypd/downloads/pdf/analysis_and_planning/year-end-2018-enforcement-report.pdf.

17. Michael D. Tanner, "The Real '1 Percent,'" *New York Post*, November 8, 2011, https://www.cato.org/publications/commentary/real-1-percent.

18. Alysse ElHage, "Don't Overlook Marriage in the Fight to End Child Poverty," Institute for Family Studies, September 19, 2016, https://ifstudies.org/blog/dont-overlook-marriage-in-the-fight-to-end-child-poverty.

19. "List of Ethnic Groups in the United States by Household Income," Wikipedia, https://en.wikipedia.org/wiki/List_of_ethnic_groups_in_the_United_States_by_household_income.

20. "Kimberlé Crenshaw," Discover the Networks, https://www.discoverthenetworks.org/individuals/kimberle-crenshaw/.

21. Ilanik Chernick, "Louis Farrakhan Loses Twitter Verification after 'Satanic Jew' Rant," *Jerusalem Post*, June 12, 2018, https://www.jpost.com/Diaspora/Louis-Farrakhan-loses-Twitter-verification-right-after-Satanic-Jew-rant-559738.

22. "Derrick Bell," Discover the Networks, https://www.discoverthenetworks.org/individuals/derrick-bell.

23. Jonathan Haidt, "The Age of Outrage," *City Journal,* December 17, 2017.

24. Rachel Frommer, "Alan Dershowitz Derides Theory of Intersectionality in Columbia Lecture," Washington Free Beacon, September 28, 2017, https://freebeacon.com/culture/alan-dershowitz-derides-theory-intersectionality-columbia-lecture/.

25. Elizabeth Harrington, "NSF Has Spent $62.5 Million on 'Intersectionality' and STEM under Current Director: 'Workshops on Allies, Inclusive Classrooms, and Microaggressions,'" *Washington Free Beacon,* December 3, 2018, https://freebeacon.com/issues/nsf-spent-62-5-million-intersectionality-stem-current-director/.

26. James Damore, "Google's Ideological Echo Chamber: How Bias Clouds Our Thinking about Diversity and Inclusion," July 2017, https://web.archive.org/web/20170809220001/https://diversitymemo-static.s3-us-west-2.amazonaws.com/Googles-Ideological-Echo-Chamber.pdf.

27. Daniel Greenfield, "The Google Gulag: The Internet Cannot Remain in the Hands of a Corporation That Hates Free Speech," FrontPageMag, August 9, 2017, https://www.frontpagemag.com/fpm/267519/google-gulag-daniel-greenfield.

28. "The Gender-Equality Paradox in Science, Technology, Engineering, and Mathematics Education," Wikipedia, https://en.wikipedia.org/wiki/Gender-equality_paradox; Gijsbert Stoet and David C. Geary, "The Gender-Equality Paradox in Science, Technology, Engineering, and Mathematics Education," *Psychological Science,* February 14, 2018, https://journals.sagepub.com/doi/10.1177/0956797617741719.

29. "White Supremacy," Google Dictionary, https://www.google.com/search?client=firefox-b-1-d&q=GOOGLE+DICTIONARY#dobs=WHITE%20SUPREMACY.

30. "White Supremacy," Wikipedia, https://en.wikipedia.org/wiki/White_supremacy.

31. David Pietrusza, "The Ku Klux Klan in the 1920s," CNX, https://cnx.org/contents/P9mavqYZ@4/%F0%9F%94%8E-The-Ku-Klux-Klan-in-the-1920s.

32. Ibid.

33. Deirdre Washington, "Pelosi: 'White Supremacist' Bannon Making America 'Less Safe,'" CNN, Politics, February 3, 2017, https://www.cnn.com/2017/02/02/politics/pelosi-steve-bannon-white-supremacist/index.html.

34. Thomas Sowell, *Discrimination and Disparities*, rev. ed. (New York: Basic Books, 2019).

35. "2016 Democratic Party Platform," https://democrats.org/wp-content/uploads/2018/10/2016_DNC_Platform.pdf.

36. See, e.g., David Horowitz, "The Road to Nowhere" in *Ruling Ideas*, vol. 9 of *The Black Book of the American Left* (Los Angeles: Second Thought Books, 2018).

Chapter 3: A Racist Culture

1. See Thomas Chatterton Williams's review of Coates's next book, *We Were Eight Years in Power*: "How Ta-Nehisi Coates Gives Whiteness Power," *New York Times*, October 6, 2017, https://www.nytimes.com/2017/10/06/opinion/ta-nehisi-coates-whiteness-power.html. Chatterton is black.
2. Ta Nehisi Coates, "Black Pathology and the Closing of the Progressive Mind," *The Atlantic*, March 21, 2014, https://www.theatlantic.com/politics/archive/2014/03/black-pathology-and-the-closing-of-the-progressive-mind/284523/.
3. Don Cox, *Just Another Nigger: My Life in the Black Panther Party* (Berkeley, California: Heyday, 2019).
4. David Horowitz, *Radical Son: A Generational Odyssey*, 1997 *Odyssey* (New York, New York: Touchstone, 1997); see also Horowitz, "Black Murder Inc.," in *My Life and Times*, vol. 1 of *The Black Book of the American Left* (New York: Encounter, 2013).
5. George Packer, "George Packer Responds to Ta-Nehisi Coates," *The Atlantic*, September 15, 2017, https://www.theatlantic.com/notes/2017/09/ta-nehisi-coates-george-packer-white-president/539976/.
6. Ta-Nehisi Coates, *We Were Eight Years in Power* (London: One World, 2017), 113.
7. Ibid., 42
8. Tucker Carlson, *Ship of Fools* (New York: Free Press, 2018), Kindle edition, loc. 1954.
9. Ibid., loc. 1942.
10. Randall Kennedy, "Ta-Nehisi Coates's Caricature of Black Reality," *The American Prospect*, November 19, 2015, http://prospect.org/article/ta-nehisi-coatess-caricature-black-reality.
11. Quoted in Carlson, *Ship of Fools*, loc. 1989.
12. Ibid.
13. For a statistical refutation of this claim, see chapter 11 below.
14. Ta-Nehisi Coates, *Between the World and Me* (London: One World, 2015), 83.
15. Ibid., 110–11.
16. Ibid.
17. Ta-Nehisi Coates, "The Case for Reparations," *The Atlantic*, June 2014, https://www.theatlantic.com/magazine/archive/2014/06/the-case-for-reparations/361631/.

18. Manuel Roig-Franzia, "With *Atlantic* Article on Reparations, Ta-Nehisi Coates Sees Payoff for Years of Struggle," *Washington Post*, https://www.washingtonpost.com/lifestyle/style/with-atlantic-article-on-reparations-ta-nehisi-coates-sees-payoff-for-years-of-struggle/2014/06/18/6a2bd10e-f636-11e3-a3a5-42be35962a52_story.html.

19. I have written extensively on this subject and was the center of a national controversy when I opposed reparations in 2001. See David Horowitz, *Uncivil Wars: The Controversy over Reparations for Slavery* (New York: Encounter, 2001); David Horowitz, *Progressive Racism* (New York: Encounter, 2016); and David Horowitz, *Ruling Ideas*, vol. 9 of *The Black Book of the American Left* (Los Angeles: Second Thought Books, 2018).

20. Randall Robinson, *The Debt: What America Owes to Blacks* (New York: Dutton Adult, 2000), 8.

21. Kevin Grant, "Socialist Professor Addresses Student Audience on Reparations and Race Relations," Arizona State Press, April 24, 2001. Dyson is a professor at DePaul University and was flown in at university expense to provide a rebuttal to a case against reparations that I had been invited by students to present.

22. According to Henry Louis Gates Jr., "How Many Slaves Landed in the U.S.?," PBS, https://www.pbs.org/wnet/african-americans-many-rivers-to-cross/history/how-many-slaves-landed-in-the-us/.

23. Zora Neale Hurston, *Dust Tracks on a Road*, excerpted at http://larryslibrary.blogspot.com/2017/12/zora-neale-hurston-excerpt.html.

24. E.g., Cory Booker and Julián Castro, Democrat senators and candidates for their party's 2020 presidential nomination, called slavery "America's original sin"—without any dissent from their colleagues.

25. David Horowitz, "Anatomy of a Lynching: The Political Uses of Race," FrontPageMag, October 24, 2016, https://www.frontpagemag.com/fpm/264592/anatomy-lynching-david-horowitz.

26. Jim Wallis, "Slavery Never Ended. It Just Evolved.," HuffPost, December 18, 2016, https://www.huffingtonpost.com/jim-wallis/slavery-never-ended-it-ju_b_8837844.html; also see the website of the Equal Justice Initiative at https://eji.org/.

27. Quoted in Carlson, *Ship of Fools*, loc. 1974.

Chapter 4: A Poisonous Protest

1. Cody Derespina, "Ta-Nehisi Coates, Who Called 9/11 Responders 'Menaces of Nature,' to Speak at West Point," Fox News, March 7, 2017, https://www.foxnews.com/us/ta-nehisi-coates-who-called-9-11-responders-menaces-of-nature-to-speak-at-west-point.

2. "Video Shows NYC Protestors Chanting for 'Dead Cops,'" NBC New York, December 15, 2020, https://www.nbcnewyork.com/news/local/eric-garner-manhattan-dead-cops-video-millions-march-protest/2015303/.

3. For an extensive analysis of these events, see Heather Mac Donald, *The War on Cops: How the Attack on Law and Order Makes Everyone Less Safe* (New York: Encounter, 2017).

4. "Hands Up Don't Shoot," Wikipedia, https://en.wikipedia.org/wiki/Hands_up,_don%27t_shoot.

5. For details on the organization and its founders, see "Black Lives Matter (BLM)," Discover the Networks, www.discoverthenetworks.org.

6. Brian Amaral, "Another Anniversary Passes with N.J. Trooper's Convicted Killer at Large," NJ.com, March 29, 2019, https://www.nj.com/middlesex/index.ssf/2015/05/trooper_werner_foerster_was_killed_42_years_ago_to.html.

7. Talon Archives, "#BlackLivesMatter Assata Shakur Chant," August 7, 2016, https://www.youtube.com/watch?v=SNayoOysBLY.

8. Ibid.

9. For other examples, see "Black Lives Matter (BLM)," Discover the Networks.

10. Khaleda Rahman, "'F*** You, You Filthy White F****!' Black Lives Matter Protesters Scream Epithets at White Students Studying in Dartmouth Library," *Daily Mail*, November 16, 2015, https://www.dailymail.co.uk/news/article-3321190/F-filthy-white-s-Black-Lives-Matter-protesters-scream-epithets-white-students-studying-Dartmouth-library.html; "Dartmouth Students Lead Profane Black Lives Matter Protest," *Dartmouth Review*, November 14, 2015, https://www.campusreform.org/?ID=6990.

11. Nicholas Fandos, "Protesters Confront Candidates on Race at Netroots Nation Conference," *New York Times*, July 19, 2015, https://www.nytimes.com/2015/07/19/us/protesters-confront-candidates-on-race-at-netroots-nation-conference.html.

12. Ibid.

13. Larry Elder, "The Truth about Cops Killing Blacks," WND, July 6, 2016, https://www.wnd.com/2016/07/the-truth-about-cops-killing-blacks/#LWc1WAIoIYWi4UVq.99. See also Mac Donald, *The War On Cops*, chapter 13 "Black and Unarmed," for a further breakdown of the statistics.

14. Jamiles Larty, "Obama on Black Lives Matter: They Are 'Much Better Organizers Than I Was,'" *Guardian*, February 18, 2016, https://www.theguardian.com/us-news/2016/feb/18/black-lives-matter-meet-president-obama-white-house-justice-system.

15. Alex Seitz-Wald, "DNC Passes Resolution Supporting Black Lives Matter," MSNBC, August 28, 2015, http://www.msnbc.com/msnbc/dnc-passes-resolution-supporting-black-lives-matter.

16. Matthew Vadum, "Dems Officially Endorse Anti-Cop BlackLivesMatter Movement: As Police Are Stalked and Killed in the Streets," FrontPageMag, September 2, 2015, https://archives.frontpagemag.com/fpm/dems-officially-endorse-anti-cop-blacklivesmatter-matthew-vadum/.

17. "Black Lives Matter (BLM)," Discover the Networks, https://www.discoverthenetworks.org/organizations/black-lives-matter-blm/.

18. "Obama Defends Black Lives Matter Movement," PBS News Hour, October 23, 2015, https://www.pbs.org/newshour/politics/obama-defends-black-lives-matter-movement.

19. Matt Pearce and Jaweed Kaleem, "12 Officers Shot, 5 Fatally, by Snipers in Dallas during Protest over Police Shootings," *Los Angeles Times*, July 8, 2016, https://www.latimes.com/nation/la-na-dallas-shooting-20160707-snap-story.html.

20. Carlson, *Ship of Fools*, loc. 2005.

21. Nickarama, "Video: Black Lives Matter Activist Shouts: 'Kill All White Babies!'" Weasel Zippers, July 18, 2016, https://www.weaselzippers.us/284283-video-black-lives-matter-activist-shouts-kill-all-white-babies/.

22. Carlson, *Ship of Fools*. Also see Mac Donald, *The War on Cops*, on the support for Black Lives Matter in the mainstream media.

23. Rich Morin, et al., "Behind the Badge: Amid Protests and Calls for Reform, How Police View Their Jobs, Key Issues and Fatal Encounters between Blacks and Police," Pew Research Center, January 11, 2017, http://www.pewsocialtrends.org/2017/01/11/behind-the-badge/; Aamer Medhani, "'Ferguson Effect': 72% of U.S. Cops Reluctant to Make Stops," *USA Today*, January 11, 2017, https://www.usatoday.com/story/news/2017/01/8911/ferguson-effect-study-72-us-cops-reluctant-make-stops/96446504/.

24. Martin Kaste, "Murder Rate Spike Could be 'Ferguson Effect,'" NPR, June 15, 2016, https://www.npr.org/2016/06/15/482123552/murder-rate-spike-attributed-to-ferguson-effect-doj-study-says.

25. Will Racke, "The FBI's Latest Report Suggests the 'Ferguson Effect' Is Real," Daily Caller, October 1, 2017, https://dailycaller.com/2017/10/01/the-fbis-latest-report-suggests-the-ferguson-effect-is-real/.

26. See "Black Lives Matter," Discover the Networks, https://www.discoverthenetworks.org/organizations/black-lives-matter-blm/; Valerie Richardson, "Black Lives Matter Cashes in with $100 Million from Liberal Foundations," *Washington Times*, August 16, 2016, https://www.washingtontimes.com/news/2016/aug/16/black-lives-matter-cashes-100-million-liberal-foun/.

27. Nat Hentoff, "The Sadist as Revolutionary," *Dissent,* Spring 1987, 2–3. Hentoff was a well-known libertarian leftist.

28. "Lessons from Fidel: Black Lives Matter and the Transition of El Comandante," Black Lives Matter Global Network, November 27, 2016, https://medium.com/@BlackLivesMatterNetwork/lessons-from-fidel-black-lives-matter-and-the-transition-of-el-comandante-c11ee5e51fb0.

29. "Huey Newton," Discover the Networks, https://www.discoverthenetworks.org/individuals/huey-newton/; Patrick Oppmann, "Admitted Hijacker Dreams of Home after 43 Years Hiding Out in Cuba," CNN, April 9, 2015, https://www.cnn.com/2015/04/09/americas/us-cuba-fugitive-charlie-hill/.

30. Robert Spencer, "2015: Black Lives Matter Visits 'Palestine,' Links Jihad against Israel to Race War in US," Jihad Watch, July 8, 2016, https://www.jihadwatch.org/2016/07/2015-black-lives-matter-visits-palestine-links-jihad-against-israel-to-race-war-in-us.

31. "2015 Black Solidarity Statement with Palestine," http://www.blackforpalestine.com/read-the-statement.html; Renee Lewis, "Black Activists Endorse Boycott of Israel," Al Jazeera, August 19, 2015, http://america.aljazeera.com/articles/2015/8/19/black-activists-endorse-bds-movement.html; Liat Collins, "My Word: BDS's Binding Ties with Terrorists," *Jerusalem Post,* February 8, 2019, https://www.jpost.com/Opinion/My-word-BDSs-binding-ties-with-terrorists-580068.

32. Sandra Tamari and Tara Thompson, "From Ferguson to Palestine, We See Us" HuffPo, October 16, 2015, https://www.huffingtonpost.com/sandra-tamari/from-ferguson-to-palestine_b_8307832.html.

33. Bridget Johnson, "Obama: 'Longstanding Tradition' of 'Contentious and Messy' Protest Needed in the United States," PJ Media, July 7, 2016, https://pjmedia.com/news-and-politics/2016/07/11/obama-longstanding-tradition-of-contentious-and-messy-protest-needed-in-america/m.

Chapter 5: A Public Hanging

1. "Sexism," Wikipedia, https://en.wikipedia.org/wiki/Sexism.

2. Thomas Sowell, *Discrimination and Disparities,* rev. ed. (New York: Basic Books, 2019).

3. Erica Chenoweth, "This Is What We Learned by Counting the Women's Marches," *Washington Post,* February 7, 2017, https://www.washingtonpost.com/news/monkey-cage/wp/2017/02/07/this-is-what-we-learned-by-counting-the-womens-marches/?utm_term=.570233ffbd81.

4. *Emily Crockett,* "The 'Women's March on Washington,' Explained," Vox, November 1, 2016, https://www.vox.com/ identities/2016/11/21/13651804/women-march-washington-trump-inauguration.

5. Jackie Kucinich, "A Record Number of Women Were Just Elected, but the Women's March Is Imploding," Daily Beast, November 20, 2018, https://www.thedailybeast.com/a-record-number-of-women-were-just-elected-but-the-womens-march-is-imploding; Leah McSweeney and Jacob Siegel, "Is the Women's March Melting Down?," *Tablet,* December 10, 2018, https://www.tabletmag.com/jewish-news-and-politics/276694/is-the-womens-march-melting-down.

6. Samantha Cooney, "Women's March C-President Bob Bland Says White Women Need to 'Take a Seat' after Charlottesville," *Time,* August 15, 2017, http://time.com/4900380/ bob-bland-womens-march-charlottesville/.

7. Bari Weiss, "When Progressives Embrace Hate," *New York Times,* August 1, 2017, https://www.nytimes.com/2017/08/01/opinion/womens-march-progressives-hate.html.

8. Nick Kangadis, "Belafonte on Trump Presidency: 'Welcome to the Fourth Reich,'" MRC TV, December 6, 2016, https://www.mrctv.org/ blog/belafonte-trump-presidency-welcome-fourth-reich. This was in reference to the Trump presidency, but Belafonte used the same phrase to, for example, describe America during the Bush presidency. See David Horowitz, *Indoctrination U: The Left's War against Academic Freedom* (New York: Encounter, 2007), chapter 5, "Dangerous Professors."

9. Ibid.

10. "Carmen Perez," Discover the Networks, https://www. discoverthenetworks.org/individuals/carmen-perez.

11. Jack Heretik, "Convicted Terrorist Deported, Upsetting Women's March Organizers," Washington Free Beacon, September 21, 2017, https:// freebeacon.com/issues/ convicted-terrorist-deported-upsetting-womens-march-organizers/.

12. Critical Voices, "Linda Sarsour's Powerful Speech at the Women's March on Washington," Youtube, January 21, 2017, https://www. youtube.com/watch?v=DnaT8JxUTYo.

13. Associated Press, "Madonna: 'Thought about Blowing Up White House," Youtube, January 22, 2017, https://youtu.be/o9oqmm3qRuo.

14. Rebecca Shabad, "Schumer: I'm Going to Fight the Kavanaugh Nomination 'with Everything I've Got," NBC News, July 10, 2018, https://www.nbcnews.com/politics/congress/schumer-kavanaugh-i-m-going-fight-nomination-everything-i-ve-n890246.

15. Sheryl Gay Stolberg and Adam Liptak, "Kavanaugh Portrayed as a Hopeless Partisan as Hearings on Supreme Court Nominee Open," *New York Times*, September 4, 2018, https://www.nytimes.com/2018/09/04/us/politics/kavanaugh-confirmation-supreme-court.html; "'You're Out of Order': Protests on Day 1 of Kavanaugh Hearings," *New York Times*, https://www.nytimes.com/video/us/politics/100000006085845/kavanaugh-supreme-court-protests.html; Doug Stanglin and Caroline Simon, "'Rise Up, Women!' Angry Crowds Flood Capitol Hill to Protest Brett Kavanaugh Nomination," *USA Today*, September 28, 2019, https://www.usatoday.com/story/news/2018/09/28/brett-kavanaugh-hearing-protesters-christine-blasey-ford/1453524002/.

16. Jim Huffman, "Opinion: The Orchestrated Disruptions of Kavanaugh's Hearings Demonstrated Neither Democracy nor Free Speech," Daily Caller, September 18, 2018, https://dailycaller.com/2018/09/18/disruptions-kavanaugh-democracy-free-time/.

17. Brian Flood, "'The View' Host Joy Behar Says 'White Men' Are Protecting 'Probably Guilty' Brett Kavanaugh," Fox News, September 19, 2018, https://www.foxnews.com/entertainment/the-view-host-joy-behar-says-white-men-are-protecting-probably-guilty-brett-kavanaugh.

18. Ian Schwartz, "Sen. Merkley: 'Crew of White Republican Men' Treat Women as If They Are the Problem," RealClearPolitics, October 4, 2018, https://www.realclearpolitics.com/video/2018/10/04/sen_merkley_crew_of_white_republican_men_treat_women_as_if_they_are_the_problem.html.

19. Emily Baumgaertner, "Justice Kavanaugh's Law Clerks Are All Women, a First for the Supreme Court," *New York Times*, October 9, 2018, https://www.nytimes.com/2018/10/09/us/politics/kavanaugh-women-law-clerks.html.

20. A. P. Dillon, "Cutting to the Chase: Just the Ford-Mitchell Transcript," Lady Liberty, September 29, 2018, https://ladyliberty1885.com/2018/09/29/just-ford-mitchell-transcript/.

21. Margot Cleveland, "Christine Blasey Ford's Changing Kavanaugh Assault Story Leaves Her Short on Credibility: Put Aside Christine Blasey Ford's Emotional Performance. Her Testimony Revealed Her as a Witness Whose Memories Change at Her Convenience.," *USA Today*, October 3, 2018, https://usatoday.com/story/opinion/2018/10/03/christine-blasey-ford-changing-memories-not-credible-kavanaugh-column/1497661002/.

22. Bre Payton, "Sex Crimes Prosecutor Details 12 Massive Inconsistencies in Kavanaugh Accuser's Story," The Federalist, October 10, 2018, http://thefederalist.com/2018/10/01/sex-crimes-prosecutor-details-12-massive-inconsistencies-kavanaugh-accusers-story/.

23. Dillon, "Cutting to the Chase."

24. Emma Brown, "California Professor, Writer of Confidential Brett Kavanaugh Letter, Speaks Out about Her Allegation of Sexual Assault," Washington Post, September 16, 2018, https://www.washingtonpost.com/investigations/california-professor-writer-of-confidential-brett-kavanaugh-letter-speaks-out-about-her-allegation-of-sexual-assault/2018/09/16/46982194-b846-11e8-94eb-3bd52dfe917b_story.html.

25. "Read the Letter Christine Blasey Ford Sent Accusing Brett Kavanaugh of Sexual Misconduct," CNN, September 16, 2018, https://www.cnn.com/2018/09/16/politics/blasey-ford-kavanaugh-letter-feinstein/index.html.

26. Melissa Quinn, "Christine Blasey Ford Scrubbed Social Media Profile before Sending Letter Detailing Alleged Sexual Assault: Book," Washington Examiner, July 8, 2019, https://www.washingtonexaminer.com/policy/courts/christine-blasey-ford-scrubbed-social-media-profile-before-sending-letter-detailing-alleged-sexual-assault-book.

27. "Believe Women," Wikipedia, https://en.wikipedia.org/wiki/Believe_women.

28. Click on Detroit Local 4 WDIV, "Sen. Kamala Harris to Christine Blasey Ford: 'You Are Not on Trial,'" Youtube, September 27, 2018, https://www.youtube.com/watch?v=6jrweFqnn1c.

29. Denver 7—the Denver Chanel, "Sen. Klobuchar Asks, Dr. Ford, 'Can You Tell Us What You Don't Forget about That Night?" September 27, 2018, Youtube, https://www.youtube.com/watch?v=C1U-tQKs9SU.

30. "Read the Letter Christine Blasey Ford Sent Accusing Brett Kavanaugh of Sexual Misconduct."

31. Thomas Lipscomb, "Documents Raise Questions about Ford's Double-Door Story," RealClear Politics, October 2, 2018, https://www.realclearpolitics.com/articles/2018/10/02/records_raise_questions_about_fords_double-door_story__138225.html.

32. Ibid.

33. Senator Richard Blumenthal, "Senator Blumenthal Questioning Judge Kavanaugh A . . .," Facebook, https://www.facebook.com/SenBlumenthal/videos/senator-blumenthal-questioning-judge-kavanaugh-about-sexual-assault-allegations/337558956991877/.

34. Raymond Hernandez, "Richard Blumenthal's Words on Vietnam Service Differ from History," New York Times, May 17, 2010, https://www.nytimes.com/2010/05/18/nyregion/18blumenthal.html.

35. "Researcher Uncovers Christine Blasey Ford's 'Hidden' 80's-Era High School Social Life," Tennessee Star, September 22, 2018, http://

tennesseestar.com/2018/09/22/researcher-uncovers-christine-blasey-fords-hidden-80s-era-high-school-social-life/.

36. Jessica McBride, "Christine Blasey Ford's Politics: She's a Democrat," heavy.com, September 17, 2018, https://heavy.com/news/2018/09/christine-blasey-ford-politics-democrat/.

37. "Full Remarks: Kavanaugh's Opening Statement," Politico, September 27, 2018, https://www.politico.com/story/2018/09/27/brett-kavanaugh-hearing-opening-statement-849484.

38. "Full Transcript: Brett Kavanaugh's Opening Statement to the Senate Judiciary Committee," *Politico,* September 26, 2018, https://www.politico.com/story/2018/09/26/kavanaugh-testimony-transcript-843105.

39. Natasha Korecki and Marianne Levine, "Third Kavanaugh Accuser Steps Forward," *Politico*, September 26, 2018, https://www.politico.com/story/2018/09/26/third-kavanaugh-accuser-steps-forward-843086.

40. Lindsey Graham, "Graham Questions Judge Kavanaugh," Youtube, September 27, 2018, https://youtu.be/ZBcJVpM87tc.

Chapter 6: Progressive Character Assassins

1. Nomani, "George Soros's March on Washington: Saturday's Protests and Unlawful Disruptions Were Brought to Us by a Well-Funded Network," *Wall Street Journal*, October 7, 2018, https://www.wsj.com/articles/george-soross-march-on-washington-1538951025.

2. Ibid.

3. Sophie Tatum, "More than 300 Protesters Arrested as Kavanaugh Demonstrations Pack Capitol Hill," CNN, October 5, 2018, https://www.cnn.com/2018/10/04/politics/kavanaugh-protests-us-capitol/index.html.

4. Emily Baumgaertner, "Justice Kavanaugh's Law Clerks Are All Women, a First for the Supreme Court," *New York Times*, October 9, 2018, https://www.nytimes.com/2018/10/09/us/politics/kavanaugh-women-law-clerks.html.

5. See David Horowitz, *The Professors: The 101 Most Dangerous Academics in America* (Washington, D.C.: Regnery, 2006).

6. Heather Mac Donald, *The Diversity Delusion: How Race and Gender Pandering Corrupt the University and Undermine Our Culture* (New York: St. Martin's Press, 2018), Kindle edition, loc. 350.

7. Ibid., loc 149.

8. Ibid.

9. Ibid., loc. 186.

10. Ibid., loc. 199.

11. Ibid., loc. 312.

12. Ibid., loc 324, 350.

13. Ibid., loc 265.

14. "Report: 9 of 10 American Colleges Restrict First Amendment Rights on Campus," World Tribune, December 16, 2018, https://www.worldtribune.com/report-9-of-10-american-colleges-restrict-first-amendment-rights-on-campus/.

15. Asra Q. Nomani, "George Soros's March on Washington," *Wall Street Journal*, October 8, 2018, https://www.wsj.com/articles/george-soross-march-on-washington-1538951025.

16. Ibid.

17. Tim Hains, "Maxine Waters: 'God Is on Our Side,' If You See a Member of the Trump Cabinet 'Push Back,'" RealClearPolitics, June 25, 2018, https://www.realclearpolitics.com/video/2018/06/25/maxine_waters_god_is_on_our_side.html.

18. "Antifa," Discover the Networks, https://www.discoverthenetworks.org/organizations/antifa/.

19. Madison Park and Kyung La, "Berkeley Protests of Yiannopoulos Caused $100,000 in Damage," CNN, February 2, 2017, https://www.cnn.com/2017/02/01/us/milo-yiannopoulos-berkeley/index.html; Valerie Richardson, "11 Arrested As Milo Cuts Short Berkeley Speech Costing $800,000 over Antifa Concerns," *Washington Times*, September 24, 2017, https://www.washingtontimes.com/news/2017/sep/24/milo-yiannopoulos-berkeley-speech-cut-short-over-a/.

20. "Antifa Mob Attacks Tucker Carlson's Home," *The Rush Limbaugh Show*, November 8, 2018, https://www.rushlimbaugh.com/daily/2018/11/08/antifa-mob-attacks-tucker-carlsons-home/.

21. Ibid.

22. Jenna Amatulli, "Here Are the Advertisers Boycotting Tucker Carlson's Show: The Fox News Host Is Facing Backlash after Suggesting That Immigrants Make Our Country 'Poorer and Dirtier and More Divided' on 'Tucker Carlson Tonight,'" HuffPo, December 18, 2018, https://www.huffingtonpost.com/entry/advertisers-boycotting-tucker-carlson-tonight_us_5c1913d2e4b08db990580994.

23. Jack Martin and Eric A. Ruark, "The Financial Burden of Illegal Immigration on United States Taxpayers," FAIR (Federation for American Immigration Reform), February 2011, https://www.fairus.org/sites/default/files/2017-08/USCostStudy_2010.pdf.

24. John Nolte, "'No Empathy': Vox's Matt Yglesias Defends 'Terrorizing' Tucker Carlson's Family," Breitbart, November 8, 2018, https://www.breitbart.com/politics/2018/11/08/vox-matt-yglesias-defends-terrorizing-tucker-carlsons-family/.

25. Amatulli, "Here Are the Advertisers."

Chapter 7: Progressive Blacklists

1. "Southern Poverty Law Center (SPLC)," Discover the Networks, https://www.discoverthenetworks.org/organizations/southern-poverty-law-center-splc/; David Montgomery, "The State of Hate: Researchers at the Southern Poverty Law Center Have Set Themselves Up as the Ultimate Judges of Hate in America. But Are They Judging Fairly?," *Washington Post Magazine*, November 18, 2018, https://www.washingtonpost.com/news/magazine/wp/2018/11/08/feature/is-the-southern-poverty-law-center-judging-hate-fairly/.

2. John Perazzo, "The Hate Group That Tracks Down 'Hate Groups': The Despicable Southern Poverty Law Center," FrontPageMag, January 9, 2017, https://www.frontpagemag.com/fpm/265403/hate-group-tracks-down-hate-groups-john-perazzo.

3. Ibid.

4. Kenneth Robinson, "Hate: The Elephant in the Room," HuffPo, June 24, 2013, https://www.huffingtonpost.com/kenneth-robinson/hate-the-elephant-in-the-_b_3094855.html.

5. Ibid.

6. "Black Lives Matter Is Not a Hate Group," Southern Poverty Law Center, July 19, 2016, https://www.splcenter.org/news/2016/07/19/black-lives-matter-not-hate-group.

7. Calvin Freiburger, "60 Groups Consider Suing Southern Poverty Law Center After It Pays $3.4M in Defamation Settlement," LifeSiteNews, June 20, 2018, https://www.lifesitenews.com/news/3.4-million-defamation-win-inspires-60-groups-to-consider-suing-anti-christ.

8. Ben Shreckinger, "Has a Civil Rights Stalwart Lost Its Way? The Southern Poverty Law Center—Led by Charismatic, Swashbuckling Founder Morris Dees—Is Making the Most of the Trump Era. But Is It Overstepping Its Bounds?," *Politico*, June 28, 2017, https://www.politico.com/magazine/story/2017/06/28/morris-dees-splc-trump-southern-poverty-law-center-215312.

9. Mark Pulliam, "Provocateur Journalism: CNN Uncritically Publishes a List of 'Hate Groups' Compiled by the Discredited Southern Poverty Law Center," *City Journal*, August 17, 2017, https://www.city-journal.org/html/provocateur-journalism-15400.html.

10. Lee Smith, "A New Blacklist from the Southern Poverty Law Center Marks the Demise of a Once-Vital Organization: 15 Prominent Writers and Thinkers Are Labeled 'Anti-Muslim Extremists'—Why?," *Tablet*, October 30, 2016, https://www.tabletmag.com/jewish-news-and-politics/216494/southern-poverty-law-center-blacklist; the author is on the list.

11. Ibid.

12. Glenn Harlan Reynolds, *The Judiciary's Class War* (New York: Encounter Broadsides, 2013), Kindle edition, loc. 234.

13. Montgomery, "The State of Hate."

14. Fred Lucas, "Domestic Terrorist Says He Targeted FRC after Finding It on Southern Poverty Law Center Website," CNS News, April 25, 2013, https://www.cnsnews.com/news/article/domestic-terrorist-says-he-targeted-frc-after-finding-it-southern-poverty-law-center.

15. "David Horowitz," Southern Poverty Law Center, https://www.splcenter.org/fighting-hate/extremist-files/individual/david-horowitz.

16. "The Godfather," Southern Poverty Law Center, https://www.splcenter.org/fighting-hate/intelligence-report/2014/godfather.

17. David Horowitz, "Jew Hatred at USC" in *Islamo-Fascism and the War against the Jews*, vol. 6 of *The Black Book of the American Left* (New York: Encounter, 2014), part 1, chapter 16 p., 143.

18. David Horowitz, "A Malignant Cause" in *Islamo-Fascism and the War against the Jews*, vol. 6 of *The Black Book of the American Left*, part 3, chapter 10, 312.

19. For a sample, see David Horowitz, "Dartmouth Nightmare: It's Worse Than You Might Think," FrontPageMag, November 9, 2018, https://www.frontpagemag.com/fpm/271895/dartmouth-nightmare-david-horowitz.

20. Letter dated October 12, 2018 from Seth D. Berlin, Ballard Spahr, LLP, attorney for Common Cause. I have omitted two of Berlin's slanders because it would be too tedious to correct his gross misrepresentations of the facts in my text. Suffice it to say that I am not opposed to gay marriage, as Berlin claims without evidence, and that I did not "mock a children's book for referring to feminism and transgendered individuals." I objected to a book called *A Is for Activist* because it was used to teach kindergarteners and first graders the alphabet, while promoting leftwing agendas. David Horowitz, "Why We Need a Convention of the States: An Opportunity to Make America Free Again," FrontPageMag, August 31, 2018, https://www.frontpagemag.com/fpm/271179/why-we-need-convention-states-david-horowitz.

21. "What is frightening about *Roe* is that this super-protected right, is not inferable from the language of the Constitution, the framers' thinking respecting the specific problem in issue, any general value derivable from the provisions they included, or the nation's governmental structure. . . . It is bad because it is bad constitutional law, or rather because it is not constitutional law, and gives almost no sense of an obligation to try to be." John Hart Ely, "The Wages of Crying Wolf: A Comment on *Roe v.*

Wade," *Yale Law Journal,* April 1973, https://digitalcommons.law.yale.
edu/cgi/viewcontent.cgi?article=6179&context=ylj.

22. Bob Moser, "The Reckoning of Morris Dees and the Southern Poverty
Law Center," *New Yorker,* March 21, 2019, https://www.newyorker.
com/news/news-desk/
the-reckoning-of-morris-dees-and-the-southern-poverty-law-center.

23. See Mark Bray, *Antifa: The Anti-Fascist Handbook* (Brooklyn, New
York: Melville House, 2017).

24. Allum Bokhari, "Bokhari: The Terrifying Rise of Financial Blacklisting,"
Breitbart, January 2, 2019, https://www.breitbart.com/tech/2019/01/02/
bokhari-the-terrifying-rise-of-financial-blacklisting/.

25. Horowitz, "Why We Need a Convention of the States"; a video of the
speech is available at PRWatch, "David Horowitz at 2018 ALEC
Conference in New Orleans," YouTube, September 13, 2018, https://
www.youtube.com/watch?v=Mlm-zYw8k_I. /; www.frontpagemag.com/
fpm/271179/why-we-need-convention-states-david-horowitz; a video of
the speech can be viewed here: https://www.youtube.com/
watch?v=Mlm-zYw8k_I.

26. For documentation see www.stopk12indoctrination.org, a website for
which I am responsible.

27. Washington Free Beacon, "Donald Trump Destroys Rosie O'Donnell
during Debate," YouTube, August 6, 2015, https://www.youtube.com/
watch?v=s9lcr-wsYOk.

28. I have had to reconstruct my remarks and those of Chris Taylor, as there
is no transcript of the session.

29. Chris Taylor, "ALEC in Disarray,"PRWatch, August 13, 2018, https://
www.prwatch.org/news/2018/08/13381/alec-disarray.

30. Jay Riestenberg, "Coalition Letters to ALEC," Common Cause, August
28, 2018, https://www.commoncause.org/resource/coalition-letters-to-
alec-corporate-funders-over-david-horowitz-involvement-in-alec/. The
text of the speech, containing my unexceptional comments about Black
Lives Matter and CAIR's Islamist propaganda in K–12 schools, can be
read at Horowitz, "Why We Need a Convention of the States."

31. "Broad Coalition Calls on Corporations to Drop Funding for ALEC
over Horowitz Speeches," PRWatch, August 27, 2018, https://www.
prwatch.org/news/2018/08/13390/
broad-coalition-calls-corporations-drop-funding-alec-over-horowitz-
speeches.

32. Lee Fang and Nick Sergey, "Verizon Leaves Right-Wing Legislative
Group ALEC over Its invitation to Anti-Muslim Activist David
Horowitz: The Infamous Anti-Muslim Activist David Horowitz Is
Becoming a Political Liability for Republicans," The Intercept,

September 15, 2018,https://theintercept.com/2018/09/15/
verizon-alec-david-horowitz/.

33. Lee Fang and Nick Sergey, "Charles Koch Ramps Up Investment in
ALEC As the Lobbying Group Loses Corporate Funders over Far-Right
Ties: Major Corporate Donors Said They Would Not Be Giving to the
GOP-Allied Lobbying Group, Citing Its Ties to Far-Right Figure David
Horowitz," The Intercept, November 29, 2018, https://theintercept.
com/2018/11/29/alec-corporate-funders-charles-koch/.

34. John Wagner and Vanessa Williams, "DeSantis Says Florida Voters
Would 'Monkey This Up' If They Elect Gillum as Governor,"
Washington Post, August 29, 2018, https://www.washingtonpost.com/
powerpost/desantis-says-florida-voters-would-monkey-this-up-if-they-
elect-gillum-as-governor/2018/08/29/e4cbc5c6-ab96-11e8-8a0c-
70b618c98d3c_story.html.

35. Ibid.

36. Beth Reinhard and Emma Brown, "GOP Candidate for Fla. Governor
Spoke at Racially Charged Events," *Washington Post*, September 9,
2018, https://www.washingtonpost.com/investigations/gop-candidate-
for-fla-governor-spoke-at-racially-charged-events/2018/09/09/c6d3a63c-
b114-11e8-a810-4d6b627c3d5d_story.html.

37. David Horowitz, "Character Assassins at the Washington Post: And the
Fake News Media," FrontPageMag, Septempber 24, 2018, https://www.
frontpagemag.com/fpm/271403/character-assassins-washington-
post-david-horowitz.

38. Kim Hart, "Exclusive Poll: Most Democrats See Republicans as Racist,
Sexist," Axios, November 12, 2018, https://www.axios.com/poll-
democrats-and-republicans-hate-each-other-racist-ignorant-evil-
99ae7afc-5a51-42be-8ee2-3959e43ce320.html.

39. Gary Saul Morson, "Leninthink," *New Criterion*, October 2019, https://
newcriterion.com/issues/2019/10/leninthink.

40. Harold Rosenberg, "Black and Pistachio," *New Yorker*, June 15, 1963,
https://www.newyorker.com/magazine/1963/06/15/black-and-pistachio.

41. Saul Alinsky, *Rules for Radicals: A Practical Primer for Realistic
Radicals* (New York: Vintage Books, 1989), 134.

42. Horowitz, "Why We Need a Convention of the States," https://
conventionofstates.com/news/
horowitz-a-convention-of-states-can-make-american-free-again.

Chapter 8: Orwellian Seditions

1. John Murawski, "Disputed *NY Times* '1619 Project' Already Shaping
Schoolkids' Minds on Race," RealClearInvestigations, January 31, 2020,
https://www.realclearinvestigations.com/articles/2020/01/31/

disputed_ny_times_1619_project_is_already_shaping_kids_minds_on_race_bias_122192.html.

2. Daniel Buck, "7 Reasons to Say Goodbye to Teachers Unions: I Stand with Teachers, Not Unions," Foundation for Economic Education, January 2, 2019, https://fee.org/articles/7-reasons-to-say-goodbye-to-teachers-unions/.

3. Thaddeus G. McCotter, "The Mountebank Left Is Banking on You: Introducing the 1619 Project," American Greatness, August 16, 2019, https://amgreatness.com/2019/08/16/the-mountebank-left-is-banking-on-you/.

4. "The 1619 Project," *New York Times Magazine*, August 14, 2019, https://www.nytimes.com/interactive/2019/08/14/magazine/1619-america-slavery.html.

5. Nikole Hannah-Jones, "Our Democracy's Founding Ideals Were False When They Were Written. Black Americans Have Fought to Make Them True," *New York Times Magazine*, August 14, 2019, https://www.nytimes.com/interactive/2019/08/14/magazine/black-history-american-democracy.html.

6. Ibid.

7. Nell Irvin Painter, "How We Think about the Term 'Enslaved' Matters," *The Guardian*, August 14, 2019, https://www.theguardian.com/us-news/2019/aug/14/slavery-in-america-1619-first-ships-jamestown.

8. Kevin Sieff, "An African Country Reckons with Its History of Selling Slaves," *Washington Post*, January 29, 2018, https://www.washingtonpost.com/world/africa/an-african-country-reckons-with-its-history-of-selling-slaves/2018/01/29/5234f5aa-ff9a-11e7-86b9-8908743c79dd_story.html; Lilian Diarra, "Ghana's Slave Castles: The Shocking Story of the Ghanian Slave Coast," The Culture Trip, January 24, 2017, https://theculturetrip.com/africa/ghana/articles/ghana-s-slave-castles-the-shocking-story-of-the-ghanaian-cape-coast/.

9. "Slavery," The National Museum: The Royal Navy, https://www.nmrn.org.uk/research/slavery.

10. Murray N. Rothbard, "The Brutality of Slavery," Mises Institute, November 14, 2018, https://mises.org/library/brutality-slavery; https://www.gilderlehrman.org/history-resources/teaching-resource/historical-context-american-slavery-comparative-perspective.

11. Steven Mintz, "Historical Context: American Slavery in Comparative Perspective," The Gilder Lehrman Institute of American History, https://www.statista.com/statistics/1010169/black-and-slave-population-us-1790-1880/.

12. Hannah-Jones, "Our Democracy's Founding Ideals Were False."

13. C. Bradley Thompson, *America's Revolutionary Mind: A Moral History of the American Revolution and Declaration That Defined It* (New York: Encounter, 2019).

14. "Northwest Ordinances," Britannica, https://www.britannica.com/event/Northwest-Ordinances.

15. "Slave States and Free States," Wikipedia, https://en.wikipedia.org/wiki/Slave_states_and_free_states.

16. Hannah-Jones, "Our Democracy's Founding Ideals Were False."

17. Andrew Malcolm, "Obama Declares Racism Inhabits Americans' DNA," Investors Business Daily, May 3, 2015, https://www.investors.com/politics/columnists/obama-racism-is-in-american-dna/.

18. Tom Mackaman, "An Interview with Historian James Oakes on the *New York Times'* 1619 Project," World Socialist Web Site, November 18, 2019, https://www.wsws.org/en/articles/2019/11/18/oake-n18.html.

19. Shawn, "*NY Times* Publisher Defends 1619 Project after His Own Columnist Rips It to Shreds," Fix This Nation, October 12, 2020, http://www.fixthisnation.com/conservative-breaking-news/ny-times-publisher-defends-1619-project-after-his-own-columnist-rips-it-to-shreds/.

20. Allen C. Guelzo, "Preaching a Conspiracy Theory: The 1619 Project Offers Bitterness, Fragility, and Intellectual Corruption—Not History," *City Journal*, December 8, 2019, https://www.city-journal.org/1619-project-conspiracy-theory.

21. Walter Williams, "How Seeing 'Racism' Everywhere Keeps Black Americans Blind to Real Problems," Yellow Hammer, https://yellowhammernews.com/blind-to-real-problems/.

22. "The 1619 Project," Wikipedia, https://en.wikipedia.org/wiki/The_1619_Project.

23. Ellen Lai, "Nikole Hannah-Jones Named 2017 MacArthur 'Genius' Grant Winner," The City Uniersity of New York Craig Newmark Graduate School of Journalism, October 11, 2017, https://www.journalism.cuny.edu/2017/10/nikole-hannah-jones-named-2017-macarthur-genius-grant-winner/; Jeff Barrus, "Nikole Hannah-Jones Wins Pulitzer Prize for 1619 Project," Pulitzer Center, May 4, 2020, https://pulitzercenter.org/blog/nikole-hannah-jones-wins-pulitzer-prize-1619-project.

24. Jordan Davidson, "In Racist Screed, NYT's 1619 Project Founder Calls 'White Race' 'Barbaric Devils' 'Bloodsuckers,' Columbus 'No Different Than Hitler,'" The Federalist, June 25, 2020, https://thefederalist.com/2020/06/25/in-racist-screed-nyts-1619-project-founder-calls-white-race-barbaric-devils-bloodsuckers-no-different-than-hitler/.

25. I became aware of this course in the Social Work Department of Kansas State University when I was asked by state legislators to testify on the curricula of their schools of higher education.

26. Paul Kengor, "Debunking Howard Zinn's Amerikkka: Mary Grabar Does the Job Matt Damon Refused to Do," *American Spectator,* September 11, 2019, https://spectator.org/ debunking-howard-zinns-amerikkka.

27. Ronald Radosh, "Howard Zinn: Fake Historian," Law & Liberty, January 16, 2020, https://www.lawliberty.org/2020/01/16/ howard-zinn-fake-historian/.

28. Howard Zinn, *A People's History of the United States* (New York: Harper Perennial Modern Classics, 2015), 23.

29. Ibid., 646.

30. Ibid., 59.

31. Ibid., 73.

32. David Horowitz and Jacob Laksin, *One-Party Classroom: How Radical Professors at America's Top Colleges Indoctrinate Students and Undermine Our Democracy* (New York: Crown Forum, 2009).

33. Ron Grossman, "Strong Words," *Chicago Tribune,* January 1, 1993, https://www.chicagotribune.com/news/ct-xpm-1993-01-01-9303152231-story.html. This section on Chomsky and the previous section on Zinn are drawn from my essay, "The Mind of the Left" in *Progressives,* vol. 2 of *The Black Book of the American Left* (Los Angeles: Second Thought Books, 2014).

34. Ibid.

35. Noam Chomsky, *Propaganda and the Public Mind: Interviews by David Barsamian (Cambridge: South End Press, 2001), x.* In the endpapers of the volume the *New York Times* is quoted praising Chomsky as "an exploder of received truths" and *The Guardian* (London) as calling him "[o]ne of the radical heroes of our age. . . . A towering intellect. . . ."

36. Interview, September 19, 2001, qtd. in Dinesh D'Souza, *The Enemy at Home: Responsibility for 9/11* (New York: Doubleday, 2007), 231.

37. Ibid., 79.

38. Noam Chomsky, *What Uncle Sam Really Wants* (Odonian Press, 1992), 8, 18, 29, 31, 32, 56–58.

39. Ibid, 32.

40. Paul Kengor, "Obama's Prairie Fire Companion," *American Spectator,* September 28, 2010, https://spectator.org/obamas-prairie-fire-companion/; on Ayers as the ghost writer for Obama's first book, *Dreams of My Father,* see Jack Cashill, "More Proof Ayers Ghosted Obama's 'Dreams,'" WND, September 25, 2008, https://www.wnd.

com/2008/09/76166/; see also Stanley Kurtz, *Radical-in-Chief: Barack Obama and the Untold Story of American Socialism* (New York: Simon & Schuster, 2010).

41. Bill Ayers, *Fugitive Days: Memoirs of an Antiwar Activist* (Boston: Beacon Press, 2001), 256.

42. Jeane Kirkpatrick, "'Blame America First,' GOP Convention Speech—1984," Speakola, https://speakola.com/political/ jeane-kirkpatrick-blame-america-first-gop-1984.

43. David Horowitz, *The Great Betrayal,* vol. 3 of *The Black Book of the American Left,* (Los Angeles: Second Thought Books, 2013), and David Horowitz, *The Left in Power: Clinton to Obama,* vol. 7 of *The Black Book of the American Left* (Los Angeles: Second Thoughts Books, 2015).

44. David Horowitz, *Unholy Alliance: Radical Islam and the American Left* (Washington, D.C.: Regnery, 2004).

45. I have described these events in three books: Horowitz, *Unholy Alliance*; David Horowitz and Ben Johnson, *Party of Defeat: How Democrats and Radicals Undermined America's War on Terror Before and After 9/11* (Dallas: Spence Publishing, 2008); David Horowitz, *The Great Betrayal,* vol. 3 of *The Black Book of the American Left* (Los Angeles: Second Thought Books, 2013).

46. Stanley Kurtz, *Radical in Chief: Barack Obama and the Untold Story of American Socialism* (New York: Simon & Schuster, 2010); Paul Kengor, *The Communist: Frank Marshall Davis—The Untold Story of Barack Obama's Mentor* (New York: Mercury Ink, 2012).

47. "Frank Marshall Davis," Discover the Networks, https://www. discoverthenetworks.org/individuals/frank-marshall-davis/.

48. Stanley Kurtz, David Horowitz, and Jacob Laksin, "The Making of a President" in *The New Leviathan: How the Left-Wing Money-Machine Shapes American Politics and Threatens America's Future* (New York: Crown Forum, 2012), chapter 2.

49. TED-Ed, "The Atlantic Slave Trade: What Too Few Told You," Anthony Hazard," YouTube, December 22, 2014, https://www.youtube.com/ watch?v=oKxDdxzXokI.

Chapter 9: The Anti-Trump Resistance

1. The "Resistance" and its consequences, including impeachment, are described in David Horowiztz, *Blitz: Trump Will Smash the Left and Win* (New York: Humanix Books, 2020).

2. Lisa Hagen, "Pelosi Calls for Articles of Impeachment: The House Speaker in a Televised Statement Said She's Asking for the House Judiciary to Draft Articles of Impeachment.," *U.S. News & World*

Report, December 5, 2019, https://www.usnews.com/news/national-news/articles/2019-12-05/pelosi-calls-for-articles-of-impeachment.

3. Letter from Pat A. Cipollone to Nancy Pelosi, Adam B. Schiff, Eliot L. Engel, and Elijah E. Cummings, October 8, 2019, https://assets. documentcloud.org/documents/6459967/PAC-Letter-10-08-2019.pdf.

4. Dan Gallo, "Flashback: What Nadler Said about Impeaching a President in 1998: Then, He Was a Rank-and-File Member of the powerful House Judiciary Committee He Now Chairs," NBC News, December 4, 2019, https://www.nbcnews.com/politics/trump-impeachment-inquiry/ flashback-what-nadler-said-about-impeaching-president-1998-n1095141.

5. Edwin Mora, "Senate Impeachment Trial: Schiff Says Trump's 'Misconduct Cannot Be Settled at the Ballot Box," Breitbart, January 23, 2020, https://www.breitbart.com/politics/2020/01/23/senate-impeachment-trial-schiff-says-trumps-misconduct-cannot-decided-ballot-box/.

6. Jarrett Stepman, "The Left Lost on Kavanaugh, So Now They Want to Abolish the Senate," The Daily Signal, October 11, 2018, https://www. dailysignal.com/2018/10/11/ the-left-lost-on-kavanaugh-so-now-they-want-to-abolish-the-senate/.

7. Alex Seitz-Wald, "Democrats to Introduce Constitutional Amendment to Abolish Electoral College," NBC News, April 1, 2019, https://www. nbcnews.com/politics/2020-election/senate-dems-introduce-constitutional-amendment-abolish-electoral-college-n989656. On the alleged racism of the Electoral College, see Eliza Relman, "Ocasio-Cortez Calls the Electoral College a Racist 'Scam'—an Argument That a Growing Number of Democrats Are Making Going into 2020," Business Insider, August 20, 2019, https://www.businessinsider.com/ alexandria-ocasio-cortez-calls-electoral-college-racist-scam-2019-8.

8. Nancy Pelosi, "A Republic, If You Can Keep It," Facebook, September 28,2019, https://www.facebook.com/NancyPelosi/ videos/a-republic-if-you-can-keep-it/384051012267935/.

9. Cited in "A Republic, Madam, If You Can Keep It," Locks Law Firm, https://www.lockslaw.com/ blog/2016/07/22/a-republic-madam-if-you-can-keep-it.

10. Ibid.

11. Julia Musto, "Carrie Severino Slams Schumer's 'Totally Unacceptable' Attack on Justices Kavanaugh and Gorsuch," Fox News, March 7, 2020, https://www.foxnews.com/media/carrie-severino-chuck-schumer-threatening-comments-totally-unacceptable.issues uestion. atement.

12. Ibid.

13. Ian Hatchett, "MSNBC's O'Donnell: The Senate Is American Democracy's 'Most Serious Structural Flaw," Breitbart, February 1,

2020, https://www.breitbart.com/clips/2020/02/01/msnbcs-odonnell-the-senate-is-american-democracys-most-serious-structural-flaw/.

14. Curtis Houck, "O'Donnell: 'Obama Is the Most Noble Man' to Ever Be President above Genocidal Racists like Abraham Lincoln," NewsBusters, November 10, 2016, https://www.newsbusters.org/blogs/nb/curtis-houck/2016/11/10/odonnell-obama-most-noble-man-ever-be-president-above-genocidal.

15. Shane Croucher, "Beto O'Rourke: Donald Trump 'Poses a Moral Threat to People of Color," *Newsweek*, September 13, 2019, https://www.newsweek.com/beto-orourke-trump-white-supremacist-mortal-danger-people-color-2020-debate-1459088.

16. *Washington Examiner* (@dcexaminer), "'The United States didn't inherit slavery from anybody. We created It.' —Senator @TimKaine," Twitter, June 16, 2020, 1:57 p.m., https://twitter.com/horowitz39/status/1272956331901587456?s=20.

17. Ken Blackwell, "Tim Kaine's Radical Roots," *The Hill*, September 9, 2016, https://thehill.com/blogs/pundits-blog/presidential-campaign/295229-tim-kaines-radical-roots.

18. Jason Riley, "The Myth of Voter Suppression," PragerU, December 2, 2019, https://www.prageru.com/video/the-myth-of-voter-suppression/.

19. Bruce Hendry, "Democrat Voter Fraud in Minnesota," FrontPageMag, March 9, 2020, https://www.frontpagemag.com/fpm/2020/03/democrat-voter-fraud-minnesota-bruce-hendry/.

20. I describe this process in detail in David Horowitz, *The Professors: The 101 Most Dangerous Academics in America* (Washington, D.C.: Regnery, 2006).

21. Mitchell Langbert, et al., "Faculty Voter Registration in Economics, History, Journalism, Law, and Psychology," Econ Journal Watch 13, no. 3 (September 2016): 422–51, https://econjwatch.org/articles/faculty-voter-registration-in-economics-history-journalism-communications-law-and-psychology.

22. See Horowitz, *The Professors* and David Horowitz and Jacob Laksin, *One-Party Classroom: How Radical Professors at America's Top Colleges Indoctrinate Students and Undermine Our Democracy* (New York: Crown Forum, 2009).

23. Max Boot, "Fox News Has Completed Its Transformation into Trump's State TV," Business Insider, August 13, 2017, https://www.businessinsider.com/fox-news-has-completed-its-transformation-into-trumps-state-tv-2017-8; Douglas Perry, "Fox News Reportedly Killed a Sordid Stormy Daniels Story before the 2016 Election," *Pittsburgh Post-Gazette*, March 5, 2019, https://www.post-gazette.com/news/

nation/2019/03/04/Fox-News-reportedly-killed-the-Stormy-Daniels-story-in-2016-it-has-played-it-down-ever-since/stories/201903040132; "Fox News Is Already Trash-Talking Mueller's Congressional Testimony—That Won't Happen for 3 Weeks," Daily Kos, June 26, 2019, https://www.dailykos.com/stories/2019/6/26/1867464/-FOX-News-is-Already-Trash-Talking-Mueller-s-Congressional-Testimony-That-Won-t-Happen-for-3-Weeks.

24. Lauren Finer, "Kamala Harris Asks Twitter CEO Jack Dorsey to Consider Suspending Trump's Account," CNBC, October 2, 2019, https://www.cnbc.com/2019/10/02/kamala-harris-asks-twitter-ceo-to-consider-suspending-trumps-account.html.

25. Tony Badran, "U.S. Kills Quassem Soleimani," *Tablet*, January 3, 2020, https://www.tabletmag.com/jewish-news-and-politics/296383/us-kills-qassem-soleimani.

26. "Democratic Presidential Candidates Criticize Trump for Ordering Soleimani Strike," NPR, January 6, 2020, https://www.npr.org/transcripts/794044686; Robert Mackey, "Republicans Attack Democrats for Saying Qasem Soleimani Was Assassinated, and Reporters Play Along," The Intercept, January 9, 2020, https://theintercept.com/2020/01/09/republican-reporters-want-democrats-stop-saying-qassim-suleimani-assassinated/.

27. Ibid.

28. Robert Spencer, "174 House Dems: Convicted Terrorists Must Not Be Barred from Working for TSA," FrontPageMage, March 12, 2020, https://www.frontpagemag.com/fpm/2020/03/174-house-dems-convicted-terrorists-must-not-be-robert-spencer/.

29. Ibid.

Chapter 10: The Invisible War

1. Eva Fu, "Exclusive: China Had COVID-Like Patients Months before Official Timeline," *Epoch Times*, October 13, 2020, https://www.theepochtimes.com/china-saw-covid-19-like-patients-months-before-official-timeline-internal-documents_3537965.html; Jeanna Bryner, "1st Known Case of Coronavirus Traced Back to November in China," Live Science, March 14, 2020, https://www.livescience.com/first-case-coronavirus-found.html.

2. Marc A. Thiessen, "China Should Be Legally Liable for the Pandemic Damage It Has Done," *Washington Post*, April 9, 2020, https://www.washingtonpost.com/opinions/2020/04/09/china-should-be-legally-liable-pandemic-damage-it-has-done/.

3.   Zhao Yusha, "Controversial Baibuting Speaks Up on Banquet," *Global Times*, April 25, 2020, https://www.globaltimes.cn/content/1186702.shtml.

4.   Paul Mirengoff, "Hold China Accountable and Remember That Freedom Abroad Matters," PowerLine, March 19,2020, https://www.powerlineblog.com/archives/2020/03/hold-china-accountable-and-remember-that-freedom-abroad-matters.php.

5.   Eric Levenson, "Officials Keep Calling the Coronavirus Panic a 'War': Here's Why," CNN, April 2, 2020, https://www.cnn.com/2020/04/01/us/war-on-coronavirus-attack/index.html; Julie Hinds, "Coronavirus Comparisons to World War II Are Rampant. Are We Ready to Be Greatest Generation?," *Detroit Free Press*, March 29, 2020, https://www.freep.com/story/entertainment/movies/julie-hinds/2020/03/29/fair-compare-coronavirus-pandemic-world-war-ii/2916429001/; "Markey Calls for Wartime Mobilization on Coronavirus Gear: Senator Urges Trump Administration to Invoke Defense Protection Act," *Boston Globe*, March 15, 2020, https://www.bostonglobe.com/2020/03/15/nation/markey-calls-wartime-mobilization-coronavirus-gear/.

6.   Tom McCarthy, "Democrats Focus on Ukraine 'Cover Up' as Marathon Impeachment Case Wraps," *The Guardian*, January 24, 2020, https://www.theguardian.com/us-news/2020/jan/24/trump-impeachment-trial-democrats-focus; Amanda Prestigiacomo, "Limbaugh Points Out Exactly Where Democrats' Impeachment Effort Fell Apart," The Daily Wire, November 15, 2019, https://www.dailywire.com/news/limbaugh-points-out-exactly-where-democrats-impeachment-effort-fell-apart.

7.   Nicholas Fandos and Michael D. Shear, "Trump Impeachment for Abuse of Power and Obstruction of Congress," *New York Times*, December 18, 2019, https://www.nytimes.com/2019/12/18/us/politics/trump-impeached.html.

8.   Haley Byrd, Manu Raju, and Phil Mattingly, "Nancy Pelosi Won't Commit to Sending Articles of Impeachment to Senate," CNN, December 18, 2019, https://www.cnn.com/2019/12/18/politics/nancy-pelosi-sending-impeachment-articles-senate/index.html.

9.   Benjamin Siegel, et al., "Articles of Impeachment Delivered to Senate, Triggering Historic Trial of President Donald Trump: Speaker Nancy Pelosi Said the House Was Holding the President 'Accountable,'" ABC News, January 15, 2020, https://abcnews.go.com/Politics/trump-impeachment-live-updates-house-votes-send-articles/story?id=68277959.

10. "First Travel-Related Case of 2019 Novel Coronavirus Detected in United States," Centers for Disease Control, January 21, 2020, https://

www.cdc.gov/media/releases/2020/p0121-novel-coronavirus-travel-case.
html.

11. Michael Levenson, "Scale of China's Wuhan Shutdown Is Believed to Be
without Precedent: In Sealing Off a City of 11 Million People, China Is
Trying," *New York Times*, January 22, 2020, https://www.nytimes.
com/2020/01/22/world/asia/coronavirus-quarantines-history.html.

12. Berkeley Lovelace Jr. and Will Feuer "WHO Declares China
Coronavirus That's Killed More than 200 a Global Health Emergency,"
CNBC, January 30, 2020, https://www.cnbc.com/2020/01/30/who-
declares-china-coronavirus-a-global-health-emergency.html.

13. Jack Davis, "Trump Bans Travel from China, Orders 1st Quarantine in
50 Years," Western Journal, February 1, 2020, https://www.
westernjournal.com/
trump-bans-travel-china-orders-1st-quarantine-50-years/.

14. "Joe Biden Calls Trumps Travel Restrictions 'Hysterical Xenophobia,"
Air News, April 15, 2020, https://www.air.tv/
watch?v=ggkXUdBvS46p4SRIAgm_4w.

15. Nicole Narea and Catherine Kim, "Read the Full Text of Trump's State
of the Union Address: President Donald Trump Addressed Congress
Tuesday Night for His State of the Union Address," Vox, February 4,
2020, https://www.vox.com/2020/2/4/21123394/
state-of-the-union-full-transcript-trump.

16. Liz Plank, "Nancy Pelosi Tears Up Trump's State of the Union Speech in
Possible 2020 Tipping Point: Why Was Pelosi So Angry? Maybe It Was
the Fact That Trump Is Totally Getting Away with Undermining the
Election. Or Maybe It Was All the Lying," NBC News, February 5,
2020, https://www.nbcnews.com/think/opinion/
nancy-pelosi-tears-trump-s-state-union-speech-possible-2020-
ncna1130776.

17. "The Wuhan Coronavirus: Assessing the Outbreak, the Response, and
Regional Implications," U.S. House of Representatives Committee on
Foreign Affairs, February 5, 2020, https://foreignaffairs.house.
gov/2020/2/
the-wuhan-coronavirus-assessing-the-outbreak-the-response-and-
regional-implications.

18. Matthew J. Belvedere, "Trump Says He Trusts China's Xi on
Coronavirus and the US Has It 'Totally under Control,'" CNBC,
January 22, 2020, https://www.cnbc.com/2020/01/22/trump-on-
coronavirus-from-china-we-have-it-totally-under-control.html.

19. MSNBC, "'Not Up to the Job': Fmr. AG Holder on Trump's Failed
Coronavirus Response /All In / MSNBC," YouTube, May 12, 2020,
https://youtu.be/4blElpobLHg.

20. Ed Markey, "Donald Trump Is a pathological liar. . . .," Facebook, April 10, 2020, https://www.facebook.com/EdMarkeyforMA/posts/2276192159151105; Paul Krugman, "Trump's Coronavirus Response Was beyond Incompetent: He Wasn't Oblivious to the Danger. He Just Didn't Care," *New York Times*, September 10, 2020, https://www.nytimes.com/2020/09/10/opinion/donald-trump-coronavirus.html; Kimmy Yam, "After Trump's COVID-19 Diagnosis, Anti-Asian Tweets and Conspiracies Rose 85%: Report," NBC News, October 15, 2020, https://www.nbcnews.com/news/asian-america/after-trump-s-covid-19-diagnosis-anti-asian-tweets-conspiracies-n1243441; Joseph Ax, "Obama Assails Trump as Unfit, Says Biden Will Preserve U.S. Democracy," Reuters, August 20, 2020, https://news.trust.org/item/20200820024605-qz2ux/.

21. Tom Pappert, "Flashback: Biden Called Trump's COVID-19 China Travel Ban 'Xenophobia': Biden Claimed Trump Was Doing Too Much to Combat the Virus before Claiming That He's Not Doing Enough," National File, May 26, 2020, https://nationalfile.com/flashback-biden-opposed-trumps-chinese-coronavirus-travel-ban-as-xenophobia/.

22. Caitlin Obrysko and Susannah Luthi, "Trump Labels Himself 'a Wartime President' Combatting Coronavirus: 'Now It's Our Time. We Must Sacrifice Together, Because We Are All in This Together, and We Will Come Through Together,' the President Said," *Politico*, March 18, 2020, https://www.politico.com/news/2020/03/18/trump-administration-self-swab-coronavirus-tests-135590.

23. Arlette Saenz, "Pro-Biden Group Hits Trump's Coronavirus Response in Nationwide TV Ad," CNN, March 25, 2020, https://www.cnn.com/2020/03/25/politics/biden-trump-coronavirus/index.html.

24. Ibid.

25. Hope Yen, "AP Fact Check: Biden Distorts Trump's Words on Virus 'Hoax,'" Associated Press, September 17, 2020, https://apnews.com/article/election-2020-virus-outbreak-ap-fact-check-politics-joe-biden-1eea443cca46df5f18e61b7c34549da2; Liz Alesse, "Did Trump Try to Cut the CDC's Budget As Democrats Claim?: Analysis: The Allegations Come amid the Emergency over the COVID-19 Crisis," ABC News, February 28, 2020, https://abcnews.go.com/Politics/trump-cut-cdcs-budget-democrats-claim-analysis/story?id=69233170; Scott Paul, "Why Can't America Make Enough Masks or Ventilators? The President Has Promoted Himself as a Champion of American Manufacturing, but Now He Avoids Addressing Its Shortcomings.," *New York Times*, April 14, 2020, https://www.nytimes.com/2020/04/14/opinion/coronavirus-industry-manufacturing.html.

26. Yen, "AP Fact Check."

27. Fred Lucas, "The Truth about the Charge That Trump 'Eliminated' White House Pandemic Office before Coronavirus," The Daily Signal, March 24, 2020, https://www.dailysignal.com/2020/03/24/ the-truth-about-the-charge-that-trump-eliminated-white-house-pandemic-office-before-coronavirus/.

28. Susan Berry, "USA Today: 'True'—'No Indication' Obama Administration Replenished Mask Supply," Breitbart, April 5, 2020, https://www.breitbart.com/politics/2020/04/05/ usa-today-true-no-indication-obama-admin-replenished-mask-supply/.

29. Greg Re, "Obama Administration Repeatedly Sought Millions in CDC Funding Cuts, Despite Biden's Attacks on Trump's Preparedness," Fox News, March 27, 2020, https://www.foxnews.com/politics/ obama-admin-repeatedly-sought-millions-in-cdc-funding-cuts.

30. Faiz Siddiqui, "The U.S. Forced Major Manufacturers to Build Ventilators. Now They're Piling Up Unused in a Strategic Reserve," *Washington Post*, August 18, 2020, https://www.washingtonpost.com/ business/2020/08/18/ventilators-coronavirus-stockpile/; "President Trump's Historic Coronavirus Response," White House, August 10, 2020, https://www.whitehouse.gov/briefings-statements/ president-trumps-historic-coronavirus-response/.

31. Lisa Friedman and Brad Plumer, "Trump's Response to Virus Reflects a Long Disregard for Science: The President's COVID-19 Response Has Extended the Administration's Longstanding Practice of Undermining Scientific Expertise for Political Purposes," *New York Times*, April 28, 2020, https://www.nytimes.com/2020/04/28/climate/trump-coronavirus-climate-science.html.

32. Trump War Room—Text TRUMP to 88022 (@Trump WarRoom), "Dr. Fauci says President Trump has 'never' gone against the science-based advice. . . .," Twitter, March 26, 2020, 2:31 p.m., @https://twitter.com/ TrumpWarRoom/status/1243244272335413249?s=20; John Nolte, CNN Analyst Joe Lockhart Attacked Dr. Deborah Birx as a Trump 'Kool-Aid' Drinker after She Tamped Down a Number of Coronavirus Alarmist Theories. This Included a Sexist Attack on Her as a 'Stepford Doc': Birx, of Course, Is the White House Coronavirus Response Coordinator, Who Along with Dr. Anthony Fauci, Has Become a Household Name in the Wake of the Chinese Virus Pandemic," Breitbart, March 27, 2020, https://www.breitbart.com/the-media/2020/03/27/ nolte-cnn-analyst-joe-lockhart-belittles-dr-birx-as-stepford-doc/.

33. David Horowitz, "The Democrats' Twisted Approach to the Virus: Trump Is Deadlier than the Virus," FrontPageMag, April 17, 2020,

https://www.frontpagemag.com/fpm/2020/04/
democrats-twisted-approach-virus-david-horowitz/.

34. "Chinese Media: Defunding World Health Organization Is 'Genocide,'"
    Breitbart, April 16, 2020, https://www.newsbreak.com/
    news/1548129188071/
    chinese-media-defunding-world-health-organization-is-genocide.

35. Olivia Beavers, "Pelosi Says Trump Decision on WHO Will Be 'Swiftly
    Challenged,'"*The Hill*, April 15, 2020, https://thehill.com/homenews/
    house/492936-pelosi-says-trump-decision-on-who-will-be-swiftly-
    challenged.

36. Timothy Bella, "Bill Gates: Trump Halting Funding to World Health
    Organization," *Washington Post*, April 15, 2020, https://www.
    washingtonpost.com/nation/2020/04/15/
    who-bill-gates-coronavirus-trump/.

37. Gregg Re, "Trump Announces US Will Halt Funding to World Health
    Organization over Coronavirus Response," Fox News, April 14, 2020,
    https://www.foxnews.com/politics/
    trump-announces-funding-to-world-health-organization-who-halted.

38. "Tedros Adhanom Ghebreyesus," Discover the Networks, https://www.
    discoverthenetworks.org/individuals/tedros-adhanom-ghebreyesus/.

39. Bradley A. Thayer and Lianchao Han, "China and the WHO's Chief:
    Hold Them Both Accountable for Pandemic," *The Hill*, March 17, 2020,
    https://thehill.com/opinion/international/487851-china-and-the-whos-chief-hold-
    them-both-accountable-for-pandemic.

40. John Bowden, "Hillary Clinton: Trump Using 'Racist' Rhetoric to
    Distract from Failures," *The Hill*, March 17, 2020, https://thehill.com/
    blogs/blog-briefing-room/
    news/488251-hillary-clinton-trump-using-racist-rhetoric-to-distract-
    from.

41. Ibid.

42. John Hayward, "Chinese Lawyers Sue America on Conspiracy Theory
    Virus Came from U.S.," Breitbart, March 27, 2020, https://www.
    breitbart.com/national-security/2020/03/27/
    chinese-lawyers-sue-america-on-conspiracy-theory-virus-came-from-
    u-s/.

43. Kyle Olson, "Chinese Ambassador Lauds Hillary Clinton's Attack on
    President Trump: 'Justice Always Speaks Loudly,'" Breitbart, March 21,
    2020, https://www.breitbart.com/politics/2020/03/21/chinese-
    ambassador-lauds-hillary-clintons-attack-on-president-trump-justice-
    always-speak-loudly/.

44. J. Edward Moreno, "Schiff Drafting Legislation to Set Up 9/11-Style
    Commission to Review Coronavirus Response," *The Hill*, April 1, 2020,

https://thehill.com/homenews/house/490591-schiff-drafting-legislation-to-set-up-9-11-style-commission-to-review.

45. Tim Hains, "Pelosi Will Need 'After-Action Review' of Trump Coronavirus Response; 'As the President Fiddles, People Are Dying,'" RealClearPolitics, March 29, 2020, https://www.realclearpolitics.com/video/2020/03/29/pelosi_will_need_after-action_review_of_trump_coronavirus_response_his_denial_at_the_beginning_was_deadly.html.

46. Ibid.

47. "Pelosi Tours San Francisco's Chinatown to Quell Coronavirus Fears," KPIX CBS SF BayArea, February 24, 2020, https://sanfrancisco.cbslocal.com/2020/02/24/coronavirus-speaker-house-nancy-pelosi-tours-san-franciscos-chinatown/.

48. Philip Rucker, Yasmeen Abutaleb, and Ashley Parker, "As the Coronavirus Spins Out of Control, Trump Issues Directives—but Still No Clear Plan," *Washington Post*, July 15, 2020, https://www.washingtonpost.com/politics/trump-coronavirus-pandemic-no-plan/2020/07/15/7581bea4-c5df-11ea-a99f-3bbdffb1af38_story.html.

49. "Well Done, Cuomo! NYC Has the Worst COVID-19 Death Rate Than [sic] Any Nation on Earth," Patriot for America, July 14, 2020, https://patriotforamerica.com/2020/07/14/well-done-cuomo-nyc-has-the-worst-covid-19-death-rate-than-any-nation-on-earth/.

50. Justin Hart (@justin_hart), "Don't blame me! I'm not the one. . . .," Twitter, July 16, 2020, 10:28 a.m., https://twitter.com/justin_hart/status/1283770522426212352?s=20.

51. Valerie Richardson, "CNN Quiet As Biden Claims Nobody Would Have Died of Virus If Trump Had 'Done His Job': Biden Claims 'All the People Would Still Be Alive' at Town Hall in Moosic, Pennsylvania," *Washington Times*, September 18, 2020, https://www.washingtontimes.com/news/2020/sep/18/cnn-mum-biden-claims-nobody-would-have-died-if-tru/.

52. Kaanita Iyer, Gracie Todd, Luciana Perez Uribe, and Aneuerin Canham-Clyne, "Biden Readies Sweeping Policy Changes on COVID, Economy, Immigration, and More," WJZ13 CBS Baltimore, November 14, 2020, https://baltimore.cbslocal.com/2020/11/14/biden-readies-sweeping-policy-shifts-on-covid-economy-immigration-and-more/.

53. Josh Dawsey and Yasmeen Abutaleb, "A Whole Lot of Hurt: Fauci Warns of COVID-19 Surge, Offers Blunt Assessment of Trump's Response," *Washington Post*, October 31, 2020, https://www.washingtonpost.com/politics/the-latest-fauci-says-whole-lot-of-hurt-for-us-from-virus/2020/11/01/fd183898-1c51-11eb-ad53-4c1fda49907d_story.html; The Recount (@therecount), "Biden: 'The Truth Is. . . .,'"

Twitter, November 1, 2020, 6:21 p.m., https://twitter.com/therecount/
status/1323042470280728576.

Chapter 11: A Totalitarian Insurrection

1. Richard Sander and Stuart Taylor, *Mismatch: How Affirmative Action
    Hurts Students It's Inteded to Help, and Why Universities Won't Admit
    It* (New York: Basic Books, 2012).
2. David Horowitz, *The Professors: The 101 Most Dangerous Academics
    in America* (Washington, D.C.: Regnery, 2006); David Horowitz and
    Jacob Laksin, *One-Party Classroom: How Radical Professors at
    America's Top Colleges Indoctrinate Students and Undermine Our
    Democracy* (New York: Crown Forum, 2009); David Horowitz,
    *Reforming Our Universities: The Campaign for an Academic Bill of
    Rights* (Washington, D.C.: Regnery, 2010).
3. Elizabeth Warren (@ewarren), "We cannot just say that criminal justice.
    . . ," Twitter, February 7, 2020, 10:04 p.m., https://twitter.com/ewarren/
    status/1225978767346143237.
4. James Madison, *The Federalist* No. 10, Bill of Rights Institute, 1787,
    https://billofrightsinstitute.org/founding-documents/primary-source-
    documents/the-federalist-papers/federalist-papers-no-10/.
5. Burgess Everett and Marianne Levine, "Dems Warm to Expanding
    Supreme Court: A Series of White House Hopefuls Are Expressing New
    Interest in Remaking the Courts—Payback for Republican Aggression
    during the Obama Presidency," *Politico*, March 18, 2018, https://www.
    politico.com/story/2019/03/18/2020-democrats-supreme-court-1223625.
6. CBS News, "Kamala Harris Calls on Twitter to Suspend Trump's
    Account," YouTube, October 2, 2019, https://www.youtube.com/
    watch?v=LVP6W9__maA.
7. "Hate Crime," Wikipedia, https://en.wikipedia.org/wiki/Hate_crime.
8. Bruce Bawer, "If You're White, You're Racist. Period. So Says Robin
    DiAngelo, Who Proves That Whites Can Be Race Hustlers, Too,"
    FrontPageMag, June26, 2020, https://www.frontpagemag.com/
    fpm/2020/06/if-youre-white-youre-racist-period-bruce-bawer/.
9. Matt Taibbi, "The Left Is Now the Right: We Laughed at the Republican
    Busybody Who Couldn't Joke, Declared War on Dirty Paitings, and
    Peered through Your Bedroom Window. Now That Person Has
    Switched Sides, and Nobody's Laughing," TK News, July 20, 2020,
    https://taibbi.substack.com/p/the-left-is-now-the-right.
10. Ibram X. Kendi, *How to Be an Anti-Racist* (London: One World, 2019),
    Kindle edition, loc. 394.
11. I have written several books on this subject, including *The Professors:
    The 101 Most Dangerous Academics in America*; Horowitz and Laksin,

One-Party Classroom: How Radical Professors at America's Top Colleges Indoctrinate Students and Undermine Our Democracy; and Horowitz, *Reforming Our Universities: The Campaign for an Academic Bill of Rights.*

12. Kendi, *How to Be an Antiracist*, loc. 335.
13. Mark Bray, *Antifa: The Anti-Fascist Handbook* (Brooklyn, New York: Melville House, 2017).
14. Kendi, *How to Be an Antiracist*, loc. 338.
15. Kendi, *How to Be an Antiracist*.
16. "Obesity and African Americans," U.S. Department of Health and Human Services Office of Minority Health, https://minorityhealth.hhs.gov/omh/browse.aspx?lvl=4&lvlid=25.
17. Richard Sander and Stuart Taylor Jr., Mismatch: How Affirmative Action Hurts Students It's Intended to Help, and Why Universities Won't Admit It (New York,New York: Basic Books, 2012).
18. Kendi, *How to Be an Antiracist*, loc. 357–58.
19. Thomas Sowell, *Discrimination and Disparities* (New York: Basic Books, 2019).
20. "Selected Characteristics of People at Specified Levels of Poverty," United States Census Bureau, https://data.census.gov/cedsci/table?q=poverty%20and%20marriage&tid=ACSST1Y2019.S1703&hidePreview=false.
21. Roger Clegg, "Percentage of Births to Unmarried Women," Center for Equal Opportunity, February 26, 2020, http://www.ceousa.org/issues/1354-percentage-of-births-to-unmarried-women.
22. Sara Rimer, "Jack Dorsey, Twitter and Square Cofounder, Donates $10 Million to BU Center for Antiracist Research: Gift from Tech CEO's Small Start Philanthropic Initiative Comes with No Strings Attached, Less than Two Months after Leading Scholar Ibram X. Kendi Launches Center," BU Today, August 20, 2020, https://www.bu.edu/articles/2020/jack-dorsey-bu-center-for-antiracist-research-gift/.
23. Joy Pullman, "Study: Up to 95 Percent of 2020 U.S. Riots Are Linked to Black Lives Matter: A Report Accompanying the Data Project, However, Reads Like an Upscale Attempt to Blame the Police for Criminals' Decision to Steal, Kill, and Destroy," The Federalist, September 16, 2020, https://thefederalist.com/2020/09/16/study-up-to-95-percent-of-2020-u-s-riots-are-linked-to-black-lives-matter/; Emma Colton, "Conservatives Point Out That Princeton Study on Protests Reveals Violence Was Found at Hundreds of Demonstrations," *Washington Examiner*, November 27, 2020, https://www.washingtonexaminer.com/news/conservatives-point-out-that-princeton-study-on-protests-reveals-violence-was-found-at-hundreds-of-demonstrations.

24. Associated Press, "Boston's Peaceful Protests Turn Violent at Night," VOA News, May 31, 2020, https://www.voanews.com/usa/bostons-peaceful-protests-turn-violent-night; Michele Munz, et al., "Peaceful Day of Protests Turn Violent at Night As Ferguson Is Damaged," *St. Louis Post-Dispatch*, May 31, 2020, https://www.stltoday.com/news/local/crime-and-courts/peaceful-day-of-protests-turns-violent-at-night-as-ferguson-is-damaged/article_547e9980-f6b1-5df9-852a-88ae68833b84.html; Jessica M. Goldstein, "Peaceful Protests Turn Violent by Nightfall in St. Louis," Think Progress, September 17, 2017, https://archive.thinkprogress.org/peaceful-protests-turn-violent-by-nightfall-in-st-louis-fc91c1bf1574/.

25. See the definitive analysis by George Parry, a former prosecutor who specializes in police brutality cases: "Who Killed George Floyd," *The American Spectator*, August 6, 2020, https://spectator.org/george-floyd-death-toxicology-report/.

26. Ibid.

27. John Hinderaker, "Keith Ellison Endorses Political Violence," The American Experiment, January 4, 2020, https://www.americanexperiment.org/2018/01/keith-ellison-endorses-political-violence/.

28. "Exclusive: A New Start Turns to a Tragic End for George Floyd, Who Moved to Minneapolis Determined to Turn His Life Around after Being Released from Prison in Texas," *Daily Mail*, May 28, 2020, https://www.dailymail.co.uk/news/article-8366533/George-Floyd-moved-Minneapolis-start-new-life-released-prison-Texas.html.

29. George Parry, "Who Killed George Floyd?"; Shayndi Raice and Erin Ailworth, "Derek Chauvin's Lawyers File Motion to Dismiss Charges in George Floyd's Death: Former Minneapolis Police Officer Knelt on Floyd's Neck for about Nine Minutes," *Wall Street Journal*, August 28, 2020, https://www.wsj.com/articles/george-floyds-death-likely-caused-by-drug-overdose-argue-derek-chauvins-lawyers-11598668982.

30. Mike Carter, "Medics Can't Reach Shooting Victims in Seattle Protest Zone," Firehouse, June 21, 2020, https://www.firehouse.com/operations-training/ems/news/21142977/medics-cant-reach-shooting-victims-in-seattle-protest-zone.

31. Jonathan Turley, "University of Massachusetts Nursing Dean Fired for Saying Everyone's Life Matters," JonathanTurley.org, July 2, 2020, https://jonathanturley.org/2020/07/02/university-of-massachusetts-nursing-dean-fired-for-saying-everyones-life-matters/.

32. Cassandra Fairbanks, "Young White Mother Killed by Black Lives Matter Mob for Allegedly Saying 'All Lives Matter,' National Media

Fully Ignores," The Gateway Pundit, July 11, 2020, https://www.
thegatewaypundit.com/2020/07/
young-white-mother-killed-black-lives-matter-mob-allegedly-saying-
lives-matter-national-media-fully-ignores/.

33. Seth McLaughlin, "Harris Heralds 'New Coalition of Conscience' in
First VP Outing," *Washington Times*, August 12, 2020, https://www.
washingtontimes.com/news/2020/aug/12/
kamala-harris-heralds-new-coalition-conscience-vp-/.

34. Michael Ruiz, "Minnesota Gov. Walz Asks Trump for Disaster
Declaration after George Floyd Riots Trigger over $500M in Damages:
Governor's Office Says It Has Fully Mobilized the National Guard for
the First Time since World War II," Fox News, July 2, 2020, https://
www.foxnews.com/politics/
minnesota-gov-walz-trump-disaster-declaration-george-floyd-riots-
500m-damages.

35. "Tucker Carlson on Democrats' Ties to Funding of Riots," In the News,
September 6, 2020, http://itnshow.com/2020/09/06/tucker-carlson-on-
democrats-ties-to-funding-of-riots/; Joe Vaughan, "Who's Funding the
American Race Riots? Democrats and Celebrities," The Post Millennial,
September 4, 2020, https://thepostmillennial.com/
who-funded-the-american-race-riots-democrats-and-celebrities.

36. Frankel Jeremy (@FrankelJeremy), "Trump Denies Minnesota
Governor's Request. . . .," Twitter, July 12, 2020, 6:25 p.m., https://
twitter.com/FrankelJeremy/status/1282440924933562369?s=20.

37. John Perazzo, "Exposing the Lies of Black Lives Matter: Where Black
Racism and Marxism Are Dressed Up as 'Social Justice,'"
FrontPageMag, July 2, 2020, https://www.frontpagemag.com/
fpm/2020/07/exposing-lies-black-lives-matter-john-perazzo/.

38. "2016 Presidential Candidates on the Black Lives Matter Movement,"
Ballotpedia, https://ballotpedia.
org/2016_presidential_candidates_on_the_Black_Lives_Matter_
movement.

39. Jodi M. Brown and Patrick A. Langan, "Policing and Homicide, 1976–
98: Justifiable Homicide by Police; Police Officers Murdered by Felons,"
U.S. Department of Justice, Bureau of Justice Statistics, March 2001,
http://bjs.ojp.usdoj.gov/content/pub/pdf/ph98.pdf; Perazzo, "Exposing
the Lies."

40. "2018: Crime in the United States," Department of Justice Federal
Bureau of Investigations, https://ucr.fbi.gov/crime-in-the-u.s/2018/crime-
in-the-u.s.-2018/topic-pages/tables/table-43.

41. Perazzo, "Exposing the Lies."

42. Roland J. Fryer Jr., "An Empirical Analysis of Racial Differences in Police Use of Force," National Bureau of Economics Research, January 2018, https://www.nber.org/papers/w22399.

43. Heather Mac Donald, "There Is No Epidemic of Racist Police Shootings," *National Review*, July 31, 2019, https://www.nationalreview.com/2019/07/white-cops-dont-commit-more-shootings/.

44. Heather Mac Donald, "Academic Research on Police Shootings and Race," *Washington Post*, July 19, 2016, https://www.washingtonpost.com/news/volokh-conspiracy/wp/2016/07/19/academic-research-on-police-shootings-and-race/.

45. "National Crime Victimization Survey, 2012–13," U.S. Department of Justice Bureau of Justice Statistics, Special Tabulation, table 10, in Edwin S. Rubinstein, "The Color of Crime: Race, Crime, and Justice in America," New Century Foundation, 2016, https://www.amren.com/wp-content/uploads/2016/03/Color-Of-Crime-2016.pdf; Perazzo, "Exposing the Lies."

46. Perazzo, "Exposing the Lies"; Rachel E. Morgan and Barbara A. Oudekerk, "Criminal Victimization 2018," U.S. Department of Justice Bureau of Justice Statistics, September 2019, https://www.bjs.gov/content/pub/pdf/cv18.pdf, table 14; Heather Mac Donald, "A Platform of Urban Decline: Democratic Presidential Candidates Believe America Is Racist, Yet They Ignore the Evidence on Crime and Ensure That Racial Disparities Persist," City Journal, September 23, 2019, https://www.city-journal.org/democratic-candidates-racism-crime.

47. Mac Donald, "A Platform of Urban Decline."

48. "2016 Presidential Candidates on the Black Lives Matter Movement."

49. "Reverend Al Sharpton's Eulogy at George Floyd Memorial Service," Rev, June 4, 2020, https://www.rev.com/blog/transcripts/reverend-al-sharpton-eulogy-transcript-at-george-floyd-memorial-service.

50. "Black Lives Matter Holds Rally Supporting Individuals Arrested in Chicago Looting Monday," NBC 5 Chicago, August 10, 2020, https://www.nbcchicago.com/news/local/black-lives-matter-holds-rally-supporting-individuals-arrested-in-chicago-looting-monday/2320365/.

51. Barbara Sprunt, "'Scared Confused, and Angry': Protester Testifies about Lafayette Park Removal," NPR, June 29, 2020, https://www.npr.org/2020/06/29/884609432/scared-confused-and-angry-protester-testifies-about-lafayette-park-removal.

52. "Emancipation Memorial," Wikipedia, https://en.wikipedia.org/wiki/Emancipation_Memorial.

53. Brie Stimson, "Kaepernick Denounces 4th of July as 'Celebration of White Supremacy': 'You Enslaved Our Ancestors,' the NFL Free Agent Writes in a Twitter Message Posted Saturday," Fox News, July 5, 2020, https://www.foxnews.com/sports/kaepernick-denounces-4th-of-july-as-celebration-of-white-supremacy.

54. Libby Emmons and Barrett Wilson, "As the Fourth of July Approaches, the New York Times Compares America to Nazi Germany and Tries to Cancel Mount Rushmore: You Read That Right—the Gray Lady Seems Bent on Dismantling the Country by Churning Out Sophomoric Hot Takes That Would Make Even Brian Stelter Blush," The Post Millennial, July 1, 2020, https://thepostmillennial.com/as-the-fourth-of-july-approaches-the-new-york-times-compares-america-to-nazi-germany-and-tries-to-cancel-mount-rushmore.

55. The Associated Press and MPR Staff, "Council Advances Plan to Dismantle Minneapolis Police Department," MPR News, June 26, 2020, https://www.mprnews.org/story/2020/06/26/minneapolis-council-puts-plan-to-dismantle-police-in-motion.

56. Donald Trump, "Biden Says Police Have 'Become the Enemy' and Calls for 'Cutting' Police Funding: 'Yes, Absolutely!" YouTube, July 8, 2020, https://www.youtube.com/watch?v=_HzifzNAEDoDonald.

57. "Acting Secretary Wolf Condemns the Rampant Long-Lasting Violence in Portland," Department of Homeland Security, July 16, 2020, https://www.dhs.gov/news/2020/07/16/acting-secretary-wolf-condemns-rampant-long-lasting-violence-portland.

58. "DHS Chief: Democrat Leaders Told Us to Leave When We Offered to Secure Portland. We're Not Leaving. 'That Is Just Not Going to Happen on My Watch.,'" The Daily Wire, July 17, 2020, https://www.dailywire.com/news/dhs-chief-democrat-leaders-told-us-to-leave-when-we-offered-to-secure-portland-were-not-leaving.

59. Benjamin Fearnow, "Pelosi Calls Out Trump Admin over Portland Unrest: 'We Live in a Democracy Not a Banana Republic,'" Newsweek, July 19, 2020, https://www.newsweek.com/pelosi-calls-out-trump-admin-over-portland-unrest-we-live-democracy-not-banana-republic-1518902.

60. Collin Jones, "Nancy Pelosi Spreads Far-Left Hoax about 'Unidentified Stormtroopers' on Portland Streets: Speaker Nancy Pelosi Took to Twitter on Friday to Push a Conspiracy Theory That Trump Has Deployed Unidentified Stormtroopers to Kidnap and Assault Protesters and Rioters in Portland," The Post Millennial, July 18, 2020, https://thepostmillennial.com/nancy-pelosi-spread-far-left-hoax-about-unidentified-stormtroopers/.

61. Ibid. See also the reporting of Andy Ngo on Twitter at @MrAndyNgo.

62. Joshua Caplan, "Bernie Sanders: Trump Advocating for 'Armed Violence' against Black Communities," Breitbart, May 30, 2020, https://www.breitbart.com/politics/2020/05/30/bernie-sanders-trump-advocating-for-armed-violence-against-black-communities/#.

63. Louis Casiano, "81% of Black Americans Want Police to Maintain or Increase Local Presence, Poll Reveals," Fox News, August 5, 2020, https://www.foxnews.com/us/81-black-americans-police-retain-increase-presence.

64. I have analyzed the Green New Deal in *Blitz: Trump Will Smash the Left and Win* (New York: Humanix Books, 2020).

Chapter 12: Heading towards the Abyss

1. "Read the Full Transcript from the First Presidential Debate between Joe Biden and Donald Trump," *USA Today*, September 30, 2020, https://www.usatoday.com/story/news/politics/elections/2020/09/30/presidential-debate-read-full-transcript-first-debate/3587462001/.

2. "Executive Order on Combatting Race and Sex Stereotyping," White House, September 22, 2020, https://www.whitehouse.gov/presidential-actions/executive-order-combating-race-sex-stereotyping/.

3. Ibid.

4. Ibid.

5. "Read the Full Transcript."

6. Ibid.

7. Chrisopher F. Rufo, "The Truth About Critical Race Theory: Trump Is Right. Training Sessions for Government Employees Amounted to Political Indoctrination," *Wall Street Journal*, October 4, 2020, https://www.wsj.com/articles/the-truth-about-critical-race-theory-11601841968; Christopher F. Rufo, "Cult Programming in Seattle," *City Journal*, July 8, 2020, https://www.city-journal.org/seattle-interrupting-whiteness-training; Christopher F. Rufo, " Obscene Federal 'Diversity Training' Scam Prospers—Even under Trump," *New York Post*, July 16, 2020, https://nypost.com/2020/07/16/obscene-federal-diversity-training-scam-prospers-even-under-trump/.

8. Mark M. Smith, *Debating Slavery: Economy and Society in the Antebellum American South* (Cambridge, 1988), chapter 6; Robert Fogel and Stanley Engermann, *Time on the Cross: The Economics of American Negro Slavery* (New York, New York, 1974), 59 ff., 109 ff., 153, and 144 ff.

9. Christopher F. Rufo, "The Truth about Critical Race Theory," The Dale Yeager Blog, October 6, 2020, https://daleyeagerdotcom.wordpress.com/2020/10/06/the-truth-about-critical-race-theory/.

10. Ibid.

11. "Sure, We'll Have Fascism in This Country, and We'll Call It Anti-Fascism," Quote Investigator, https://quoteinvestigator.com/2017/03/04/anti-fascism/.

12. Kavita Das, "The Diversity Industry Is Worth Billions. But What Do We Have to Show for It? A New Book Out Today, 'Diversity, Inc.,' Looks beyond the Corporate Hype to Reveal If There's Been Any Progress Toward Equality," Fast Company, October 22, 2019, https://www.fastcompany.com/90419581/the-diversity-industry-is-worth-billions-but-what-do-we-have-to-show-for-it.

13. "Diversity Primer," Diversity Best Practices, September 29, 2009, https://wwwdiversitybestpractices.com/publications/diversity-primer; Bill de la Cruz, "Are Diversity Equity Inclusion Practitioners Selling Modern Day Snake Oil?," LinkedIn, June 5, 2020, https://www.linkedin.com/pulse/diversity-equity-inclusion-practitioners-selling-day-snake-bill/?articleId=6674522927133786112.

14. Leon Trotsky, *How the Revolution Armed*, vols. 4–5, trans. Brian Pearce (Oak Park, Michigan: New Park Publications, 1979), 125.

15. David Horowitz and Jacob Laskin, *One-Party Classroom: How Radical Professors at America's Top Colleges Indoctrinate Students and Undermine Our Democracy* (New York, New York: Crown Forum, 2009).

16. Priyamvada Rana, "Who Owns Yelp? Internet Slams Website for Going to War against Racism: Yelp Will Place a New 'Business Accused of Racist Behavior Alert' on Their Yelp Page to Inform Users about Businesses That Have Been Accused of Racist Conduct," Meaww, October 9, 2020, https://meaww.com/who-owns-yelp-why-company-anti-racist-business-accused-of-racist-behavior-alert-slammed-delete-app; Jenny Gross, "Yelp Says It Will Mark Pages of Businesses Accused of Racist Conduct," *New York Times*, October 9, 2020, https://www.nytimes.com/2020/10/09/business/yelp-racism.html.

17. Allum Bokhari, *#Deleted: Big Tech's Battle to Erase the Trump Movement and Steal the Election* (New York: Center Street, 2020).

18. Ibid., 18.

19. Ibid.

20. Allum Bokhari, "Exclusive: Facebook's Process to Label You a 'Hate Agent' Revealed," Breitbart, June 13, 2019, https://www.breitbart.com/tech/2019/06/13/exclusive-facebooks-process-to-label-you-a-hate-agent-revealed/. See also Jessica Roy, "How 'Pepe the Frog' Went from Harmless to Hate Symbol," *Los Angeles Times*, October 11, 2016, https://www.latimes.com/politics/

la-na-pol-pepe-the-frog-hate-symbol-20161011-snap-htmlstory.html;
   "Okay Hand Gesture: Racist Hand Signs," Anti-Defamation League
   (ADL), https://www.adl.org/education/references/hate-symbols/
   okay-hand-gesture.
21. Bokhari, "Exclusive: Facebook's Process"; Allum Bokhari, "Daily Beast
   Says Facebook Helped Them Dox Trump Supporter," Breitbart, June 2,
   2019, https://www.breitbart.com/tech/2019/06/02/
   daily-beast-says-facebook-helped-them-dox-trump-supporter/.
22. Bokhari, *Deleted*, 31–32.
23. Ibid.
24. Ibid.

Coda: Love against Hate

1. "Federal Elections 2008: Election Results for the U.S. President, the U.S.
   Senate and the U.S. House of Representatives," Federal Election
   Commission, July 2009, https://www.fec.gov/resources/cms-content/
   documents/federalelections2008.pdf; https://www.amazon.com/s?k=the+
   plot+against+the+president+lee+smith&i=stripbooks&crid=23FL50JL2E
   1S9&sprefix=The+Plot+%2Cstripbooks%2C194&ref
   =nb_sb_ss_ts-a-p_4_9.
2. Daniel Greenfield, "An Election between Love and Hate: Why Are
   President Trump's Rallies Packed While Biden's Rallies Are Deserted?"
   FrontPageMag, October 29, 2020, https://www.frontpagemag.com/
   fpm/2020/10/election-between-love-and-hate-daniel-greenfield/.
3. Ibid.
4. Alison Durkee, "Biden Campaign Deploys 600 Lawyers So Trump Can't
   'Steal This Election,'" *Forbes*, July 2, 2020, https://www.forbes.com/
   sites/alisondurkee/2020/07/02/biden-campaign-deploys-600-
   lawyers-so-trump-cant-steal-this-election/?sh=6431c2c61e00.
5. Holly Otterbein, "Why Biden Didn't Do Better in Big Cities: He Failed to
   Produce the Massive Big-City Margins Some Democrats Expected. One
   Reason Is That Trump Surpassed His 2016 Performance in Many
   Cities," *Politico*, November 15, 2020, https://www.politico.com/
   news/2020/11/15/big-cities-biden-election-436529.
6. "2020 U.S. House of Representatives Elections," Wikipedia, https://
   en.wikipedia.org/wiki/2020_United_States_House_of_
   Representatives_elections#cite_note-Undecided-2.
7. Michael Lee, "Republicans Won All 27 House Races Listed as 'Toss-
   Ups'—and Then Some," *Washington Examiner*, November 19, 2020,
   https://www.washingtonexaminer.com/news/
   republicans-won-all-27-house-races-listed-as-toss-ups-and-then-some.

8. Charles Creitz, "Patrick Basham Explains Why Biden Victory 'Not Statistically Impossible, but . . . Statistically Implausible': Key 'Non-Polling Metrics' Indicated That Trump Would Win Second Term, Democracy Institute Founding Director Tells 'Life, Liberty, & Levin,'" Fox News, December 6, 2020, https://www.foxnews.com/politics/2020-presidential-election-joe-biden-donald-trump-patrick-basham-mark-levin.

9. For the voting records of each of these counties, see Suzanne Downing, "How Could the 'Bellwether Counties' Get It So Wrong?" Must Read Alaska, November 6, 2020, https://mustreadalaska.com/how-could-the-bellwether-counties-get-it-so-wrong/.

10. Daniel Horowitz, "New Analysis Shows Biden Winning Mail-In Ballots By Nearly Impossible Margins," The Blaze, November 30, 2020, https://www.theblaze.com/op-ed/horowitz-new-analysis-shows-biden-winning-nearly-impossible-margins-on-mail-in-ballots-in-pennsylvania.

11. Simon Lewis and Joseph Tanfani, "Special Report: How a Small Group of U.S. Lawyers Pushed Voter Fraud Fears into the Mainstream," Reuters, September 9, 2020, https://www.reuters.com/article/us-usa-election-voter-fraud-special-repo/special-report-how-a-small-group-of-u-s-lawyers-pushed-voter-fraud-fears-into-the-mainstream-idUSKBN2601GZ.

12. "Millions of Mail Ballots Have Not Been Returned as Window Closes," *Washington Post*, October 28, 2020, https://www.washingtonpost.com/politics/2020/10/28/mail-ballots-postal-service/.

13. "Most Countries of the World Ban Mail-In Voting Due to Fraud & Vote Buying," Independant Sentinel, August 9, 2020, https://www.independentsentinel.com/most-countries-of-the-world-ban-mail-in-voting-due-to-fraud-vote-buying/.

14. Ibid.

15. John R. Lott, "Why Do Most Countries Ban Mail-In Ballots?: They Have Seen Massive Vote Fraud Problems," Social Science Research Network, August 9, 2020, https://papers.ssrn.com/sol3/papers.cfm?abstract_id=3666259. The Google search index is so politically biased that one has to go through five pages of references before coming to an article that acknowledges that this is a real problem.

16. Ibid.

17. "Pew: One in Eight Voter Registrations Inaccurate; 51 Million Citizens Unregistered," Press Releases and Statements, Pew, February 14, 2012, https://www.pewtrusts.org/en/about/news-room/press-releases-and-statements/2012/02/14/

pew-one-in-eight-voter-registrations-inaccurate-51-million-citizens-unregistered.

18. Economic War Room with Kevin Freeman, "Dr. Shiva Ayyadurai, MIT PhD Testimony," YouTube, https://www.youtube.com/watch?v=nwHa1p fyJjc&feature=youtu.be.

19. Ibid.

20. Peter Navarro, "The Immaculate Deception," Navarro Report, December 15, 2020, https://www.docdroid.net/QhVNwFw/ the-immaculate-deception-121520-1-pdf.

21. Ibid., 6.

Index